Beginning JSON

T0211256

Ben Smith

Apress®

Beginning JSON

ISBN-13 (pbk): 978-1-4842-0203-6

ISBN-13 (electronic): 978-1-4842-0202-9

Managing Director: Welmoed Spahr
Lead Editor: Ben Renow-Clarke
Technical Reviewer: Victor Sumner
Editorial Board: Steve Anglin, Mark Beckner, Ewan Buckingham, Gary Cornell, Louise Corrigan, Jim DeWolf, Jonathan Gennick, Robert Hutchinson, Michelle Lowman, James Markham, Matthew Moodie, Jeff Olson, Jeffrey Pepper, Douglas Pundick, Ben Renow-Clarke, Dominic Shakeshaft, Gwenan Spearing, Matt Wade, Steve Weiss
Coordinating Editor: Christine Ricketts
Copy Editor: Michael G. Laraque
Compositor: SPi Global
Indexer: SPi Global
Artist: SPi Global

Distributed to the book trade worldwide by Springer Science+Business Media New York, 233 Spring Street, 6th Floor, New York, NY 10013. Phone 1-800-SPRINGER, fax (201) 348-4505, e-mail orders-ny@springer-sbm.com, or visit www.springeronline.com. Apress Media, LLC is a California LLC and the sole member (owner) is Springer Science + Business Media Finance Inc (SSBM Finance Inc). SSBM Finance Inc is a Delaware corporation.

For information on translations, please e-mail rights@apress.com, or visit www.apress.com.

Apress and friends of ED books may be purchased in bulk for academic, corporate, or promotional use. eBook versions and licenses are also available for most titles. For more information, reference our Special Bulk Sales–eBook Licensing web page at www.apress.com/bulk-sales.

Any source code or other supplementary material referenced by the author in this text is available to readers at www.apress.com. For detailed information about how to locate your book's source code, go to www.apress.com/source-code/.

To my wife, for her patience with the late evenings and stay-at-home weekends,
as well as for her constant encouragement

Contents at a Glance

Contents

About the Author

Ben Smith is an accomplished technical experience director with many years of experience leading web development for well-known digital agencies. His list of contributions to the community has earned him a place as an Adobe Community Professional. It should be apparent from his background as an author, speaker, and a judge for the Favourite Website Awards (FWA) that he is passionate about the Web. He attributes his growth to experimentation and experience.

About the Technical Reviewer

Victor Sumner is a senior software engineer at D2L Corporation, where he helps to build and maintain an integrated learning platform. As a self-taught developer, he is always interested in emerging technologies and enjoys working on and solving problems that are outside his comfort zone.

When not at the office, Victor has a number of hobbies, including photography, horseback riding, and gaming. He lives in Ontario, Canada, with his wife, Alicia, and their two children.

Acknowledgments

This book could not have been written without a loving and patient wife, an understanding circle of friends, and a great team of editors and reviewers. My sincerest thanks to them all.

Introduction

Programming is not at all a linear path. Often, you find yourself facing a fork in the road. In choosing one path, you are likely to find, after a period of time, that you go back and travel down the other. While it is assumed that you are familiar with HTML, CSS, and JavaScript, this book makes no further assumptions regarding your experience. Therefore, it attempts to provide a thorough explanation for everything you will read in it.

While JSON is the essence of this book, it is not the sole topic discussed. While that may sound counterproductive, it is a much-needed requirement. JSON can be devised in isolation, but it would serve little purpose. What makes JSON so impactful is that it interacts with the many tools of the developer. For this reason, this book covers a wide range of implementations—from libraries to software.

CHAPTER 1

■ ■ ■

JavaScript Basics

JavaScript is a scripting language that has been known to be a finicky beast. Many well-known developers have forged their names in the annals of the web-development community, having discovered special techniques and hidden gems to tame said beast. The topic of this book, JSON, is one such gem. You will learn more about that in Chapter 4.

JSON is simply a data-interchange format and, therefore, does not directly require immediate knowledge of the JavaScript language. However, this book does not only discuss the composition of JSON. It also discusses how to incorporate it within an application. For this reason, this book employs JavaScript extensively to demonstrate the many ways to work with JSON. There are plenty of great books that reveal the ins and outs of the JavaScript language. This chapter solely acts as a primer to the upcoming chapters.

JavaScript History

The year is 1995, and Netscape seeks to add dynamic behavior as well as the capability to automate parts of a web page within its browser. It was at this point in time that Brendan Eich was hired to incorporate the functional scripting language Scheme into the Netscape Navigator browser.[1] However, Netscape had also been in discussion with other software/hardware companies. In a mad dash for the finish line, Eich had prototyped the scripting language that would soon become what is known today as JavaScript.

The incorporation of this new dynamic behavior within the browser became a game-changer. This had a direct impact on how developers programmed for the Web. Furthermore, this incorporation, as an innovation, encouraged Internet users to adopt Navigator as the preferred browser. In order to compete with the new dynamic, and with the browser wars on the rise, Microsoft was quick to incorporate a scripting language of its own into Internet Explorer.

Microsoft's scripting dialect was developed to be compatible with the scripting language of Netscape. However, to ensure the language remained uniform, Netscape submitted its dialect to the Ecma International for standardization. Thus were the beginnings of the ECMA-262 specification. ECMA-262 is the name for this scripting language's specification. The name *ECMAScript* is the union of *Ecma* International and Java*Script*. To reference ECMAScript is to reference the specification rather than the language itself.

---

[1]Wikipedia, "JavaScript," http://en.wikipedia.org/wiki/JavaScript, modified January 2015.

JavaScript Essentials

At its core, JavaScript is a text-based scripting language, whereby sequences of Unicode characters are strung together. That said, what makes JavaScript more than a sequence of characters is its adherence to the rules that govern how the JavaScript engine interprets said sequence into a particular application. The set of rules that defines the valid sequencing of characters is known as Syntax. Listing 1-1 reveals a syntactically correct, albeit simple, JavaScript application.

Listing 1-1. A Valid JavaScript Program

```
1 var welcomeMessage = "Hello World";
2  //Lines denoted with '//' are used to leave comments
3  console.log( welcomeMessage );  //prints to the console Hello World
4  console.log("A");    //prints the character A
5  console.log( 2+5 ); //prints the number 7
6
7  console.log("goodbye" + " " + "all"); //prints goodbye all.
```

Listing 1-1 reveals seven lines composed of a sequence of Unicode-encoded characters. However, as the characters of Listing 1-1 adhere to the ECMAScript specification, what Listing 1-1 reveals is technically a JavaScript application.

Values

Because many languages heavily influenced JavaScript, the values used by JavaScript may appear familiar. While there are many values used by the JavaScript language, there are two categories for which these values are distinguished. Those two categories are the primitive and non-primitive types. Non-primitive types are otherwise known as Objects and are the topic of Chapter 2.

Primitive Types

A primitive type represents the set of all basic building blocks for which data can be represented. These are referred to as *primitive* because they are rudimentary. This is, of course, in contrast to non-primitive types.

There are five primitive types in JavaScript, as depicted in Figure 1-1. These five types are number, string, Boolean, undefined, and null.

Figure 1-1. *The five primitive types in JavaScript*

The Number Type

The number type represents the set of all possible numeric values recognized by the JavaScript language. Such representations are shown in Figure 1-2. Possible number values include fractions as well as whole numbers, and each can possess a negative or positive value. Additionally, fractions can be written using scientific notation. Listing 1-2 reveals a variety of valid JavaScript numeric values.

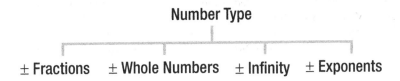

Figure 1-2. *Valid representations of the number type*

Listing 1-2. Valid Number Values

```
4
16
3.402823669209385e+38
-1
```

The String Type

The string type represents the set of all possible string values whereby a string value is a finite representation that includes 0 or more Unicode characters. As outlined in Figure 1-3, while the character encoding is strictly regarded as that of Unicode, string values can also be representative of ASCII character encoding. This is because ASCII is a subset of the Unicode character set. Examples of possible string values can be found in Listing 1-3.

Figure 1-3. *Valid encodings of the string type*

Listing 1-3. Valid String Values

```
"this is a string value";
"string";
"s";
"";   //An empty String
```

Because a program is made up of text, a string value is differentiated from our program by delimiting its value with quotations. In Listing 1-3, I have wrapped each string value within double quotes. However, it is entirely valid to utilize singular quotes as well.

Because quotations mark the beginning and end of a string value, it will be imperative that your string does not employ the same outer quotes to nest quotes such as the following: "Mike said and I quote, "let me tell you a secret"". Nesting quotations with the same characters used to signify a string will confuse the engine, resulting in the likelihood of an error. Because the engine reads in a left-to-right, top-to-bottom manner, the first nested quotation encountered will be interpreted as the terminating quotation. This means that what was expected to be a quote by Mike is instead treated as an invalid statement.

Nesting quotations within string values are perfectly acceptable, providing they do not cause the engine to believe the string ends prematurely, as in the preceding example. There are two possible ways to accomplish this.

Alternate Quotations

Because you can alternate between singular and double quotes, whichever you use to delimit a string value, you can use the alternate variation to add grammar to your string. Listing 1-4 revisits the preceding example with the use of alternating quotations.

Listing 1-4. Alternating Use of Quotes

```
'Mike said and I quote, "let me tell you a secret".';  //  ' is used to delimit a string
"Mike said and I quote, 'let me tell you a secret'.";  //  " is used to delimit a string
```

As you can see from Listing 1-4, you can use one pair of quotes to signify a string and an alternate form to establish proper English grammar within. The engine will interpret this as a string within a string and move on.

Escaped Quotations

The second method of incorporating quotes within a string is to ensure that the engine does not treat our inner quotations as string delimiters. In order to accomplish this, we must escape our inner quotation marks.

The escape character instructs the engine to interpret the subsequent character differently from how it would otherwise be viewed. This is opposed to being interpreted as a delimiter that would otherwise be used to mark the end or beginning of a string value. Escaping a character is easily accomplished by prefixing the character you wish to escape with a backslash (\).

The use of the escaped quotation allows our strings to employ quotations indiscriminately. Examples can be seen in Listing 1-5.

Listing 1-5. Nested Escaped Quotations

```
"Mike said and I quote, \"let me tell you a secret\".";
'Mike said and I quote, \'let me tell you a secret\'.';
```

▪ **Note**   The escape character informs the engine to interpret a character differently.

4

The Boolean Type

A Boolean type represents a logical value consisting of only two possible values. Those values, as illustrated in Figure 1-4, are either true or false. While these are two possible values that can be assigned, a Boolean type is commonly returned as the evaluation of a condition. Such an evaluation may be the comparison between two numbers, as seen in Listing 1-6.

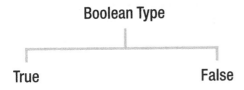

True   **False**

Figure 1-4. Valid values of the Boolean type

Listing 1-6. Boolean Expressions

```
var bol = false; //assigns bol a false value
(10<9);          //evaluates to false;
(10>9);          //evaluates to true;
```

Boolean values are great for incorporating decision making within your application. Determining whether an expression evaluates to true or false allows an application to react accordingly. We will revisit this when I discuss conditional statements.

undefined Type

The undefined type is the value used to represent when an identifier has not yet been assigned a value. When a reference to a variable is evaluated, if it has yet to be assigned a value, the value of undefined is returned.

Listing 1-7 reveals two lines of code. The first line is used to declare a variable labeled name (**line 1**). The declaration of our variable informs the JavaScript engine to allocate a portion of memory that our application can use to store data. The variable's identifier name provides us a textual means to refer to said allocation. As we have not yet assigned any data to our variable, the subsequent line returns the value of undefined (**line 2**).

Listing 1-7. An Undefined Variable

```
1 var name;
2 console.log(name)    //returns undefined;
```

null Type

The null type represents the intentional absence of a value. This is contrary to the undefined value, which represents no value as having been set. The null type is a value used explicitly to represent an empty or nonexistent reference.

Listing 1-8, assigns the value of null to the name identifier, to explicitly denote the intentional absence of a value.

Listing 1-8. null Assignment

```
var name = null;
console.log(name)    //returns null;
```

Expressions

Simply stated by the Mozilla Developer Network, "An *expression* is any valid unit of code that resolves to a value."[2] The value to which an expression resolves is either that of a primitive type or that of an object. Two possible forms of expressions can be viewed in Listing 1-9.

Listing 1-9. Contrasting Expressions

```
1 var name = "ben";
2             2+5;
```

Listing 1-9 demonstrates two different types of expressions. The first represents the assignment of a literal value to a variable (**line 1**) where name represents the identifier to which the string literal ben is assigned. The second regards the operation of two operands (**line 2**).

■ **Note** The operand is the datum being operated on.

An expression either returns a value, causes a side effect, or both. The determining factor is the operator employed.

Operators

There are a variety of operators within the JavaScript language that can be used to fashion an expression. The operator utilized directly impacts the outcome of the value. I will take this opportunity to discuss the various operators utilized throughout this book.

Assignment Operator

The assignment operator is used to set the value of an expression to that of an identifier. In order to devise an assignment, the JavaScript language relies on the use of the equal (=) operator. Listing 1-10 makes use of the assignment operator to assign a primitive value to a variable.

Listing 1-10. Assigning Values to Variables

```
1 var bolValue = true;
2 var name = "ben";
```

Once a value is assigned, it can be obtained by referencing the appropriate identifier. It's important to note that identifiers are case-sensitive, meaning that if you use all lowercase characters to label a variable, it must always be referred to in lowercase. To do otherwise would cause an error.

---

[2]MDN: Mozilla Developer Network, "Expressions and operators," https://developer.mozilla.org/en-US/docs/Web/JavaScript/Guide/Expressions_and_Operators, last updated November 27, 2014.

Arithmetic Operators

The arithmetic operators are operators that are concerned with mathematical operations. The operators that make up this category can be viewed in Table 1-1.

Table 1-1. *Arithmetic Operators*

Arithmetic Operator	Operator
Addition Operator	+
Subtraction Operator	-
Division Operator	/
Multiplication Operator	*

As you may suspect, arithmetic operators are used to perform mathematical operations on numerical values, as shown in Listing 1-11.

Listing 1-11. Arithmetic Operations

```
4+9;  // evaluates to 13
8-2;  // evaluates to 6
3*7;  // evaluates to 21
2/1;  // evaluates to 2
```

However, what might not be expected is that the addition operator serves two purposes. The first purpose concerns the summation of numbers; the second is used to join two string values together. As long as the two operands used in conjunction with the additional operator are of numeric value, they will be added together. However, if at least one operand is a string value, both operands will be coerced into their string representations and joined end-to-end, as demonstrated in Listing 1-12.

Listing 1-12. String Concatenation

```
1 'Hello' + 'World'; // evaluates to "Hello World"
2 "" + 'Welcome';    // evaluates to "Welcome"
3 true + '';         // evaluates to "true"
4 3 + '3';           // evaluates to "33"
```

Listing 1-12 demonstrates the union of strings when used with the addition operator. While lines 1 and 2 may be easily accepted, lines 3 and 4 may not be. As previously stated, the addition operator can only be used on numbers or strings. If both operands are numbers, then it's easy for the engine to know which operation to perform. However, if at least one operand is a string value, then no matter what data type the other operand is, it will always be converted into a string.

Line 3 seeks to add a Boolean value with an empty string, which results in the coercion of true into that of a string. Then, as both operands are viewed as strings, they are joined together and returned as the singular string value. Similarly, line 4 seeks to add the number 3 with that of the string '3', resulting in the string value "33".

Comparison Operators

Comparison operators are used to compare two operands (see Table 1-2). The evaluated value, which will always be that of a Boolean value, is a direct reflection as to whether or not the comparison is true. It is important to point out that few comparison operators compare operands without implicit type coercion.

Table 1-2. *Comparison Operators*

Comparison Operator	Operator	Description
Less Than	<	Used to determine whether the left operand is less than the right
Greater Than	>	Used to determine whether the left operand is greater than the right
Less Than or Equal	<=	Used to determine whether the left operand is less than or equal to the right
Greater Than or Equal	>=	Used to determine whether the left operand is greater than or equal to the right
Equals	==	Used to determine whether the left operand is equal to the right
Does Not Equal	!=	Used to determine whether the left operand does not equal the right
Strictly Equals	===	Compares the equality of two operands without allowing type coercion to occur
Does Not Strictly Equal	!==	Compares the inequality of two operands without allowing type coercion to occur

Listing 1-13 reflects the evaluation between two operands. As demonstrated by Listing 1-13, the comparison operators have two modes: one is the strict comparison between two operands; the other is a more lax comparison.

Listing 1-13. Comparing Operands

```
3<=3;    // evaluates to true:  after type coercion, 3 is less than or equal to 3
3=='3';  // evaluates to true:  after type coercion, '3' and '3' are found to be equal
3==3;    // evaluates to true:  after type coercion, 3 and 3 are found to be equal
3===3;   // evaluates to true:  3 and 3 are the same
3==='3'; // evaluates to false: 3 does not equal '3'
3!='3';  // evaluates to false: 3 and '3' are equal
3!=='3'; // evaluates to true:  3 does not equal '3'
```

When the comparison is lax, the two operands are coerced behind the scenes to the same type. Regardless of whether the operand is that of a string or a number, both will be coerced into the same data type before they are compared.

However, the use of a strict comparison operator ensures that both operands are compared without the use of type conversion. This is essential for determining whether two operands are similar in both value as well as type.

The typeof Operator

The typeof operator evaluates the type of any datum. The value returned reflects one of the six data types (see Listing 1-14) used by the JavaScript language.

Listing 1-14. Determining Data Types

```
1 typeof 3;                //outputs number
2 typeof "hello world";    //outputs string
3 typeof true;             //outputs boolean
4 typeof (new Object());   //outputs object
5 var emptyVariable;
6 typeof emptyVariable;    //outputs undefined
```

Listing 1-14 demonstrates how the typeof operator can be used to identify to which data type the value in question belongs.

The instanceof Operator

While the typeof operator is used to determine the type of some value, instanceof is used to test whether an instance is a subclass for a given object type. The instanceof operator returns a Boolean value, indicating whether or not the instance is the descendant, directly or otherwise, of a particular object. Use of the instanceof operator is demonstrated in Listing 1-15.

Listing 1-15. Classifying Instances

```
1 var array = new Array();
2 var xhr = new XMLHttpRequest();
3
4 console.log( xhr instanceof Array);              //outputs false
5 console.log( array instanceof XMLHttpRequest);   //outputs false
6 console.log( array instanceof Array);            //outputs true
7 console.log( xhr instanceof XMLHttpRequest);     //outputs true
8 console.log( xhr instanceof Object);             //outputs true
9 console.log( array instanceof Object);           //outputs true
```

Listing 1-15 employs the instanceof operator to determine whether two instances, array and xhr, evaluate as members of each other's object type. Because xhr is an instance of the XMLHttpRequest Object, and array is an instance of the Array Object type, they both output false when compared against each other's object type.

From there, each instance is compared against its own object type, which evaluates to that of true. This is because our array is an instance of the Array Object type, while xhr is indeed a member of the XMLHttpRequest Object type.

One final thing to point out is that both our xhr and array instances are in fact members of the Object type. This is because both the Array and XMLHttpRequest Objects are direct descendants of the Object itself. This will be discussed in more detail in Chapter 2.

The ! Operator

The NOT operator, signified by the exclamation (!) token, is used to invert a Boolean value, as seen in Listing 1-16.

Listing 1-16. Inversing a Boolean Value

```
console.log( !true );    // outputs false
var someVal = !false;    // assigns the value true;
```

Statements

While expressions are concerned with the evaluation of values, statements are concerned with the actions of an application. A statement can be as simple as displaying the sum of two numbers or as complex as generating the histogram of a photograph.

A statement may exist on a line of its own or be composed of multiple statements. A general rule of thumb is that each new line of code represents a statement. However, what truly distinguishes a statement is the explicit use of line terminators.

■ **Note**   While expressions and statements are two separate categories in the JavaScript syntax, the reality is that the two will often be intertwined. In other words, the two do not always occur independently.

Line Terminators

The use of a semicolon (;) explicitly signifies the end of a statement. This ensures that if multiple statements are found on a single line, they are interpreted as entirely separate statements. If a semicolon is not found at the end of a valid statement, the engine will instead interpret carriage returns and line breaks as statement terminators. When these implicit line terminators are encountered, the engine inserts semicolons behind the scenes to comply with the syntax.

Listing 1-17 reveals four lines of code. The first two lines represent two separate statements. While they do not explicitly end with a semicolon, they do employ line breaks, which is seen by the engine as a line terminator. When the JavaScript interpreter reads these two lines, it will automatically add semicolons to the end of both lines 1 and 2, making them valid statements.

Listing 1-17. Statements Require Terminators

```
1 console.log('a')                     //valid statement
2 console.log('b')                     //valid statement
3 console.log('a'); console.log('b');  //2 valid statements on 1 line
4 console.log('a')  console.log('b');  //1 invalid statement
```

Line 3, on the other hand, is a condensed way of writing the preceding two statements. Rather than occupy two lines of code, the explicit use of semicolons after each statement informs the interpreter that multiple statements occur on the same line.

Line 4, on the other hand, possesses two statements without explicit use of the ; delimiter. This results in the engine executing an *invalid* statement leading to a syntax error.

▨ **Tip** It's best to clearly identify your statements by ending them with a ;.

Control Statements

Control statements are used to add decision making to an application. Depending on the evaluation of an expression, an application can determine whether or not to execute a particular statement. Table 1-3 reveals two keywords that are used by this book to devise control statements.

Table 1-3. *Control Statements*

Control Statements	Description
if	Executes a statement if a logical condition is true
else	An optional clause to execute a statement if a logical condition is true

The if statement is used to execute a statement if and when an expression evaluates to true. On the other hand, if the expression evaluates to false, the indicated statement will be skipped, as seen in Listing 1-18.

Listing 1-18. Controlling Flow with if

```
1 var bol = false;
2 if( bol ) console.log('condition is met');
```

Listing 1-18 demonstrates a typical use of the if statement. Listing 1-18 begins by assigning false to a variable labeled bol (**Line 1**). The subsequent line represents our control, which outlines the following condition: if bol evaluates as true, then perform the subsequent statement (**Line 2**). Unfortunately, as bol evaluates to false, the condition is not met, and, therefore, the statement does not execute.

Whereas the statement in Listing 1-18 will cease to be executed, the else clause can be paired with that of the if statement. As you may have anticipated, the else clause will execute a statement in the case that a condition is not met. Listing 1-19 appends the else statement to our earlier demonstration.

Listing 1-19. Controlling Flow with if/else

```
1 var bol=false;
2 if( bol ) console.log('condition is met');
3 else console.log('condition is not met');    // condition is not met
```

Running Listing 1-19 results in the execution of line 3.

11

Block Statements

Although a statement can only ever comprise one task, it is quite possible to group a series of statements to be performed. A grouping of statements is known as a *block statement*. A block statement is delimited with the pair of curly brackets, as seen in Listing 1-20.

Listing 1-20. Grouping Statements Within a Block

```
{
  statement1;
  statement2;
  statement3;
}
```

As revealed by Listing 1-20, a statement block can hold any number of statements within. You may notice that while each enclosed statement within the block is concluded with a semicolon, the block statement itself does not require them. The statement block is an extremely important aspect of the language, because it can be inserted wherever a statement is considered valid. Listing 1-21 revisits our control statements from Listing 1-19 and incorporates the use of a block statement.

Listing 1-21. Substituting Block Statements for Statements

```
1 var bol=false;
2 if( bol ) {  console.log('condition is met'); alert('condition is met'); }
3 else {  console.log('condition is not met'); alert('condition is not met'); }
```

Truthy/Falsy

Any valid JavaScript value will evaluate to that of a Boolean value when used as the expression of a control statement. While the evaluation returns either true or false, the values that evaluate to true or false are not as cut and dry. Those that evaluate to true are referred to as *truthy* values. While those that evaluate to false are referred to as *falsy* values.

The simplest way to contrast the truthy values from those that are falsy is to recognize which values are falsy. Listing 1-22 reveals the falsy values of the JavaScript language.

Listing 1-22. Demonstrates All Falsy Values

```
if('');           // An empty string
if(0);            // the number 0
if(null);         // a value of null
if(false)         // a value of false
if(undefined);    // a value of undefined
if(NaN);          // a value of NaN
```

Any value not displayed in Listing 1-22 represents a truthy value.

Loop Statements

The JavaScript language does possess a few loop statements, which enable a statement to occur as long as a particular condition is met.

The for loop

One loop that is used extensively throughout this book is the for loop. The for loop is commonly used to execute a statement for as long as a condition remains true. The syntax for the for loop can be seen in Listing 1-23.

Listing 1-23. The Syntax of a for Loop

```
for( initialization ; condition ; operation ) statement;
```

As revealed in Listing 1-23, a for loop requires an initialization, a condition, and, last, an operation that either increments or decrements the initialized value.

As long as the condition remains true, the provided statement will be executed. However, the moment the condition is no longer met, the loop will terminate and the engine will move on to the next statement in the application. Listing 1-24 employs a for loop to execute a statement, as long as the variable i remains less than 10.

Listing 1-24. An Iterative Statement Can Reference the Current Index

```
1 for( var i=0; i<10 ; i++ ) console.log( i ); // logs out 0, 1, 2, 3, 4, 5, 6, 7, 8, 9
```

The for/in loop

The second form of a loop that will be used by this book is the for/in loop. The for/in loop is used to enumerate the members possessed by an object instance (see Listing 1-25).

Listing 1-25. Iterating All Owned Enumerable Keys of an object

```
1 var carA = new Object();
2     carA.wheels=4;
3     carA.color="blue"
4     carA.make="Volvo";
5 for( var member in carA ) console.log( member );
```

Listing 1-25 possesses a variable labeled carA, which is assigned a non-primitive value. To be more specific, carA is assigned the value of an object. An object can be thought of as a container used to group common variables together. In this case, the particular variables are grouped together to represent a vehicle. As revealed in Listing 1-25, the variables used in the collection are the following: wheels, color, and make. These properties are used to add specifics to our vehicle.

The for/in loop is used to iterate all identifiers contained within the chosen instance. Executing the preceding listing results in the following output:

```
wheels
color
make
```

Declarations

JavaScript declarations are used to register text identifiers that can be referenced throughout a program.

Variables

For all intents and purposes, JavaScript variables can be thought of as a named pointer that remains a symbolic link to a particular location in memory. The name for which the pointer is provided is known as an identifier. An identifier is a case-sensitive label used as a means to refer to its particular storage location. Only by declaring a variable can a value be assigned, retained, and later referenced.

In the JavaScript language, variables are declared via the keyword var, as demonstrated in Listing 1-26.

Listing 1-26. Declaring Three Variables

```
1 var name = "ben";
2 var age = 36;
3 var sayName = function(){ return this.name };  //function expression
```

Listing 1-26 declares three variables and provides each with a concise yet meaningful identifier. Identifiers should reflect something meaningful and befit the data for which they are assigned.

Functions

Technically, functions are not statements but are used to perform specific actions. Functions are a special form of object, which allows functions to be treated as values. Listing 1-27 reveals the syntax of a function.

Listing 1-27. The Syntax of the Function Declaration

```
function Identifier ( FormalParameterListopt ) { //statements; }
```

As outlined in Listing 1-27, a function is defined by using the function keyword. The identifier, which follows the declaration, registers the function with the provided label. This ensures that an application can refer to the function at any point in time throughout the application.

Following the identifier is a pair of parentheses, which are used to hold any number of optional identifiers separated with the use of a comma. These identifiers are used as labels for the parameters that you may wish to provide to the body of a function.

The final component of the function declaration is the statement block to be executed when the function is executed. Listing 1-28 declares a function labeled sayName.

Listing 1-28. Invoking the sayName Function with a Parameter

```
1 function sayName (name){
2   return "Hello " + name;
3 };
4 console.log( sayName("Ben") ); // Hello Ben
```

Listing 1-28 employs a function declaration to devise a function that is capable of accepting an arbitrary value whose identifier reflects that of name. This identifier represents the identity for the parameterized value provided by the caller of the function. The body of the function can then reference this value and use it within its operation.

In the case of `sayName`, the function body references the identifier `name` and uses the addition operator to join its value and the word *Hello* together. Utilizing the keyword `return`, the evaluation is then provided back to the caller of the function. This results in the output of `Hello Ben` to the console.

Summary

This chapter has sought to provide an overview of the many upcoming chapters, in which the JavaScript language will be relied on extensively to employ, explain, and devise JSON. While much of this chapter has focused on statements, operators, and primitive types that will be used in this book, the next chapter focuses on the non-primitive types of the language, otherwise known as objects.

Key Points from This Chapter

- JavaScript is a text-based language made up of Unicode and ASCII characters.
- ECMAScript refers to the specification of the language.
- JavaScript possesses two categories of data types: primitive and non-primitive.
- Primitive values can be numbers, strings, Boolean, `undefined`, and `null`.
- `undefined` represents the lack of value.
- `null` is used to denote intentional absence of value.
- Expressions resolve to a value.
- Operators are used to fashion expressions.
- The addition operator serves two purposes.
- Strict comparison operators prevent the occurrence of type coercion.
- Non-strict comparison operators rely on type coercion before comparing two operands.
- The `typeof` operator is used to determine the type of datum.
- The `instanceof` operator is used to determine the Object type of an instance.
- Statements should be terminated explicitly.
- Statement blocks can group multiple statements.
- Identifiers are case-sensitive text-based labels.
- Functions are named blocks of code that can be provided parameters.

CHAPTER 2

■ ■ ■

Special Objects

JavaScript is an object-oriented language, which is a programming paradigm that acknowledges the compartmentalization of data encapsulated within an "object." But what exactly is an object? To put it plainly, it is a classification used to represent a generalized/generic form. This lack of specificity makes it possible to classify an object as anything that exists. This affords an object-oriented language a means to address any and all non-primitive types.

This is extremely beneficial to an object-oriented language, which employs the Object—due to its general classification—thereby encompassing everything within a singular classification. The object is the singular classification that unifies any and all more specific objects within the language, thereby devising a hierarchical system. No matter how unique or specific the possessed behaviors of an object may be considered, they can always be regarded as an object.

Objects

Absolutely everything is an object. It's true that an object can be grouped into a particular category with regard to its particular attributes. This categorization is considered the classification of an object. The greater the emphasis on the particular set of behaviors an object possesses, the further its classification from that of the generalized object. Simultaneously, the emphasis placed on the specific traits, attributes, and/or behaviors of an object can be used to place it within a subclassification. However, the inverse will always hold true. In JavaScript, all classifications, in their most generalized form, are objects.

Before we go any further, it is worth noting the repeated use of the words *Object* and *object(s)*. These two terms are not being used interchangeably. Throughout this book, I have done my best to ensure that *Object* and *object* remain properly distinguished in the sentences in which I refer to them. *Object* and *object* refer to two separate concepts, as you will, I hope, come to learn. The term *Object* regards a built-in type of the JavaScript language, whereas the term *object* refers to an instance of a said *Object* type.

Objects Are Collections

What classifies all objects in the JavaScript language is that at their most atomic unit, they are simply collections of string value pairs. Technically speaking, all objects are associative arrays. Simply, what this means is that an object has the capability to retain a value for any given identifier. Furthermore, as a collection of strings, it can hold many identifiers.

Quite commonly, these identifiers are referred to as *properties*, *members*, and even *keys*. Regardless of how they are referred to, these identifiers, much like variables, will map to a value. Such values can be primitive or non-primitive. Because a member can only be paired to a singular value, a member and its value are often referred to as a key/value pair. Precisely like a variable, the keys of an object can be referenced, invoked (if it's assigned value is that of a function), and even assigned a value. Unlike a variable, which can be referenced simply by the name of the identifier, a key must be accessed through the instance. This is achieved with access notation. You will learn more about how to access, assign, and invoke properties within the section "Access Notation."

░ **Note** This book uses the terms *properties*, *members*, and *keys* interchangeably.

What is so powerful about the object-oriented paradigm is its ability to devise collections of like-minded behaviors whose sole faculties are dedicated toward a specific task. The more specific the behaviors, the more specialized these objects become. Furthermore, because an object-oriented language relies on a hierarchical structure to establish relationships among all objects, any object spawned from an existing object can and will inherit its ancestor's behaviors. This helps to ensure that every descendant possesses its ancestor's behaviors. This provides all objects the ability to be classified as any of the classifications that make up their lineage. This, of course, includes their topmost ancestor, the Object.

Built-in Objects

The JavaScript language has plenty of built-in objects, many of which are used throughout this book. Because they all share a common ancestor, the Object, each of these objects, at its core, will continue to remain collections of key/value pairs. Furthermore, as direct descendants, they will indirectly possess the behaviors of their ancestor. What makes these objects specialized are the collective behaviors each possesses to facilitate the fulfillment of a specific goal. For each object, the collections of behaviors and attributes uniquely classify it as highly specialized. The Object and Array are just two of the specialized objects this book will make extensive use of.

Object

As mentioned earlier, an Object is a built-in type that defines an unordered collection of key/value pairs. The defined properties and behaviors possessed by the built-in Object facilitate this behavior. In addition to the aforementioned behavior, the Object also possesses other behaviors, which will be inherited by every descendant. One such behavior possessed and passed on by the Object is the toString behavior.

The toString identifier represents the key that directly accesses the value of a function. Because the key is paired to a function, we can follow up the reference with the parentheses (()) operator, to invoke the function. This results in the return of the string representation of the object.

░ **Note** When an identifier is mapped to a function, it is referred to as a *method* of the object.

Beyond its default behaviors, the Object acts as a template from which our application can clone and supply to it a collection of behaviors required by our application.

Creating Objects

While the Object is extremely beneficial within an object-oriented language, its sole use to a developer is the ability to provide to it a collection of behaviors. Fortunately, for this reason, the JavaScript language allows us to create instances of the Object by way of the keyword new, as demonstrated in Listing 2-1.

Listing 2-1. Creation of an object

```
var aCollection = new Object();
```

Listing 2-1 leverages the keyword new to inform the JavaScript engine to create an instance of the Object type. Upon the instantiation, an object is created, returned, and assigned to a variable, so that our application can maintain a reference to the instance. By referencing the aCollection identifier, our application can directly refer to our instance and take advantage of its possessed behaviors.

At any point in time, a reference to aCollection allows our application to access any of the key/value pairs retained by it. At this moment, the only behaviors possessed by our aCollection instance are those that are built in to the Object type. One such behavior is the toString method.

Access Notation

The JavaScript language offers two ways in which one can assign or retrieve a value from an instance. The two varieties of manner are known as dot notation and bracket notation.

Dot Notation

Dot notation represents the particular syntax for which a key/value pair can be accessed or assigned to a specified instance. *Dot* refers to the use of the operator employed to access a property of an instance. That operator is the period (.) symbol. The period itself acts as the delimiter between our instance and the key we wish to get, set, or invoke, as seen in Listing 2-2.

Listing 2-2. Dot Notation Is Used to Access a Member from an Instance

```
1 var aCollection = new Object();
2    console.log( aCollection.firstProperty ); // undefined
3    aCollection.firstProperty= "hello world";
4    console.log( aCollection.firstProperty ); // hello world
5    console.log( aCollection.toString() );    // [object Object]
```

Listing 2-2 instantiates an object and assigns it to aCollection (**line 1**). Utilizing dot notation, Listing 2-2 attempts to read a property value from our aCollection instance. The name of the property is appropriately labeled firstProperty. As the collection lacks a value for the requested property, the value undefined is returned. This value is then logged to the developer's console (**line 2**).

In order to get a value for a particular key, it must be assigned a value, lest it returns undefined. To keep things simple, Listing 2-2 assigns the string value "hello world" to the key firstProperty (**line 3**). On assignment of a value to the identified property, our aCollection instance will reflect a value for each query of firstProperty until the value is reassigned or deleted. A subsequent lookup of the firstProperty utilizing dot notation outputs the value of "hello world" to the console (**line 4**).

Last, as every object possesses the toString method, we can invoke its behavior by succeeding the key identifier with a parenthesis (**line 5**). Doing so outputs a string that represents the current object. As you can see, the output, while not all that insightful, does indeed provide a value to the console. This output is the default behavior of the built-in Object. However, because all objects are collections of key/value pairs, the toString member of aCollection can be reassigned with a function that more accurately represents our instance. Each object-type of the JavaScript language overrides the default functionality of the toString method.

Bracket Notation

The second mechanism used to assign, obtain, or invoke a key/value pair is bracket notation. Bracket notation is similar to dot notation in that it is used to query or assign a value for a given property of an instance. The most noticeable difference between bracket notation and dot notation is that bracket notation requires all keys to be referenced as string values rather than as an identifier. The reference to bracket notation regards the delimiter between the key, represented as a string value, and the instance from which it's being accessed. The string value is enclosed within an opening ([) and closing (]) bracket and immediately succeeds the instance identifier from which the key is being queried. Listing 2-3 revisits the firstProperty, only this time, it employs bracket notation to do so.

Listing 2-3. Bracket Notation Is Used to Access a Member from an Instance

```
var aCollection = new Object();
    console.log( aCollection['firstProperty'] ); // undefined
    aCollection['firstProperty']= "hello world";
    console.log( aCollection['firstProperty'] ); // hello world
    console.log( aCollection['toString']() );    // [object Object]
```

If you were to execute the preceding listing, you would arrive at precisely the same results as those of Listing 2-2. Aside from the obvious differences in syntax, you may wonder why you would use one notation over the other.

Bracket Notation vs. Dot Notation

While dot notation is certainly cleaner than bracket notation, bracket notation has a particular advantage. Bracket notation relies on string values, whereas dot notation utilizes identifiers. The key difference is that identifiers must adhere to language constraints. For example, identifiers can't start with numbers, use whitespace, or be a reserved word in the language. On the other hand, because bracket notation utilizes string values, it allows for the use of characters that otherwise would be a violation of the syntax. One such example is shown in Listing 2-4.

Listing 2-4. Comparing Notations

```
var aBracketNotationCollectionA = new Object();
    aBracketNotationCollectionA['1']="1";    // creates a key of "1" and assigns it the
                                                string value '1'
var aDotNotationCollectionB = new Object();
    aDotNotationCollectionB.1="1";           // throws a SyntaxError
```

Array

Because a collection retains a value for a given key, a value is obtained directly by referencing its key. Thus, the key is the sole conduit through which a value is reached. For this reason, the Object is known as an unordered collection. The Array is a specialized descendant of the JavaScript Object, which, on the other hand, seeks to provide an order among values.

What makes the Array special is that its collective behaviors allow for cataloging of data as an ordered list. In order to accomplish this, the Array employs the use of numbers to stand in as the key for any key/value pair. As you may have already surmised, because numbers are involved, rather than relying on dot notation, an Array requires none other than bracket notation. Listing 2-5 demonstrates the use of the array to devise an ordered collection set.

Listing 2-5. An Ordered List of the Days of the Week

```
var orderedCollection = new Array(); //instantiate an array instance
    orderedCollection[0] = 'Sunday';
    orderedCollection[1] = 'Monday';
    orderedCollection[2] = 'Tuesday';
    orderedCollection[3] = 'Wednesday';
    orderedCollection[4] = 'Thursday';
    orderedCollection[5] = 'Friday';
    orderedCollection[6] = 'Saturday';
```

As revealed by Listing 2-5, the days of the week are assigned as the value to a key, similar to an object. The difference in this case is that an Array employs bracket notation to allow for its properties to be specified as integers. With each key identified as a sequence of integers, values can be obtained in the precise order in which they are cataloged. The simplest way to obtain each value sequentially is with a for loop, as shown in Listing 2-6.

Listing 2-6. A for Loop Is Used to Read from an Ordered List

```
var daysOfTheWeek = 7;
for(var i=0; i<daysOfTheWeek; i++) console.log( orderedCollection[i] );
```

If you were to run Listing 2-6, you would undoubtedly see the days of the week printed to the console tab within the developer's toolbar. Furthermore, they would be output in the order they are assigned.

As was stated earlier, JavaScript objects are collections of string/value pairs. Although the keys of an array are numerical, behind the scenes each integer is coerced into its string representation.

As a descendant of the Object, all instances of the array possess an inherit toString method. Unlike the default value output earlier, our array instance provides a more appropriate value upon invocation, as seen in Listing 2-7.

Listing 2-7. Demonstrating the String Representation of an array

```
var orderedCollection = new Array();           //instantiate an array instance
    orderedCollection[0] = 'Sunday';
    orderedCollection[1] = 'Monday';
    orderedCollection[2] = 'Tuesday';
console.log(orderedCollection.toString());  // "Sunday,Monday,Tuesday"
```

As demonstrated in Listing 2-7, the `toString` implementation results in the joining of all user-defined values possessed by the collection in a comma-delimited string. Because our collection is ordered, the values within the returned string reflect their index within the collection.

Object Literals

Both the Array and the Object can be instantiated via the keyword new. Once either instance is created, key/value pairs can be assigned accordingly. That being said, both the Array and Object are capable of being configured without this syntactical overhead. To better illustrate this point, take a look at Listing 2-8.

Listing 2-8. Object Literals Can Be Designed with Members

```
var array= ["Sunday","Monday","Tuesday","Wednesday","Thursday","Friday","Saturday"];
    console.log( array[0] );    //outputs "Sunday"

var object= { firstProperty: "hello world" };
    console.log( object.firstProperty );    //outputs "hello world"
```

Listing 2-8 creates two object literals. The first represents the instance of the Array, while the latter represents an instance of the Object. For all intents and purposes, an object literal is just another way to arrive at an instantiated object.

While it may not appear to be the case, the instantiation of an object literal and the instantiation of an object via the keyword new create objects similarly. The most significant difference is that literals can be instantiated with a preconfigured collection of key/values pairs. Literals are referred to as such because they are instantiated as they are designed.

Utilizing this technique, we can assign key/value pairs to the object prior to its instantiation. One immediate benefit is that key/value pairs are more identifiable without the added dot/bracket notation. A second benefit is that complex collections and their structures can be defined prior to the existence of other instances. To better understand the preceding statement, consider the following complex collection in Listing 2-9.

Listing 2-9. undefined Assignment of `internalObject`

```
 1 var externalObject = new Object();
 2     externalObject.child = internalObject;
 3 var internalObject = new Array();
 4     internalObject[0] = 'Sunday';
 5     internalObject[1] = 'Monday';
 6     internalObject[2] = 'Tuesday';
 7     internalObject[3] = 'Wednesday';
 8     internalObject[4] = 'Thursday';
 9     internalObject[5] = 'Friday';
10     internalObject[6] = 'Saturday';
11
12 console.log(externalObject.child);    // outputs undefined
```

Listing 2-9 instantiates an instance of the Object and Array. As you can see, the object instance is assigned as the value to externalObject (**line 1**). Conversely, the array instance is assigned to the variable labeled internalObject (**line 3**). Because a property can be assigned any valid type in JavaScript, we will devise a complex structure where our object instance possesses a direct reference to our array instance. Used to represent this relationship is the identifier labeled child (**line 2**).

As it currently stands, externalObject.child does not possess a reference to internalObject. This is made evident by the undefined value that is printed in the console (**line 12**). The reason the value is not assigned is simply due to the fact that internalObject was undefined at the time of its assignment to externalObject.child (**line 2**). Correcting the matter in this particular example is as simple as moving the code within line 2 down to line 11, as seen in Listing 2-10.

Listing 2-10. Moved Assignment of Instance Creation

```
1 var externalObject = new Object();
2
3 var internalObject = new Array();
4    internalObject[0] = 'Sunday';
5    internalObject[1] = 'Monday';
6    internalObject[2] = 'Tuesday';
7    internalObject[3] = 'Wednesday';
8    internalObject[4] = 'Thursday';
9    internalObject[5] = 'Friday';
10   internalObject[6] = 'Saturday';
11   externalObject.child = internalObject;
12 console.log(externalObject.child);   // outputs our array as expected
```

Listing 2-10 reflects in **bold** our changes. Moving the order in which our child property is assigned does, in fact, solve our issue. Unfortunately, this reorganization of code actually decreases the continuity of keeping code organized and can soon become a maintenance nightmare. In this case, our code was subject to function vs. form, not the other way around.

A second alternative is to swap altogether the order in which both instances are created, as seen in Listing 2-11.

Listing 2-11. Reordering of Instantiations

```
1 var internalObject = new Array();
2    internalObject[0] = 'Sunday';
3    internalObject[1] = 'Monday';
4    internalObject[2] = 'Tuesday';
5    internalObject[3] = 'Wednesday';
6    internalObject[4] = 'Thursday';
7    internalObject[5] = 'Friday';
8    internalObject[6] = 'Saturday';
9 var externalObject = new Object();
10    externalObject.child = internalObject;
11
12 console.log(externalObject.child);   // outputs our array as expected
```

Listing 2-11 has solved our dilemma in the most ideal way that the new keyword can provide. Because new instantiates bare objects, you may find yourself having to resort to reordering code simply to assign key/value pairs. This is where object literals can truly shine.

Because collections can be preconfigured using literal syntax, creating nested collections is as simple as designing them. When the engine evaluates the literal, each nested collection is instantiated on demand. The end result is the same, as made evident by the output on line 4 of Listing 2-12.

Listing 2-12. Object Literals Are Created As They Are Evaluated

```
1 var externalObject = {
2         child: ["Sunday", "Monday", "Tuesday", "Wednesday", "Thursday", "Friday",
          "Saturday"]
3     };
4 console.log(externalObject.child);       // outputs our array as expected
5 console.log(externalObject.toString());  // [object Object]
```

Listing 2-12 employs the literal syntax of the object and array to configure the key/value pairs for two individual collections. Furthermore, because all literals are instantiated into objects, they are bestowed with any and all inherited behaviors. This accounts for the ability to reference the toString method of externalObject.

■ **Note**   All literals in the JavaScript language are instantiated behind the scenes.

Designing Literals

Because both Array and Object are collections of key/value pairs, the term *designing literals* simply refers to the incorporation of key/value pairs at author time. Depending on whether the literal is that of an object vs. an array, the syntax used to design a literal will vary.

The Object Literal

The syntax used to delimit an object literal is the use of the opening and closing brace ({, }) symbols. When the JavaScript engine encounters an assignment of a variable that employs the aforementioned delimiters, behind the scenes, an instance of the Object type is instantiated and returned. Listing 2-13 employs the object literal syntax to create an object instance.

Listing 2-13. Syntactical Representation of an Object Literal

```
1 var emptyObject = { };
    console.log(emptyObject.toString());  // [object Object]
```

What is important to note is that the assignment operation informs the engine to evaluate the brackets as an object literal rather than that of a statement. This is necessary as a block statement employs the use of the same tokens to delimit a block of statements.

Currently our object literal remains absent of any key/value pairs and thus will be instantiated at runtime without any custom behaviors. However this can be easily changed, as seen in Listing 2-14.

Listing 2-14. Object Literal with a Key/Value Pair

```
var literalObject = {
       firstProperty:"hello world"
    };
console.log(literalObject.firstProperty ); // "hello world"
```

As revealed by Listing 2-14, a key/value pair is configured by specifying an identifier along with its value separated by a colon (:) token. Listing 2-14 demonstrates how firstProperty is assigned the value "hello world" with literal syntax. Additionally, literals can be designed with multiple key/value pairs. Each key/value pair must remain separate from one another. This is achieved by separating each key/value pair with a comma (,). Listing 2-15 outlines an object literal that possesses three key/value pairs.

Listing 2-15. Object Literal Designed with Multiple Key/Value Pairs

```
var literalObject = {
       firstProperty : "hello world",
       name          : "iObjectA",
       toString      : function(){ return this.name; }
    };
console.log( literalObject.toString() ); // "iObjectA"
```

Listing 2-15 revisits our previous object literal from Listing 2-14. This time instead of configuring a singular key/value pair, it defines three. Note the use of the commas to separate each key/value pair. Lastly, one thing to note is that the toString method is assigned with a function that explicitly returns the name property. The use of this ensures that the identifier being referenced remains scoped to the context of our instance. Use of this is necessary because the built-in Object does not possess a name property, only our literalObject. Therefore, we must ensure the scope remains relevant to the instance invoking the behavior.

The Array Literal

The syntax used to delimit an array literal is the use of the opening and closing bracket ([,]) symbols. When the JavaScript engine encounters an assignment of a variable that employs the aforementioned delimiters, behind the scenes an instance of the Array type is instantiated and returned. Listing 2-16 employs the array literal syntax to create an empty instance of the Array type.

Listing 2-16. Syntactical Representation of an array Literal

```
var literalArray = [];
```

Currently, our literal remains absent of any key/value pairs and, thus, will be instantiated at runtime without any custom behaviors. However, this can be easily changed, as seen in Listing 2-17.

Listing 2-17. array Literal Designed with a Key/Value Pair

```
var literalArray = ["hello world"];
```

Listing 2-17 reveals an array literal that's in possession of a singular string value. You may notice that the key for which this string value is assigned appears to be missing. In fact, it is not missing at all. As you may recall, the Array represents an ordered collection. This means that each value supplied is implicitly provided an index key. In other words, when our literalArray is instantiated as an object at runtime, we can use the 0 integer and bracket notation to access "hello world", as shown in Listing 2-18.

Listing 2-18. Array Literal Value Obtainable via Bracket Notation

```
var literalArray = ["hello world"];
console.log(literalArray[0]);  // hello world
```

As with the object literal syntax, multiple values can be supplied to an ordered collection by separating multiple values with a comma, as shown in Listing 2-19. Each value is implicitly provided the next available index as its key.

Listing 2-19. Array Literal Designed with Multiple Key/Value Pairs

```
var literalArray = ["hello world","goodbye world"];
console.log(literalArray[0]);  // hello world
console.log(literalArray[1]);  // goodbye world
```

Summary

This chapter provided the fundamentals for working with JavaScript objects. Objects are of great importance not only to the language itself, but to JSON as well.

Key Points from This Chapter

- Absolutely everything is an object.
- All classifications in their most generalized form are objects.
- *Object* and *object* have two different meanings.
- *Object* (with an initial capital letter) refers to the JavaScript Object type.
- An object refers to an instance.
- objects are collections.
- Special Objects are collections of like-minded behaviors.
- All instances implicitly possess their ancestors' behaviors.
- toString returns the string representation of an object.
- new is used to create instances of a non-primitive value.
- Dot notation relies on identifiers.
- Bracket notation relies on strings.
- Objects are unordered collections.
- Arrays are ordered collections.
- Literals can be instantiated with predefined key/value pairs.
- All literals are instantiated via objects behind the scenes.
- this is used to maintain the scope of the property being accessed.

CHAPTER 3

String Manipulation

As I mentioned in Chapter 1, a JavaScript application is written entirely as a sequence of Unicode characters. This is not at all a feature exclusive to the JavaScript language. Other examples are HTML and CSS, to name just a few. Even the underlying protocol used by the World Wide Web is an entirely text-based communications protocol.

Data is often transmitted in the form of text, as it's highly interoperable. This is due to the fact that all computers have the ability to work with Unicode. One attribute that makes JSON highly interoperable is that it's composed of, and transmitted simply as, Unicode. For this reason, this book will work extensively with the creation, formation, and general manipulation of strings designed for both inbound and outbound traffic.

String Concatenation

The incorporation of the string literal makes creating strings an absolute cinch. As you may recall from Chapter 1, a string value represents a sequence of 0 or more finite Unicode characters. The reason why the definition of a string contains the word *finite* is due to the fact that JavaScript strings are immutable. In other words, a string's value is a constant. While strings themselves are immutable, entirely new strings can be created simply by joining two strings together end-to-end, using the addition operator, as shown in Listing 3-1.

Listing 3-1. Joining Strings

```
1 var str = "Hello" + " World";
2 console.log( str );  //Hello World
```

Listing 3-1 demonstrates the union between the two string literals, Hello and World, via the addition operator (**line 1**). The result of the union will be that of Hello World. This joining of strings, known as *string concatenation*, is the language's simplest means of string manipulation. It is the concatenation of strings, which invites our application to build strings on the fly.

While concatenation is solely limited to strings, we can use the addition operator to coerce primitive values into their string representations. This offers our application the ability to capture its state as a singular string value, which can later be transmitted across the Internet. Consider the demonstration in Listing 3-2.

Listing 3-2. Formatting Data

```
1 var userName = "Ben";
2 var clickedButton = false;
3 var stringRepresentation = "username="+userName +"&clickedButton=" + clickedButton;
4 console.log( stringRepresentation);  // "username=Ben&clickedButton=false"
```

Listing 3-2 employs the use of the addition operator to convert and append the existing state of an application into that of a string value. This results in the production of a string containing the Unicode characters that read as `"username=Ben&clickedButton=false"`.

The way in which our data is represented is referred to as a data format. It is the purpose of the data format to provide a structure that infers the meaning of all concatenated values. Relying on a lesser-known data format makes it difficult for the recipient to extract or analyze the individual values. This book will regard a variety of data formats similar to the preceding one, as well as JSON.

The String Object

The String object is a specialized object whose collective behaviors facilitate the manipulation of a string value. We will learn more of its behaviors in the upcoming sections.

Creating String Objects

Like all objects, a String object, is created using the keyword new followed by the constructor function of the object-type. As revealed by the syntax of the String's constructor, `String( string );`, each instance must be provided with a string value at the time of its instantiation. Listing 3-3 demonstrates the provision of the string literal "test".

Listing 3-3. Instantiating a String object

```
1 var strObject = new String( "test" );
2 console.log( strObject ) ;   //String { 0="t", 1="e", 2="s", 3="t" }
```

To keep things succinct, the string object in Listing 3-3 is provided with a string literal. However, it could have just as easily been supplied an identifier that evaluates to a string value. Upon the instance's creation, the string object is returned and assigned to the strObject variable (**line 1**). As the assignment to a variable, we can continue to reference it and its many behaviors.

As revealed by the subsequent line (**line 2**), logging out the reference to our instance shows that the provided string is no longer retained in its original form. Instead, each character of the provided string has been separated and cataloged within our collection. Exploding the string into the individual characters of which it was composed becomes the foundation from which all manipulation occurs.

The Interface of the String Object

As outlined in Table 3-1, the interface of the String object offers a wide range of utility. Furthermore, it is inheritied by each instance to allow for the manipulation and formatting of the string value for which it is provided.

Table 3-1. *String object's Interface*

Properties	Type	Description
length	Property	Returns the length of the string
toString	Method	Returns a string representation of the collection
charAt	Method	Returns the character at the specified index
indexOf	Method	Returns the position of the first occurrence of a substring
lastIndexOf	Method	Returns the last occurrence of a substring
match	Method	Matches a string with a pattern and returns all matches as an array
replace	Method	Replaces text in a string
slice	Method	Returns a section of a string, as indicated by a range
substr	Method	Returns a substring, as indicated by a start index, through a specified length
split	Method	Splits a string into substrings, using the specified separator, and returns them as an array
toUpperCase	Method	Converts all characters in the string to uppercase
toLowerCase	Method	Converts all characters in the string to lowercase

■ **Note** A substring can be a singular character or a sequence of characters.

length

The length member is the only behavior that is not a method. The sole purpose of the length property is to obtain an accurate count of how many characters are retained within the collection. Both forms of access notation can access the length member, as well as those outlined in Table 3-1. Listing 3-4 makes use of dot notation.

Listing 3-4. Obtaining a String's Length

```
1 var str = "test";
2 var strObject = new String( str );
3 console.log( strObject ) ;   //String { 0="t", 1="e", 2="s", 3="t" }
4 console.log( strObject.length );   // 4
```

Listing 3-4 begins by assigning the string literal "test" to the str variable (**line 1**). Next, we instantiate a string object and provide our str variable as the argument. The instance is then assigned as the reference to strObject (**line 2**). Utilizing our reference, we print its contents to the console (**line 3**). Last, utilizing the dot notation, we access the length property and print the resulting value to the console (**line 4**).

As you can see in Listing 3-4, the access of length results in the return of the amount of characters used to devise the original string. Understanding the total character count will be a great benefit when manipulating an ordered sequence of characters.

toString

The `toString` method, whose signature is that of `toString();`, is used to return the string representation of the value possessed by our collection. It is worth noting that the `toString` method does not return a string object, but rather the primitive-type string.

charAt

The `charAt` method, whose signature is that of `charAt( index );`, is used to return the cataloged character whose key matches the specified index. As the string object represents an ordered collection of characters, the first character's index is always 0. Obtaining a character is as simple as providing an index to the method, as seen in Listing 3-5.

Listing 3-5. Obtaining Unicode Characters

```
var str = "Hello World";
var strObject = new String( str );
console.log( strObject.charAt( 0 )); // H
console.log( strObject.charAt( 1 )); // e
console.log( strObject.charAt( 2 )); // l
```

■ **Note** As an ordered collection, the returned value of `length` -1 will always be the index to the last character in the collection.

By pairing the `charAt` and the `length` property, we can automate our efforts by way of a `for` loop, as seen in Listing 3-6.

Listing 3-6. Iterating Through a String's Characters

```
1 var str = "Hello World";
2 var strObject = new String( str );
3 var length = strObject.length;
4 for(var i=0; i<length; i++)  console.log( strObject.charAt(i) );
```

Listing 3-6 uses a `for` loop to print each sequential character (**line 3**). The loop begins with an initial variable, `i`, which is assigned the value of 0. In order to ensure that all characters are evaluated, the condition for the loop determines whether the current value of `i` is less than the total length of characters in the collection. As long as this condition evaluates to `true`, our statement is executed, and the post-operation increments `i` by a value of 1.

indexOf

While the `charAt` method aims to return a character at the specified index, the `indexOf` method provides the inverse behavior. Instead of supplying an index to obtain its corresponding character, the `indexOf` enables you to obtain the index whereby the first use of a specified subset occurs. Its signature, `indexOf(subString[, startIndex]);`, reveals that the method anticipates a possible two arguments. The first represents the `subString`, whose index we seek, while the second parameter, `startIndex`, represents an offset from which the search should begin. Because the startIndex is optional, we will only focus on the required parameter. (See Listing 3-7.)

Listing 3-7. Obtaining the First Location for a Substring

```
1 var str = "Hello World";
2 var strObject = new String( str );
3 console.log( strObject.indexOf( "H" )); // 0
```

Listing 3-7 relies on indexOf to obtain the location for the first determined substring, "H", within our string value (**line 3**). As you may have expected, the result returned and output to the console is 0. It's worth stressing that indexOf only returns the index of the first determined substring. Therefore, if the substring used happens to occur more than once in the collection, only the location of the first occurrence will be returned, as shown in Listing 3-8.

Listing 3-8. The Index of the First Matched Character 'l' is Returned

```
1 var str = "Hello World";
2 var strObject = new String( str );
3 console.log( strObject.indexOf( "l" )); // 2
```

If a sought substring does not exist within the collection, the resulting index will be that of -1. Because our ordered list can only possess a positive sequence of numbers, the evaluation of -1 offers our application the ability to determine whether or not an operation should take place via a control statement, as seen in Listing 3-9.

Listing 3-9. If the Index of -1 is Returned, the Substring is Not Present

```
1 var str = "Hello World";
2 var strObject = new String(str);
3 var index = strObject.indexOf(";");
4 if(index>-1)   //perform operation
5 else console.log("substring does not occur");
```

As shown in Listing 3-9, we can incorporate the value returned by indexOf to control the flow of our application. Listing 3-9 uses a conditional operation to determine whether the index returned is greater than -1. This signifies to our application that our collection possesses the substring being sought after, resulting in some unknown operation being performed. However, if the condition is not met, the application prints to the console "substring does not occur".

It's worth stressing that indexOf accepts multiple characters. The preceding listings have only supplied a singular character. In addition to working with individual characters, indexOf can determine the starting index for a sequence of characters. This will be very beneficial when attempting to obtain the location of a substring that has multiple occurrences. Consider an example in which we are required to find a particular occurrence in a phrase that relies on repetition. (See Listing 3-10.)

Listing 3-10. The Index of the First Matched Substring is Returned

```
1 var str = "side beside besides the ocean";
2 var strObject = new String(str);
3 var index = strObject.indexOf("side");
4 if(index>-1) console.log(index);   // 0
5 else console.log("substring does not occur");
```

lastIndexOf

While the indexOf method returns the index of the first found occurrence, lastIndexOf returns the index of the last found occurrence of a substring. Similarly, if the string does not possess the provided substring, -1 is returned as the result.

The method's signature, lastIndexOf(subString[, startIndex]);, is equal to that of indexOf. It expects at most two arguments; however, this book only employs the first. Listing 3-11 demonstrates how we can obtain the starting index for the last occurrence of "side" in our previous string.

Listing 3-11. Locating the Index of the Last Matched Substring

```
1 var str = "side beside besides the ocean";
2 var strObject = new String(str);
3 var index = strObject.lastIndexOf("side");
4 if(index>-1) console.log(index);   //14
5 else console.log("substring does not occur");
```

match

The match method, whose signature is match(pattern);, is used to locate character patterns within a string. An invocation of the match accepts a string value or a regular expression and returns an array containing all matched substrings of said search. Listing 3-12 demonstrates the provision of both parameters to the method.

Listing 3-12. Obtaining Matched Substrings

```
1 var str = "username=Ben&clickedButton=false";
2 var strObject = new String(str);
3 var stringMatches = strObject.match("username");
4 console.log(stringMatches);   // ["username"]
5 var patternMatches = strObject.match( /[^&]+/g );
6 console.log(patternMatches);  // ["username=Ben", "clickedButton=false"]
```

Listing 3-12 begins by assigning a formatted string to the str variable (**line 1**). From there, we provide it as the value to initialize our instance (**line 2**).

From there, the string "username" is provided as the pattern to locate within our string (**line 3**). This results in the return of an array containing all found matches. The array returned reveals that it has, in fact, located a match (**line 4**). Alternatively, we employ a regular expression pattern to locate any and all series of characters that do not possess the & token (**line 5**). The array returned reveals that is has, in fact, located two matches (**line 6**).

replace

The replace method, whose signature is replace(pattern, replaceText);, can be used to exchange a matching substring with that of another. Whether or not a match is found, the method will result in the return of a string value. Listing 3-13 utilizes the replace method to substitute all found occurrences of the substring "Hello" with that of "Goodbye".

Listing 3-13. Replacing Matched Substrings

```
1 var str = "Hello World";
2 var strObject = new String( str );
3 var result = strObject.replace( "Hello", "Goodbye" );
4 console.log( result );     //Goodbye World
5 console.log( strObject ); //String { 0="H", 1="e", 2="l", 3="l", 4="o", 5=" ",
  ...//truncated }
```

Listing 3-13 employs the `replace` method in order to substitute the substring "Goodbye" for all determined occurrences of the substring "Hello". You may note that I assign the resulting string to a variable labeled `result` (**line 3**). Because strings are immutable, meaning they cannot be altered, the result of the behavior produces an entirely new string. It does not attempt to alter the variable it was initially supplied. Furthermore, as illustrated on line 5, use of the behaviors possessed by our string object will not alter the initial characters cataloged by the collection.

■ **Note**   All strings returned by the methods of a string object are the creation of a new string.

---

slice

The `slice` method is used to return a substring of the collection determined by a range of indexes. The method, as revealed by its signature, `replace(start, [end]);`, requires a starting index and an optional ending index. All characters located at the starting index and up to, but not including, the ending index will be returned to the caller of the method. If the end index is not specified, the substring reflects every subsequent character beyond the starting index. Listing 3-14 demonstrates how we can extract the word *Hello* from our string literal by utilizing the `slice` method.

Listing 3-14. Extracting Substrings with `slice`

```
1 var str = 'Hello World';
2 var strObject = new String(str);
3 var index = strObject.indexOf('o'); //4;
4 var result = strObject.slice(0, index);
5 console.log(result); //Hell
6 console.log(strObject.slice(0, index + 1)); //Hello
```

Listing 3-14 demonstrates the extraction of the word *Hello* from our string with the use of the `slice` method. Because we know that *Hello* begins at index 0, we simply have to determine which index is used to signify the boundary of our substring. It is important to note that `slice` returns the sequence of characters from the start index up to, but not including, the ending index. This is why line 4 outputs `Hell` rather than `Hello`.

Because the returned substring will always be one character less than that specified, the supplied index must always reflect one position more than we seek to obtain. The solution is to add 1 to the determined index (**line 6**).

substr

The substr method is used to return a substring within a specific range. The substr method is similar to the slice method in that it can be used to obtain a substring within a given boundary. As depicted by the signature substr(start [, length]);, the substr method can accept two parameters; however, only the first is required.

The required parameter, start, signifies where the substring to extract begins. This value can be followed by an optional number of characters to include in the returned substring. The key difference between substr and slice is that the length does not indicate an index. Instead, it indicates the total number of characters (including the character at the specified start) to return in the substring. Listing 3-15 demonstrates how we can extract the word *World* from the string, utilizing the substr method.

Listing 3-15. Extracting Substrings with substr

```
1 var str = 'Hello World';
2 var strObject = new String(str);
3 var startIndex = strObject.indexOf('W'); //6;
4 var length = (new String('World')).length; //4
5 var result = strObject.substr(startIndex, length );
6 console.log(result); //World
```

Listing 3-15 begins by obtaining the starting index for our substring, 'World' (**line 3**). Once we have obtained its index, we can supply it to our substr method as the starting index. Additionally, we can provide an optional number of characters, which will determine how many subsequent characters beyond the starting point to be returned.

In this case, I have opted to supply the length of characters possessed by the substring 'World'. This is achieved by creating a second string object, supplying it with the string 'World', and obtaining its character count by way of the length attribute (**line 4**). This value is then supplied as the argument that identifies the total length of characters to include in the substring (**line 5**).

▪ **Note** If the optional parameter length is omitted, all characters, from the start index to the end of the string, will be returned.

---

split

The split method is used to split a string into substrings and return them as the values of an array. As revealed by the method's signature split(separator[, limit]);, the method expects to receive at most two arguments. The first argument, labeled separator, is required, while the latter argument, limit, remains optional. This book will only make use of the separator parameter. The separator argument is used to define the delimiters that define the boundaries of substrings captured within the provided string. Listing 3-16 contains one such string, whereby substrings are delimited by way of an ordinary comma.

Listing 3-16. Separating a Comma-Delimited String

```
1 var strObject = new String('ben,mike,ivan,kyle');
2 console.log( strObject.split(',') );  // ['ben','mike','ivan','kyle']
```

Listing 3-16 instantiates a string object and supplies it with a comma-delimited list of names (**line 1**). Next, we invoke the split method and supply it with the substring used to separate each name. In this particular case, that substring is a comma, resulting in the return of an ordered collection of all names (**line 2**).

toUpperCase

The toUpperCase method is used to convert all characters within a string to uppercase. The method does not accept any parameters, and it will be applied to an entire string, as seen in Listing 3-17.

Listing 3-17. Capitalizing All Alphabetic Characters

```
1 var strObject = new String( 'Hello World' );
2 console.log( strObject.toUpperCase() );  // HELLO WORLD
```

toLowerCase

Conversely, unlike the toUpperCase method, the toLowerCase method is used to convert all alphabetic characters within a string to lowercase, as seen in Listing 3-18.

Listing 3-18. Applying Lowercase to All Alphabetic Characters

```
1 var strObject = new String( 'Hello World' );
2 console.log( strObject.toLowerCase() );  // hello world
```

Aside from the obvious use for the toUpperCase and toLowerCase methods, there is yet another reason they will be used throughout this book. When working with text, the use of capitalization or lack thereof is to be expected. However, this makes it difficult to compare two strings within a language that is case-sensitive. Listing 3-19 compares strings that will always fail, due to the inconsistent use of letter casing.

Listing 3-19. Comparisons Are Case-Sensitive

```
1 console.log('Hello World' === 'hello world' ); //false
2 console.log('Hello world' === 'hello world' ); //false
3 console.log('HELLO WORLD' === 'Hello World' ); //false
```

While the characters used in both words may appear equal to us, they are definitely not viewed as the same by a computer. This is because computers view uppercase and lowercase letters as different Unicode values. Therefore, to ensure that casing is not an issue during the comparison of strings, we will often use toUpperCase and toLowerCase before comparing them.

The Implicit String Object

The preceding listings make explicit use of the string object, in order to tap into its many behaviors. While a string object adds great value, it comes at the cost of its syntactical overhead. Consider Listing 3-4, which required the instantiation of a string object simply to obtain the length of characters used to devise a string. To ease this burden for developers, the JavaScript language does, in fact, offer us the best of both worlds.

As mentioned in Chapter 1, primitive values are not objects and, therefore, cannot possibly possess key/value pairs. Any attempt to access a property of a string, or any primitive type for that matter, would ordinarily throw a SyntaxError. However, JavaScript seeks to reduce the syntactical overhead by allowing the behaviors of the string object to be accessed through a primitive string via access notation. Doing so prompts the engine to instantiate a string object on our behalf, using the target string as its argument. Once the instance is created, the accessed behavior is fulfilled by the instance itself. Listing 3-20 demonstrates how the interface of the string object can be accessed indirectly through a string value.

Listing 3-20. Implicit Use of the String object

```
1 var strLiteral = 'Hello World';
2 console.log( strLiteral.toLowerCase() );  // hello world
3 console.log( strLiteral.length );  // 11
4 console.log( strLiteral.substr(0 , 5 ));  // Hello
```

Listing 3-20 begins by assigning the string literal 'Hello World' to the variable strLiteral (**line 1**). From there, each subsequent line of code relies on dot notation to reference a behavior of the string object. Because the engine recognizes that a string does not possess any attributes, behind the scenes, it instantiates a string object, supplies it with the value of strLiteral, and returns the resulting value. The result is precisely the same as if we instantiated the string object ourselves, only without the syntactical overhead. For this reason, you should never have to instantiate a string object directly.

Summary

This chapter has introduced you to the behaviors of the String object, which will be employed extensively in the upcoming chapters. Each behavior covered offers our applications the necessary ability to work extensively with strings.

When it comes to string manipulation, you will find that there is no right way or wrong way to get something done. It's as the old adage goes, "There is more than one way to skin a cat."

Key Points from This Chapter

- There is a corresponding object for each primitive type.
- A data format refers to the way data is assembled.
- The addition operator is used to capture application logic within a string.
- The string primitive has pseudo members that can be accessed with access notation.
- The behaviors of the string object can be used indirectly.
- The HTTP protocol transmits text.
- The comparison between strings does not ignore case.
- Manipulating a string does not alter the original.

CHAPTER 4

Introducing JSON

The JavaScript Object Notation data format, or JSON for short, is derived from the literals of the JavaScript programming language. This makes JSON a subset of the JavaScript language. As a subset, JSON does not possess any additional features that the JavaScript language itself does not already possess. Although JSON is a subset of a programming language, it itself is not a programming language but, in fact, a data interchange format.

JSON is known as the data interchange standard, which subtextually implies that it can be used as the data format wherever the exchange of data occurs. A data exchange can occur between both browser and server and even server to server, for that matter. Of course, these are not the only possible means to exchange JSON, and to leave it at those two would be rather limiting.

History

JSON is attributed to being the creation of Douglas Crockford. While Crockford admits that he is not the first to have realized the data format,[1] he did provide it with a name and a formalized grammar within RFC 4627. The RFC 4627 formalization, written in 2006, introduced the world to the registered Internet media type application/json, the file extension .json, and defines JSON's composition. In December 2009, JSON was officially recognized as an ECMA standard, ECMA-404, and is now a built-in aspect of the standardization of ECMAScript-262, 5th edition.

Controversially, another Internet working group, the Internet Engineering Task Force (IETF), has also recently published its own JSON standard, RFC 7159, which strives to clean up the original specification. The major difference between the two standards is that RFC 7159 states that a valid JSON text must encompass any valid JSON values within an initial object or an array, whereas the ECMA standard suggests that a valid JSON text can appear in the form of any recognized JSON value. You will learn more about the valid JSON values when we explore the structure of JSON.

It is important to remember, as we get further into the structure of JSON, that as a subset of JavaScript, it remains subject to the same set of governing rules defined by the ECMA-262 standardization. You can feel free to read about the latest specification at the following URL: www.ecma-international.org/publications/files/ECMA-ST/Ecma-262.pdf. At the time of writing, the current edition of the ECMA-262 standard is 5.1; however, 6 is just around the corner.

Note While edition 5.1 is today's current standard, at the time of JSON's formalization, the ECMA-262 standard was only in edition 3.

---

[1]http://yuiblog.com/yuitheater/crockford-json.m4v.

Crockford documented JSON's grammar on http://json.org in 2001, and soon word began to spread that there was an alternative to the XML data format. With the widespread adoption of Ajax (Asynchronous JavaScript and XML), JSON's popularity began to soar, as people began to note its ease of implementation and how it rivaled that of XML. You would think that Ajax would have enforced the adoption of XML, as the *x* within the acronym strictly refers to XML. However, being modeled after SGML, a document format, XML possesses qualities that make it very verbose, which is not ideal for data transmission. One of the reasons JSON has become the de facto data format of the Web, as you will shortly see in the upcoming section, is due to its grammatical simplicity, which allows for JSON to be highly interoperable.

JSON Grammar

JSON, in a nutshell, is a textual representation defined by a small set of governing rules in which data is structured. The JSON specification states that data can be structured in either of the two following compositions:

1. A collection of name/value pairs

2. An ordered list of values

Composite Structures

As the origins of JSON stem from the ECMAScript standardization, the implementations of the two structures are represented in the forms of the object and array. Crockford outlines the two structural representations of JSON through a series of syntax diagrams. As I am sure you will agree, these diagrams resemble train tracks from a bird's-eye view and thus are also referred to as *railroad diagrams*. Figure 4-1 illustrates the grammatical representation for a collection of string/value pairs.

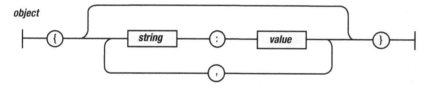

Figure 4-1. *Syntax diagram of a string/value pair collection*

As the diagram outlines, a collection begins with the use of the opening brace ({), and ends with the use of the closing brace (}). The content of the collection can be composed of any of the following possible three designated paths:

- The top path illustrates that the collection can remain devoid of any string/value pairs.

- The middle path illustrates that our collection can be that of a single string/value pair.

- The bottom path illustrates that after a single string/value pair is supplied, the collection needn't end but, rather, allow for any number of string/value pairs, before reaching the end. Each string/value pair possessed by the collection must be delimited or separated from one another by way of a comma (,).

■ **Note** String/value is equivalent to key/value pairs, with the exception that said keys must be provided as strings.

An example of each railroad path for a collection of string/value can be viewed within Listing 4-1. The structural characters that identify a valid JSON collection of name/value pairs have been provided emphasis.

Listing 4-1. Examples of Valid Representations of a Collection of Key/Value Pairs, per JSON Grammar

```
//Empty Collection Set
{};
//Single string/value pair
{"abc":"123"};
//Multiple string/value pairs
{"captainsLog":"starDate 9522.6","message":"I've never trusted Klingons, and I never
will."};
```

Figure 4-2 illustrates the grammatical representation for that of an ordered list of values. Here we can witness that an ordered list begins with the use of the open bracket ([) and ends with the use of the close bracket (]).

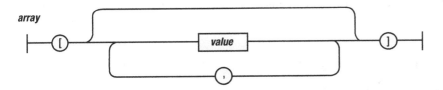

Figure 4-2. Syntax diagram of an ordered list

The values that can be held within each index are outlined by the following three "railroad" paths:

- The top path illustrates that our list can remain devoid of any value(s).

- The middle path illustrates that our ordered list can possess a singular value.

- The bottom path illustrates that the length of our list can possess any number of values, which must be delimited, that is, separated, with the use of a comma (,).

An example of each railroad path for the ordered list can be viewed within Listing 4-2. The structural tokens that identify a valid JSON ordered list have been emphasized.

Listing 4-2. Examples of Valid Representations of an Ordered List, per JSON Grammar

```
//Empty Ordered List
[];
//Ordered List of multiple values
["abc"];
//Ordered List of multiple values
["0",1,2,3,4,100];
```

You may have found yourself wondering how it came to be that the characters **[**, **]**, **{**, and **}** represent an array and an object, as illustrated in Listing 4-1 and Listing 4-2. The answer is quite simple. These come directly from the JavaScript language itself. These characters represent the Object and Array quite literally.

As was stated in Chapter 2, both an object and an array can be created in one of two distinct fashions. The first invokes the creation of either, through the use of the constructor function defined by the built-in data type we wish to create. This style of object invocation can be seen in Listing 4-3.

Listing 4-3. Using the new Keyword to Instantiate an object and array

```
var objectInstantion   = new Object();  //invoking the constructor returns a new Object
var arrayInstantiation = new Array();  //invoking the constructor returns a new Array
```

The alternative manner, which we can use to create either object or array, is by *literally* defining the composition of either, as demonstrated in Listing 4-4.

Listing 4-4. Creation of an object and an array via Literal Notation

```
var objectInstantion   = {}; //creation of an empty object
var arrayInstantiation = []; //creation of an empty array
```

Listing 4-4 demonstrates how to create both an array and an object, explicitly using JavaScript's literal notation. However, both instances are absent of any values. While it is perfectly acceptable for an array or object to exist without content, it will be more likely that we will be working with ones that possess values.

Because object literals can be used to design the composition of objects within source code, they can also be provisioned with properties as they are authored. Listing 4-5 should begin to resemble the syntax diagrams we just reviewed.

Listing 4-5. Designing an object and array via Literal Notation with the Provision of Properties

```
var objectInstantion   = {name:"ben",age:36};
var arrayInstantiation = ["ben",36];
```

■ **Note** While Listing 4-4 and Listing 4-5 illustrate the creation of objects through the use of literals, JSON uses literals to capture the composition of data.

The JSON data format expresses both objects and arrays in the form of their literal. In fact, JSON uses literals to capture all JavaScript values, except for the Date object, as it lacks a literal form.

What you may not have noticed, due to its subtlety, is that JavaScript object literals do not require its key identifiers to be explicitly defined as strings. Take, for example, the literal declaration of {name:"ben", age:36}; from Listing 4-5. It could have equally been declared as {"name":"ben", age:36};. Both declarations will create the same object, allowing our program to reference the same name property equally. Consider the code within Listing 4-6.

Listing 4-6. Object Keys Can Be Defined Explicitly or Implicitly As Strings

```
var objectInstantionA   = {name:"ben",age:36};
var objectInstantionB   = {"name":"ben",age:36};
console.log( objectInstantionA.name );  // "ben"
console.log( objectInstantionB.name );  // "ben"
```

The reason the preceding example works is because, behind the scenes, JavaScript turns every key identifier into a string. That said, it is imperative that the key of every value pair be wrapped in double quotes to be considered valid JSON. This is due to the many reserved keywords in JSON's superset and the fact that ECMA 3.0 grammar prohibits the use of keywords as the properties held by an object. The ECMA 3.0 grammar does not allow reserved words (such as *true* and *false*) to be used as a key identifier or to the right of the period in a member expression.[2] Listing 4-7 demonstrates the first JSON text used to interchange data.[3]

Listing 4-7. The Very First JSON Message Used by Douglas Crockford

```
var firstJSON = {to:"session",do:"test","message":"Hello World"}; //Syntax Error in ECMA 3
```

However, this JSON text produced an error instantly, due to the use of the reserved keyword **do** as the property name of a string/value pair. Rather than outlining all words that would then cause such syntax errors, Crockford found it simpler to formalize that all property names must be explicitly expressed as strings.

■ **Note** If you were to reference the exact preceding code expecting to arrive at a syntax error, you'll likely be confused why none is thrown. The ECMAScript, 5th edition allows for keywords to now be used with dot notation. However the JSON spec continues to account for legacy.

JSON Values

As mentioned earlier, JSON is a subset of JavaScript and does not add anything that the JavaScript language does not possess. So, naturally, the values that can be utilized within our JSON structures are represented by types, as outlined within the 3rd edition of the ECMA standard. JSON makes use of four primitive types and two structured types.

The next figure in succession, Figure 4-3, defines the possible values that can be substituted where the term *value* appears in Figures 4-1 and 4-2. A JSON value can only be a representative of string, number, object, array, true, false, and null. The latter three must remain lowercased, lest you invoke a parsing error. While Figure 4-3 does not clearly demonstrate it, all JSON values can be preceded and succeeded by whitespace, which greatly assists in the readability of the language.

[2]Allen Wirfs-Brock, "ES 3.1 'true' as absolute or relative?" https://mail.mozilla.org/pipermail/es-discuss/2009-April/009119.html, April 9, 2009.
[3]http://yuiblog.com/assets/crockford-json.zip.

value

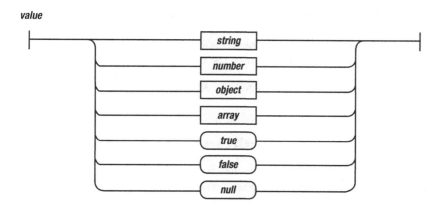

Figure 4-3. *Syntax diagram illustrating the possible values in JSON*

String literals in the JavaScript language can possess any number of Unicode characters enclosed within either single or double quotes. However, it will be important to note, as outlined in Figure 4-4, that a JSON string must always begin and end with the use of double quotes. While Crockford does not justify this, it is for interoperable reasons. The C programming grammar states that single quotes identify a single character, such as *a* or *z*. A double quote, on the other hand, represents a string literal. While Figure 4-4 appears verbose, there are only four possible paths.

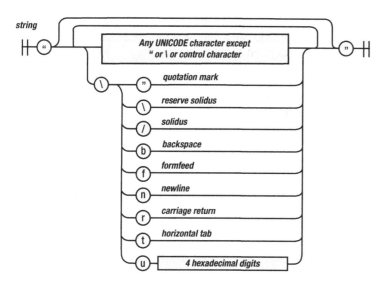

Figure 4-4. *Syntax diagram of the JSON string value*

- The topmost path illustrates that our string literal can be absent of any Unicode characters.

- The middle path illustrates that our string can possess any Unicode characters (represented in literal form), except for the following: the quotation mark, the backslash (solidus).

- The last several paths illustrate that we can insert into our string control characters with the use of a solidus (\)character preceding it. Additionally, the bottommost rung specifies that any character can be defined in its Unicode representation. To indicate that the preceding *u* character is used to identify a Unicode value, it, too, must be escaped.

- The second topmost path represents our loop, which allows the addition of any of the outlined characters.

Listing 4-8 demonstrates a variety of valid string values.

Listing 4-8. Examples of Valid String Values As Defined by the JSON Grammar

```
//absent of unicode
"";
//random unicode characters
"Σ"; or " ";
//use of escaped character to display double quotes;
" \" \" ";
//use of \u denotes a unicode value
"\u22A0"; // outputs
//a series of valid unicode as defined by the grammar
"\u22A0  \" Σ \n";
```

A solidus, better known as a *backslash*, is used to demarcate characters as having an alternate meaning. Without the use of the \, the lexer might interpret as a token what is intended to be used as a string, or vice versa. Escaping characters offers us the ability to inform the lexer to handle a character in a manner that is different from its "normal" behavior. Table 4-1 illustrates the use of the escaped literals for the prohibited characters.

Table 4-1. *Escaped Literals*

Unicode Representation	Literal	Escaped Literal	Name
u0022	"	\"	Quotation Mark
u005c	\	\\	Reverse Solidus
u002F	/	\/	Solidus
u0008	b	\b	Backspace
u000C	f	\f	Form Feed
u000A	n	\n	Line Feed
u000D	r	\r	Carriage Return
u0009	t	\t	Tab
uXXXX	uXXXX	\uXXXX	Unicode Character

The last value to discuss is that of the number. A number in JSON is the arrangement of base10 literals, in combination with mathematical notation to define a real number literal. Figure 4-5 addresses the syntactical grammar of the JSON number in great detail; however, it's rather simple when we view it step-by-step.

number

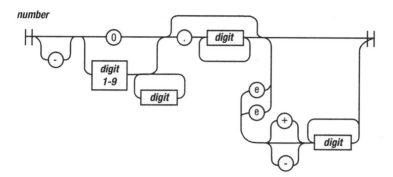

Figure 4-5. *Syntax diagram of a JSON number*

The first thing to note is that the numbers grammar does not begin or end with any particular symbolic representation, as our earlier object, array, and string examples did.

As illustrated in Figure 4-5, a JSON number must adhere to the following rules:

1. The number literal will be implicitly positive, unless explicitly indicated as a negative value.

2. Numbers cannot possess superfluous 0's.

3. Can be in the form of a whole number

   a. made up of a single BASE10 numeric literal (0-9)

   b. made. any number of BASE10 numeric literals (0-9)

4. Can be in the form of a fraction

   4.1. Made up of a singular base10 numerical literal at the 10s placement

   4.2. Made up of any base10 numerical literal per placement beyond the decimal

5. Can possess the exponential demarcation literal

   5.1. E notation can be expressed in the form of a uppercase "E" or lowercase "e"

   5.2. Immediately followed by a signed sequence of 1 or more base10 numeric literals (0-9)

Listing 4-9 reveals valid numerical values as defined by the JSON grammar.

Listing 4-9. Valid Numerical Values

```
-0.01    //valid use of 0's
00.1     //superfluous 0 produces a SyntaxError
1/3      //fraction form
.3333333333333333 //decimal form
1.2e-1 //scientific notation
```

Any of the values discussed in this chapter can be used in any combination when contained within a composite structure. Listing 4-10 illustrates how they can be mixed and matched. What is necessary is that the JSON grammar covered is followed. The examples in Listing 4-10 demonstrate proper adherence of the JSON grammar to portray data.

Listing 4-10. Examples of JSON Text Containing a Variety of Valid JSON Values

```
// JSON text of an array with primitives
[
    null, true, 8
]
// JSON text of an object with two members
{
    "first": "Ben",
    "last": "Smith",
}
// JSON text of an array with nested composites
[
    { "abc": "123" },
    [ "0", 1, 2, 3, 4, 100 ]
]
//JSON text of an object with nested composites
{
    "object": {
        "array": [true]
    }
}
```

JSON Tokens

While the Object and Array are conventions used in JavaScript, JavaScript, like many programming languages, borrowed from the C language in one form or another. While not every language explicitly implements Arrays and Objects akin to JavaScript, they do often possess the means to model collections of key/value pairs and ordered lists. These may take on the form of Hash maps, dictionaries, Hash tables, vectors, collections, and lists. Furthermore, most languages will be capable of working with text, which is precisely what JSON is based on.

At the end of the day, JSON is nothing more than a sequence of Unicode characters. However, the JSON grammar standardizes which Unicode characters or "tokens" define valid JSON, in addition to demarcating the values contained within.

Therefore, when regarding the interchange of JSON and the many languages that do not natively possess Objects and Arrays, the tokens that make up the JSON text are all that is required to interpret if any collections or ordered lists exist and apply all values in a manner required of that language. This is accomplished with six structural characters, as listed in Table 4-2.

Table 4-2. *Six Structural Character Tokens*

Token	Escaped Value	Unicode Value	Literal	Name
Array Opening	%5b	\u005b	[	Left Square Bracket
Array Closing	%5d	\u005d	]	Right Square Bracket
Object Opening	%7b	\u007b	{	Left Curly Bracket
Object Closing	%7d	\u007d	}	Right Curly Bracket
Name/Value Separator	%3a	\u003a	:	Colon
Value Separator	%2c	\u002c	,	Comma

One point to note is that JSON will ignore all insignificant whitespace before or after the preceding six structural tokens. Table 4-3 illustrates the four whitespace character tokens.

Table 4-3. *Four Whitespace Character Tokens*

Token	Name	Escaped Value	Unicode Value
Control Character	Space	%20	\u0020
Control Character	Horizontal Tab	%09	\u0009
Control Character	Line Feed/New Line	%0A	\u000A
Control Character	Carriage Return	%0D	\u000D

Because JSON is nothing more than text, you may find it rather difficult to determine whether your JSON is properly formatted or not. Furthermore, if the syntax is inaccurate to the grammar specified, then you will find that your malformed JSON causes code to come to a halt. This would be due to the syntax error that would be uncovered at the time of trying to parse said JSON. You will learn about parsing in Chapter 6.

For this reason, any attempt to devise JSON by hand should be performed with the aid of an editor. The following list of JSON editors understand the JSON grammar and are able to offer some much needed and immediate validation.

- `http://jsoneditoronline.org/`

- `http://jsonlint.com/`

The first editor, `http://jsoneditoronline.org/`, adheres to the ECMA-262 standardization and, therefore, allows your JSON text to represent a singular primitive value. Whereas the ladder follows the RFC 7159 standardization, thus requiring a JSON text to represent a structural value, i.e., array or object literal. It should be made known that the two editors mentioned previously are not the only two in existence. There are many online and offline editors, each with its own nuances. I favor the two mentioned, for their convenience.

Summary

In this chapter, I covered the history of JSON and the specifications of the JSON data format that defines the grammar of a valid JSON text. You learned that JSON is a highly interoperable format for data interchange. This is achieved via the standardization of a simplistic grammar that can be translated into any language simply by understanding the grammar.

As was demonstrated in this chapter, we can use the JSON grammar in conjunction with predetermined data to create JSON. Because we are simply working with text, it will be helpful to rely on an editor that understands JSON's grammar, for validation purposes. However, JSON can be written with a basic text editor and saved as a JSON document, using the file extension `.json`. Furthermore, as a subset of JavaScript, JSON can even be hard-coded within a JavaScript file directly. Both methods are ideal for devising configuration files for an application.

The next chapter will reveal how we can use the JavaScript language to produce JSON at runtime.

Key Points from This Chapter

- The array represents an ordered list of values, whereas the object represents a collection of key/value pairs.

- Unordered collections of key/value pairs are contained within the following opening ({) and closing (}) brace tokens.

- Ordered lists are encapsulated within opening ([) and closing (]) square bracket tokens.

- The key of a member must be contained in double quotes.

- The key of a member and its possessed value must be separated by the colon (:) token.

- Multiple values within an object or array must be separated by the comma (,) token.

- Boolean values are represented using lowercase true/false literals.

- Number values are represented using double-precision floating number point format.

- Number values can be specified with scientific notation.

- Control characters must be escaped via the reverse solidus (\) token.

- Null values are represented as the literal: null.

CHAPTER 5

▓ ▓ ▓

Creating JSON

Serialization is the process of taking a snapshot of a data structure in a manner that allows it to be stored, transmitted, and reconstructed back into a data structure at a later point in time. As serialization is merely a process rather than the utilization, its applications are mainly limited by your application's needs. This chapter will explore the serialization methods utilized by the JavaScript language and required of the JSON subset.

While serialization may seem like a mystical concept, the result of the snapshot, at the most atomic level, is nothing more than a string. The serialization process is simply the construction of said string, which often occurs behind the scenes. What is important to note is that in JavaScript, the produced string incorporates the representations of data in their literal forms. By capturing data in their literal form, each literal can be evaluated back into its respective JavaScript values.

Note   A serialized value could result in a simple-looking string, such as `"\"Hello-World\""` or `"false"`.

You learned in Chapter 4 that any C language can easily work with JSON. The most prominent reason is that all C languages possess a means to represent collections of name/value pairs, ordered lists, Booleans, and strings. Nevertheless, in the few cases in which the literals that make up the JSON subset are not inherently understood by a specific language, a translation among grammars can take place. This occurs by simply deconstructing the JSON text into a series of tokens and deriving meaningful structures that are possible within the grammar of that particular language.

Note   Grammar translation is the process of converting the syntax of one language equivalently into that of another.

Conversely, one can construct JSON from any data structure, simply by following the grammar defined by the JSON specification. In Chapter 6, you will learn more about such reconstruction. This chapter will focus on how to create a JSON text from JavaScript values.

The Serialization Process—Demystified

As was discussed in Chapter 3, all JavaScript values can be converted into their string equivalent form by adding it, via the addition operator, with another string, as seen in Listing 5-1.

Listing 5-1. Concatenating Primitive Values with Strings

```
""+1;         //produces "1"
""+true;      //produces "true"
""+null;      //produces "null"
""+undefined; //produces "undefined"
""+"Hello";   //produces "Hello"
```

While the string representations for all primitive values are captured as expected, as displayed in Listing 5-2, the same cannot be said of non-primitive values.

Listing 5-2. Concatenating Non-Primitive Values with Strings

```
""+{identifier:"Hello"};         //produces "[object Object]"
""+["Hello",["hello","World"]]; //produces "Hello,hello,World"
```

As revealed in Listing 5-2, while the JavaScript language possesses the ability to create objects out of literal forms, there is no easy way to perform the contrary. In order to deconstruct an object into that of its literal form, the members of an instance must be traversed, analyzed, and assembled piece by piece into its corresponding literal form.

To accomplish this undertaking, we must rely on the use of loops, string manipulation, and the appropriate sequencing of the necessary structural tokens, listed in Table 5-1.

Table 5-1. *The Six Structural Character Tokens*

Token	Literal	Name
Array Opening	[	Left Square Bracket
Array Closing	]	Right Square Bracket
Object Opening	{	Left Curly Bracket
Object Closing	}	Right Curly Bracket
Name/Value Separator	:	Colon
Value Separator	,	Comma

The following code in Listing 5-3 demonstrates, as succinctly as possible, a method that transforms a supplied object into that of its literal form counterpart.

Listing 5-3. Converting an object and Its Property into an object literal

```
1   var author = new Object();
2       author.name = "Ben";

3   var literal = stringify(author);

4   function stringify(structure){
       //if the structure supplied possesses the string data type
5       if(typeof structure=="string"){
6           return '"'+String(structure)+'"';
7       }
       //if the structure supplied possess the object data type
8       if(typeof structure=="object"){
9           var partial=[];
             //for each property held by our structure
10           for(var k in structure){
11               var v= structure[k];
12                   v = stringify(v);
13               partial.push(k+" : "+v);
14           }
             //if partial does not possess children capture opening/closing brackets;
15           v = (partial.length === 0)? '{}'
             //otherwise, comma delimit all values within opening/closing brackets
16           : ' { ' + partial.join(' , ')  + ' } '
17
18             return v;
19       }
20   }
21   console.log(literal);     // "{ name : "Ben" }"
22   console.log(typeof literal);    // "string"
```

Our demonstration begins (**line 1**) with the creation of an object author who is assigned a singular property name. We next supply author to the `stringify` function as the object we wish to transform into its literal representation. The `stringify` function then analyzes the data type of the structure supplied, in order to determine the appropriate course of action.

When `stringify` ascertains that the supplied structure is an object (**line 8**), the function then proceeds to traverse all members in its possession. The value of each key enumerated this way is in turn supplied to the `stringify` method, to be transformed into its literal form. Alas, this time, the data type is found to be that of a string. In order to capture said string as its literal counterpart, the function surrounds it with double quotes and returns it back to the caller of the invocation (**line 12**). From here, the current key, k, and its value, v, are sequenced together, separated by a colon (:) and stored within the array partial, so that any remaining properties can be enumerated similarly.

To keep this example short, author is in possession of one property. However, were there more properties possessed by our structure, the preceding process would be repeated until every single one is deconstructed and converted into its literal counterpart and appended to the final string representation. When there are no further properties to analyze, we determine if the length of partial is greater or equal to that of zero. If partial's length is 0, it does not possess any values, and, therefore, a string consisting of a pair of opening/closing braces is devised.

Otherwise, we create a string that joins each value with a comma separator (,) and insert it within a pair of opening/closing brace tokens. The serialized literal is then returned to the invoker (**line 3**). The demonstration ends by outputting the final representation, revealing our reverse-engineered object literal (**line 21**).

■ **Note** In the preceding example, `stringify` is only capable of converting strings and objects into their literal counterparts. Crafted for that purpose only, it is not capable of recognizing all types.

We're very close to our goal. However, this literal isn't able to be considered valid JSON, as it does not fully adhere to the JSON grammar. The key name in our key/value pair must be surrounded by double quotes. Fortunately, this is easy to remedy with strings: `partial.push('"'+ k+'"' + ": " +v);`. If we were to log our result once again, we would see the following: `"{"name":"Ben"}"`.

While the demonstration in Listing 5-1 possessed a singular member, it will not be unlikely that the data requiring serialization possesses the makeup of objects nested within objects. Four objects are used in total to represent our `author` object, as seen in Listing 5-4, and each is used to organize data. One object is used as a list, which includes the pets owned by yours truly. Another two are used to capture the names and ages of each pet. While both pets are contained within the ordered list, the ordered list itself is held as just another property on our `author` instance.

Listing 5-4. A Nested Data Structure

```
var author = new Object();
    author.name = "Ben";
    author.age  =  36;
    author.pets = [
        { name : "Waverly" , age : 3.5 },
        { name : "Westley" , age : 4 }
    ]
```

If we were to serialize `author` from Listing 5-4 using the `stringify` function outlined in Listing 5-3, each property possessed by the top-level element would be enumerated. Similarly, the value held by each key would be supplied to its own invocation of the `stringify` function as the top-level element to have its composition serialized. This process continues until all values of all structures have been analyzed, serialized, and concatenated as a valid JSON text.

■ **Note** Object properties and Array indexes represent a key.

As the `stringify` function demonstrates, transforming a JavaScript object into a valid JSON representation requires the use of identifying data types, recursion, and a heavy amount of string manipulation. Fortunately for us, the formalizer of JSON, Douglas Crockford, devised a JSON library that would conveniently produce JSON text from that of a specified datum. The JSON library is a convenient JavaScript file, which can be downloaded from the following GitHub URL: `https://github.com/douglascrockford/JSON-js/blob/master/json2.js`.

The JSON Object

As a JavaScript file, the `json2.js` library can be included in any existing application, by referencing the downloaded library within the `<head></head>` tags on each HTML page that seeks use of it. Listing 5-5 incorporates the JSON library by referencing the location of the library, relative to the top directory, within the script tag in the head of the following HTML file. In this example, the `json2.js` file has been downloaded within the `js/libs/` directory of the working directory of a project.

Listing 5-5. HTML Markup Referencing the Inclusion of the `json2.js` JavaScript Library

```
<!doctype html>
<html lang="en">
    <head>
        <meta charset="utf-8">
        <link rel="stylesheet" href="css/style.css">
        <script src="js/libs/json2.js"></script>
    </head>
    <body>
    </body>
</html>
```

When the page is viewed in a browser, and as soon as the `json2.js` file is loaded, the JSON Object declared by `json2.js` is added to the global namespace, so that the serialization method can be accessed from within any scope. Unlike the built-in objects, such as Object or Array, whose global methods can be used as a constructor to create instances of these objects via the keyword new, the JSON Object does not possess a constructor at all. Instead, the JSON Object possesses two methods, `parse` and `stringify`. However, this chapter will only discuss one of them: `stringify`.

stringify

As the name suggests, `stringify` is used for serializing JavaScript values into that of a valid JSON. The method itself accepts three parameters, `value`, `replacer`, and `space`, as defined by the signature in Listing 5-6. As I mentioned, the JSON Object is a global object that does not offer the ability to create any instances of the JSON Object. Any attempt to do so will cause a JavaScript error. Therefore, one must simply access the `stringify` method via the global JSON Object.

Listing 5-6. Syntax of the JSON `stringify` Method

```
JSON.stringify(value[, replacer [, space]]);
```

■ **Note**   The brackets surrounding the two parameters, `replacer` and `space`, is just a way to illustrate in a method definition what is optional. However, while an argument supplied to the method may be optional, you must follow the proper parameter order, as outlined by the method. In other words, to specify an argument for `space` but not `replacer`, you must supply `null` as the second argument to the `stringify` method.

---

value

The `value` parameter of the `stringify` method is the only required parameter of the three outlined by the signature in Listing 5-6. The argument supplied to the method represents the JavaScript value intended to be serialized. This can be that of any object, primitive, or even a composite of the two. As both Objects and Arrays are composite structures, the argument supplied can be in possession of any combination of objects and primitives nested within, much like our author object from Listing 5-4. Let's jump right in and serialize our author object as shown in Listing 5-7.

Listing 5-7. HTML Markup Demonstrating the Output of JSON.stringify

```
<!doctype html>
<html lang="en">
    <head>
        <meta charset="utf-8">
        <link rel="stylesheet" href="css/style.css">
        <script src="js/libs/json2.js"></script>
    </head>
    <body>
        <script>
        //obtain a reference to the body tag
        var body = document.getElementsByTagName("body")[0];

        //function log will append a value to the body for output
        function log(jsonText) {
            //surround supplied jsonText with double quotes and append a new line
            body.innerHTML += '"' + jsonText + '"<br>';
        }
        var author = new Object();
            author.name = "Ben";
            author.age  = 36;
            author.pets = [
                { name : "Waverly" , age : 3.5 },
                { name : "Westley" , age : 4 }
            ];

        var  JSONtext = JSON.stringify(author)
        log( JSONtext );
        </script>
    </body>
</html>
```

Listing 5-7 leverages the markup from Listing 5-5 and inserts within the body a script defining our author object. Immediately following, we supply author into that of JSON.stringify, which returns the following JSON text:

```
"{"name":"Ben","age":36,"pets":[{"name":"Waverly","age":3.5},{"name":"Westley","age":4}]}"
```

The produced JSON captures the data precisely as it was housed within the author object. The great thing about the serialization process is that all of the work is encapsulated behind the scenes. This allows us to remain unconcerned as to how the encoding logic works, in order to be able to use it as we just have.

Serializing structures equivalent to author will work out marvelously, as it possesses only the values that are formalized as valid values of the JSON grammar. On the other hand, as the needs of an application become more complex than that of author, you may encounter a few oddities in the way that your data is outputted.

Your program being written in JavaScript will surely take advantage of all the language has to offer, as well it should. Yet, as JSON is a subset of the JavaScript language, many objects and primitives employed by your application may not be serialized as expected. You may come to find that this is both a blessing and a curse. However, either way you see it, it will be an undeniable fact. Therefore, short of learning the inner workings of the stringify method, it will be important to understand how the serializer handles particular values it comes across, in order to be able to anticipate arriving at the expected or even necessary results.

■ **Tip** The serialization process occurs in a synchronous manner. In other words, the moment you call the `stringify` method, all remaining code that has to be executed must wait for the serialization to conclude before it can proceed. Therefore, it will be wise to keep your objects as concise as necessary during the serialization process.

EXERCISE 5-1. STRINGIFY

Let's now experiment with a few types of data structures and see what JSON text is outputted. Create an HTML file within the top root of a working directory, and within it, copy the code from Listing 5-5. Within that same directory, create a `js/` directory and a `libs/` directory within it. If you have not already downloaded `json2.js`, do so and save it within `js/libs/`. Revisit the created `.html` file and within the body tag, include the following lines of code:

```
01.  <script>
02.      //obtain a reference to the body tag
03.      var body = document.getElementsByTagName("body")[0];
04.      //function log will append a value to the body as a string value for output
05.      function log(jsonText) {
06.          //wrap all strings with double quotes and append a new line
07.          body.innerHTML += '"' + jsonText + '"<br>';
08.      }
09.
10.      log(JSON.stringify(false));
11.      log(JSON.stringify(undefined));
12.      log(JSON.stringify([undefined]));
13.      log(JSON.stringify(["undefined", false]));
14.      log(JSON.stringify({prop : undefined }));
15.      log(JSON.stringify(new Date("Jan 1 2015")));
16.
17.      var obj = new Object();
18.          obj.name = "name-test";
19.          obj.f = function() { return "function-test"  };
20.
21.      log(JSON.stringify(obj));
22.      log(JSON.stringify("this example \u000A\u000D has control characters"));
23.      log(JSON.stringify( "true" ));
24.      log( JSON.stringify( 1/0 ));
25.      log( JSON.stringify( Infinity ));
26.      log( JSON.stringify( [ function(){ return "A"} ] ));
27.
```

```
28.    var selfReference= new Array();
29.        selfReference[0]=selfReference;
30.    //because line 31 will throw an error, we must wrap it with a try catch to
       view the error
31.    try{ JSON.stringify( selfReference ) } catch(e){ log(e) };
32.  </script>
```

Once you've added the following script to your HTML file, open that .html file in your favorite browser and observe the output for each data serialized. Your results should be comparable to the results shown in the following table.

Results of the Code Produced

Exercises	Outputs
JSON.stringify(false);	"false"
JSON.stringify([undefined]);	"[null]"
JSON.stringify(["undefined" , false]);	"[\"undefined\",false]"
JSON.stringify({ prop:undefined });	"{}"
JSON.stringify(new Date("Jan 1 2015"));	"\"2015-01-01T05:00:00.000Z\""

var obj= new Object();
obj.name="name-test";
obj.f=function(){
return "function-test"
};
JSON.stringify(obj);
	"{\"name\":\"name-test\"}"

JSON.stringify("this example \u000A\u000D has control characters");	"\"this example \n\r has control characters\""
JSON.stringify("true");	"\"true\""
JSON.stringify(1/0);	"null"
JSON.stringify(Infinity);	"null"
JSON.stringify([function(){ return "A"}]);	"[null]"

var selfReference= new Array();
selfReference[0]=selfReference;
JSON.stringify(selfReference);
	TypeError: cyclic object value

As you can see from the results of our exercise, the stringify method doesn't acknowledge a few values. First and foremost, you may have realized that an undefined value is handled in one of two possible manners. If the value undefined is found on a property, the property is removed entirely from the JSON text. If, however, the value undefined is found within an ordered list, the value is converted to 'null'.

Functions are also disregarded by the `stringify` method, even functions that would return a string to the key holding it. The `stringify` method only analyzes and encodes values; it does not evaluate them. Therefore, functions when encountered by `stringify` are replaced with the `undefined` value. The rules I covered previously regarding an `undefined` value will apply to the key that now references the assigned `undefined` primitive. There is one method that will be invoked, if found to have that of a particular method name. I will talk more about this later in the `toJSON` section.

As JavaScript does not possess a date literal, `Dates` are automatically serialized as string literals, based on the (UTC) ISO encoding format.

All number values must be finite. If the number is evaluated to that of an `Infinity` or `NaN`, the number will return as the literal `'null'` value.

When the sole value serialized is that of a string value, its literal form is escaped and nested within another set of quotes.

The last takeaway from the preceding exercises is that JSON cannot handle cyclic object values, meaning that neither an array nor object can possess a value that is a reference to itself. Should you attempt to define a cyclic structure, an immediate error is thrown.

toJSON

Because dates do not possess a literal form, the `stringify` method captures all dates it encounters as string literals. It captures not only the date but time as well. Because `stringify` converts a date instance into a string, you might rationalize that it's produced by calling the `toString` method possessed by the Date object. However, `Date.toString()`, does not produce a standardized value, but, rather, a string representation whose format depends on the locale of the browser that the program is running.[1] With this output lacking a standard, it would be less than ideal to serialize this value for data interchange.

What would be ideal is to transform the contents into that of the ISO 8601 grammar, which is the standard for handling date and time interchange.

■ **Note**   A JavaScript Date Object can be instantiated with the provision of an ISO formatted string.

To enable this feature, Crockford's library also includes the `toJSON` method, which is appended to the prototype of the Date Object so that it will exist on any date. Listing 5-8 reveals the default `toJSON` function that will be inherited by any and all dates.

Listing 5-8. Default toJSON Implementation

```
Date.prototype.toJSON = function(key) {
    function f(n) {
        // Format integers to have at least two digits.
        return n < 10 ? '0' + n : n;
    }

    return this.getUTCFullYear() + '-' +
            f(this.getUTCMonth() + 1) + '-' +
```

---

[1]Microsoft, Internet Explorer Dev Center, "toString Method (Date)," `http://msdn.microsoft.com/en-us/library/ie/jj155294%28v=vs.94%29.aspx`.

```
        f(this.getUTCDate()) + 'T' +
        f(this.getUTCHours()) + ':' +
        f(this.getUTCMinutes()) + ':' +
        f(this.getUTCSeconds()) + 'Z';
};
```

When `stringify` invokes the `toJSON` method, it expects to be provided a return value. In Listing 5-8, the value being returned is a string that is devised from the concatenation of the methods possessed by the instance being analyzed. The return value can be of any value that is defined in the JSON subset. Upon returning a value, the logic within `stringify` will continue to ensure that your value is analyzed. It will do so iteratively if returned in the form of an object or, more simply, if the value returned is a primitive, it's converted into a string and sanitized. Because `stringify` continues to analyze the retuned value, the rules of Table 5-1 continue to apply.

■ **Note**   Because `toJSON` exists as a method of a Date Object, the `this` keyword remains scoped to the particular instance being analyzed. This allows the serialization logic to be statically defined, yet each instance at runtime will reference its own values.

If you are curious as to the purpose of function `f`, function `f` wraps each method and prefixes each result with 0, if the returned number is less than 10, in order to maintain a fixed number of digits. Last, each number is arranged in a sequence combined with various tokens and joined into a string, resulting in a valid grammar, according to the ISO 8601 specification.

What is important to know about the `toJSON` method is that it can be used on more than dates. For each object analyzed, the internal logic of the `stringify` method invokes said `toJSON` method, if it is in possession of one. This means we can add `toJSON` to any built-in JavaScript Object, and even to custom classes, which, in turn, will be inherited by their instances. Furthermore, we can add it to individual instances. This inherit ability to add a `toJSON` method enables each application to provide the necessary encoding that might not otherwise be possible by default, such as that of our `date`.

■ **Note**   Custom classes, when serialized, are indistinguishable from the built-in objects types.

Each call to the `toJSON` method is supplied with a key as an argument. This key references the holder of the value that `stringify` is currently examining. If the key is a property on an object, that properties label is supplied as the key to the method. If the key is the index of an array, the argument supplied will be an index. The former provides useful insight when devising conditional logic that must remain flexible or dependent on the instances context, whereas the latter is less indicative. Our `author` object possesses both a collection of key/value pairs and an ordered collection. By adding a `toJSON` method to all object instances, we can easily log the key that is provided to each `toJSON` invocation, as achieved in Listing 5-9.

Listing 5-9. Attaching the toJSON Function to the Object Will Cause All JavaScript objects to Possess It

```
Object.prototype.toJSON=function(key){
    //log the key being analyzed
    console.log(key);  //outputs the key for the current context (shown below)
    //log the scope of the method
    console.log(this); //outputs the current context (shown below)
    //return the object as is back to the serializer
    return this;
}
var author = new Object();
    author.name = "Ben";
    author.age  = 36;
    author.pets = [
            { name : "Waverly" , age : 3.5 },
            { name : "Westley" , age : 4 }
        ];

    JSON.stringify(author);

/* captured output from the above Listing */
//the author object being analyzed
//(key)      ""
//(context) Object { name="Ben", age=36, pets=[2], more...}  //truncated
//the pets object being analyzed
//(key)      pets
//(context) [Object { name="Waverly", age=3.5, toJSON=function()},
                ↪ Object { name="Westley", age=4, toJSON=function()}]
//index 0 of array being analyzed
//(key)      0
//(context) Object { name="Waverly", age=3.5, toJSON=function()}
//index 1 of array being analyzed
//(key)      1
//(context) Object { name="Westley", age=4, toJSON=function()}

"{"name":"Ben","age":36,"pets":[{"name":"Waverly","age":3.5},{"name":"Westley","age":4}]}"
```

Listing 5-9 demonstrates that each object that possesses the toJSON method is supplied with the key by which it is held. These values are logged in the order in which the properties are enumerated by the JavaScript engine. The first key that is logged from our toJSON method is that of an empty string. This is because the stringify implementation regards key/value pairs. As you can see, the immediate logging of this reveals the author object. With the return of the invoked method, stringify continues onto the next object it encounters.

■ **Note**   The key of the initial value is always that of an empty string.

The next object the `stringify` method encounters happens to be that of an array. An array, as a subtype of Object, inherits and exposes the `toJSON` method and is, therefore, invoked. The key it is passed is the identifier `pets`. Respectively, both objects contained within are invoked and provided the index to which they are ordered, those keys being 0 and 1.

The `toJSON` method provides a convenient way to define the necessary logic wherein the default behavior may fall short. While this is not always ideal, it is often necessary. However, the `toJSON` method is not the only means of augmenting the default behavior of the `stringify` method.

replacer

The second parameter, `replacer`, is optional, and when supplied, it can augment the default behavior of the serialization that would otherwise occur. There are two possible forms of argument that can be supplied. As explained within the ECMA-262 standardization, the optional `replacer` parameter is either a function that alters the way objects and arrays are stringified or an array of strings and numbers that acts as a white list for selecting the object properties that will be stringified.[2]

replacer Array

Suppose I had the following JavaScript data structure (see Listing 5-10) and decided to serialize it using the built-in JSON Object and its `stringify` method. By supplying the `author` instance as the value into the `JSON.stringify` method, I would be provided with the result displayed in Listing 5-10.

Listing 5-10. Replaced Pets Property with E-mail

```
var author = new Object();
    author.name="ben";
    author.age=35;
    author.email="iben@spilled-milk.com";

    JSON.stringify( author );
    // "{"name":"ben","age":35,"email":"iben@spilled-milk.com"}"
```

As expected, the produced JSON text reflects all of the possessed properties of the `author` object. However, suppose that e-mail addresses were not intended to be serialized by our application. We could easily delete the e-mail property and then pass `author` through `stringify`. While that would prevent the e-mail address from being serialized, this method could prove problematic if our application continued to require use of the e-mail address. Rather than delete the value from the `author` object, we could take advantage of the `replacer` method.

Were we to supply the `replacer` parameter with an array whose values outline the properties we desire `stringify` to serialize, the JSON text would only capture those key/value pairs. Listing 5-11 white lists the two properties, name and age, that our application is permitted to serialize.

Listing 5-11. Supplying a `replacer` array Can Specify What Keys to Output

```
//... continuation of Listing 5-10
JSON.stringify(author, ["name","age"] );  // "{" name":"ben","age":35"}"
```

---

[2]ECMA International, *ECMAScript Language Specification*, Standard ECMA-262, Edition 5.1, www.ecma-international.org/publications/files/ECMA-ST/Ecma-262.pdf, June 2011.

Providing an ordered list as the `replacer` argument filters the properties that are output during serialization. Any identifiers that are not specified within the `replacer` array will not become a part of the JSON text. As an additional point, the order of our white-listed properties affects the way in which they respectively occur in the serialized output. Listings 5-11 and 5-12 vary by the order of the white-listed properties supplied in the `replacer`. The results reflect the specified order in each JSON text produced.

Listing 5-12. The Order of the White-Listed Properties Determines the Order in Which They Are Captured

```
//... continuation of Listing 5-10
JSON.stringify(author, ["age","name"] ); //  "{"age":35","name":"ben"}"
```

Listing 5-11 displays name in the JSON text first, whereas in Listing 5-12, name appears last. This has to do with the fact that our `replacer` argument is an array, and an array is simply an ordered list. In this case, the ordered list just so happens to expresses our white-listed properties. The serialization process then iterates over each white-listed identifier in ascending order for each collection of name/value pairs it may come across.

White-listed properties mustn't be provided in string literal form. They can also be represented as a primitive number. However, any number the method encounters is converted into its string equivalent. This is due to the fact that keys are always stored as strings behind the scenes. This is demonstrated in Listing 5-13.

Listing 5-13. Numbers Used As Keys Are Converted to Strings

```
var yankeesLineup = new Object();
    yankeesLineup['1'] ="Jacoby Ellsbury";
    yankeesLineup['2'] ="Derek Jeter";
    yankeesLineup['3'] ="Carlos Beltran";
    yankeesLineup['4'] ="Alfonso Soriano";
    //...etc
JSON.stringify(yankeesLineup, [1,2] );
    // "{"1":"Jacoby Ellsbury","2":"Derek Jeter"}"
```

▧ **Note**   Even array indexes are converted into strings behind the scenes.

▧ **Tip**   While numbers are allowed as white-listed values, it will always be best to supply a string representation, as it will convey meaning to those who may not know that numbers are converted to strings behind the scenes. Furthermore, using numbers as a property identifier is not the best choice for a meaningful label.

---

replacer Function

The alternate form that can be supplied as the replacer is that of a function. Supplying a function to the replacer property allows the application to insert the necessary logic that determines how objects within the stringify method are serialized, much like that of the toJSON method. In fact, the replacer function and the toJSON method are nearly identical, apart from three distinguishable characteristics. The first is that one is a function and the other is a method. The second is that the replacer function is provided iteratively, the key for every property encountered. Last, the replacer function is provided the value held by each key. As you can see from the method definition in Listing 5-14, the replacer function expects to be provided with two arguments, k and v.

■ **Note**   Only properties whose values are both owned by the object being traversed, in addition to being enumerable, are discovered during the iterative process.

Listing 5-14. Signature of the replacer Function

```
var replacerFunction = function( k, v );
```

The k argument will always represent the identifier (key) per object the method seeks to encode, whereas the v parameter represents the value held by said key.

■ **Note**   If the replacer method is used in conjunction with an object that possesses a toJSON method, the value of v will be that of the result provided by the toJSON method.

The context of the toJSON method will always be that of the object for which it's defined. A method's scope is always tied to the object for which it exists. Contrary to methods, a function's scope is tied to that of where it was declared. However, within the stringify method, the scope of the replacer function supplied is continuously set to the context of each object whose key and value are being supplied as arguments. This means that the implicit this possessed by all functions will always point to the object whose keys are currently being analyzed within the stringify method.

Let's revisit our example from Listing 5-9. However, this time, rather than define a toJSON that is inherited by all objects, we will supply stringify with a replacer function. As we are not concerned with customizing the default serialization of any values for the purpose of this illustration, Listing 5-15 returns back to stringify the value, v, it has supplied to us.

Listing 5-15. Logging All Keys, Values, and Context with the replacer Function

```
var author = new Object();
    author.name = "Ben";
    author.age  =  36;
    author.pets = [
            { name : "Waverly" , age : 3.5 },
            { name : "Westley" , age : 4 }
        ];
```

```
JSON.stringify(author,
               function(k,v){
                  console.log(this);
                  console.log(k);
                  console.log(v);
                 return v;
               });
```

```
//the initial object wrapper being analyzed
//(context) Object {{...}}  //truncated
//(key)   (an empty string)
//(value) Object { name="Ben", age=36, pets=[...]} //truncated
//the author object ben property being analyzed
//(context) Object { name="Ben", age=36, pets=[...]} //truncated
//(key)     name
//(value)   Ben
//the author object age property being analyzed
//(context) Object { name="Ben", age=36, pets=[...]} //truncated
//(key)     age
//(value)   36
//the author object pets property being analyzed
//(context) Object { name="Ben", age=36, pets=[...]} //truncated
//(key)     pets
//(value)   [Object { name="Waverly", age=3.5}, Object { name="Westley", age=4}]
//the pets object 0 index being analyzed
//(context) [Object { name="Waverly", age=3.5}, Object { name="Westley", age=4}]
//(key)     0
//(value)   Object { name="Waverly", age=3.5}
//the 0 index name property being analyzed
//(context) Object { name="Waverly", age=3.5}
//(key)     name
//(value)   Waverly
//the 0 index age property being analyzed
//(context) Object { name="Waverly", age=3.5}
//(key)     age
//(value)   3.5
//the pets object 1 index being analyzed
//(context) [Object { name="Waverly", age=3.5}, Object { name="Westley", age=4}]
//(key)     1
//(value)   Object { name="Westley", age=4}
//the 1 index name property being analyzed
//(context) Object { name="Westley", age=4}
//(key)     name
//(value)   Westley
//the 1 index age property being analyzed
//(context) Object { name="Westley", age=4}
//(key)     age
//(value)   4

//JSON text "{"name":"Ben","age":36,"pets":[{"name":"Waverly","age":3.5},{"name":"Westley",
"age":4}]}"
```

While Listing 5-15 utilizes the same data structure from our to JSON example, in Listing 5-9, you will most certainly be able to perceive that the results logged in Listing 5-15 are far more plentiful. This is due to the fact that, unlike to JSON, the replacer function is triggered for each property encountered on every object.

The benefit of the keys provided to both the replacer function and to JSON is that they offer your application a means to flag a property whose value requires custom serializing. Listing 5-16 demonstrates how we can leverage a supplied key to prevent a value or values from being captured in the produced JSON text.

Listing 5-16. replacer Function Can Be Used to Provide Custom Serializing

```
var author = new Object();
      author.name = "Ben";
      author.age  =  36;
      author.pets = [
              { name : "Waverly" , age : 3.5 },
              { name : "Westley" , age : 4 }
          ];

var replacer= function(k,v){
                  //if the key matches the string 'age'
                  if(k==="age"){
                      //remove it from the final JSON text
                      return undefined;
                  } //else
                  return v;
              }
JSON.stringify(author,replacer);
// "{"name":"Ben","pets":[{"name":"Waverly"},{"name":"Westley"}]}"
```

Listing 5-16 leverages the uniqueness of the age identifier so that it can determine when to remove it from the final JSON text, by returning the value of undefined. While this is a valid example, it could have been equally satisfied by the replacer array. The takeaway is that the identifier can be extremely instrumental in the orchestration of custom serialization.

The return value, much like in the case of to JSON, can be that of any value outlined in the JSON subset. The serializer will continue to ensure that your value is iteratively analyzed if returned in the form of an object, or converted into a string and sanitized, if returned as a primitive. Furthermore, the rules of Table 5-1 will always apply to any and all returned values.

space

The third parameter, space, is also optional and allows you to specify the amount of padding that separates each value from one another within the produced JSON text. This padding provides an added layer of readability to the produced string.

The argument supplied to the parameter must be that of a whole number equal or greater to 1. Supplying a number less than 1 will have no effect on the produced JSON text. However, if the number supplied is 1 or greater, the final representation of the JSON text will display each value indented by the specified amount of whitespace from the left-hand margin. A margin is established by the inclusion of new line characters after each of the following tokens: {, }, [, and].

In other words, new line-control characters are inserted into the produced JSON after each opening/closing token, for both an array or object. Additionally, a new line character is added after each separator token. Listing 5-17 contrasts the produced JSON text with and without padding.

Listing 5-17. JSON Text with Added Padding

```
var obj={ primitive:"string", array:["a","b"] };

JSON.stringify(obj,null,0);
↪//(no padding)
  // "{"primitive":"string","array":["a","b"]}"

JSON.stringify(obj,null,8);
↪/* (8 spaces of added padding)
"{
        "primitive": "string",
        "array": [
                "a",
                "b"
        ]
}"
*/
```

The provision of the space parameter will have no effect on a JSON text if it does not possess either an array or object, regardless of the value specified. Listing 5-18 indicates that eight spaces should be applied to the produced JSON. However, because it is not in possession of either an object or array, no padding is applied.

Listing 5-18. Space Only Works on objects and arrays

```
var primitive="string";
var JSONtext= JSON.stringify( primitive , null ,8 );
console.log( JSONtext );
// ""string""
```

The added padding appended to the final JSON text will have zero impact on its conversion back into that of a JavaScript object. Additionally, the inclusion of whitespace and new line characters will not add significant weight that would slow its transmission across the Internet.

Summary

In this chapter, we covered the JSON library, which enables JavaScript structures to become serialized for storage and data interchange. This was accomplished via downloading the JSON library and referencing the JSON global object and its `stringify` method. What you may not know is that even though we downloaded the JSON library and referenced it within our `.html` files for this chapter, the odds are you did not require it.

As I mentioned in Chapter 4, JSON is incorporated within the ECMA-262, 5th edition. What this means is that any browser that aligns with ECMA 5th edition standards or greater possesses the native JSON Object as the means for both serializing and deserializing JSON. Table 5-2 lists the versions of each browser that possess the JSON Object.

Table 5-2. *Minimal Browser Versions That Possess the JSON Object*

Browser	Version
FireFox	3.5+
Chrome	5+
Safari	4.0.5+
Opera	10.5+
Internet Explorer	8+

In any browser whose version is greater or equal to what is listed, you would be successful in referring to the native JSON Object. There is absolutely zero harm in incorporating the JSON library as we have, in addition to working with a browser mentioned in the preceding table. The reason for this is because the library first checks to see if a JSON Object currently exists before creating one and attaches it to the global namespace. If one is found to exist when the library is loaded into the script, it does not take any action. Listing 5-19 demonstrates how if there isn't already a global JSON Object, one is created.

Listing 5-19. JSON Object is Instantiated Only if One Does Not Exist

```
if (typeof JSON !== 'object') {
    JSON = {};
}
```

What this means is that the library will only have an impact on browsers whose versions are below that of Table 5-2. While it's becoming increasingly less likely you will continue to cater to browsers before Internet Explorer 8, some clients continue to require it.

The benefit of having you download the JSON library rather than reference the native JSON Object is that at any point during our discussion, you possess the ability to open the JSON library and review the code within, whereas you would not be as fortunate to do so with the alternative, because, being native, it's built into the browser. Therefore, there is no code to review.

What is important to remember about this chapter is that much like in the *Matrix*, knowing the rules allows you to bend the rules in your favor.

Key Points from This Chapter

- Numbers must be finite, or they are treated as `null`.

- A value that is not recognized as a valid JSON value produces the undefined value.

- A function whose name is *not* `toJSON` is ignored.

- Properties whose values are undefined are stripped.

- If the value of an array is that of `undefined`, it is treated as `null`.

- The primitive `null` is treated as the string `null`.

- A TypeError Exception is thrown when a structure is cyclic.

- `toJSON` and the `replacer` parameter allow applications to supply necessary logic for serialization.

- `toJSON` can be defined on any built-in object and even overridden.

- A `replacer` array identifies the properties that should be serialized.

- A `replacer` function is invoked with every property in the data structure.

- `toJSON` `this` explicitly refers to the object it's defined on.

- A `replacer` function's `this` implicitly refers to the object that is currently being analyzed.

- A key is either a property possessed by an object or the index of an array.

- Custom classes are captured as ordinary objects.

In the next chapter, you will continue to learn how we can use the JSON Object's second method, `parse`, to convert JSON back into a usable JavaScript value.

CHAPTER 6

Parsing JSON

In the last chapter, I discussed how to convert a JavaScript value into a valid JSON text using JSON.stringify. In Chapter 4, you learned how JSON utilizes JavaScript's literal notation as a way to capture the structure of a JavaScript value. Additionally, you learned in that same chapter that JavaScript values can be created from their literal forms. The process by which this transformation occurs is due to the parsing component within the JavaScript engine. This brings us full circle, regarding the serializing and deserializing process.

Parsing is the process of analyzing a string of symbols, either in natural language or in computer languages, according to the rules of a formal grammar. As the grammar of JSON is a subset of JavaScript, the analysis of its tokens by the parser occurs indifferently from how the Engine parses source code. Because of this, the data produced from the analysis of the JSON grammar will be that of objects, arrays, strings, and numbers. Additionally, the three literals—true, false, and null—are produced as well.

Within our program, we will be able to refer to any of these data structures as we would any other JavaScript value. In this chapter, you will learn of the manners by which we can convert valid JSON into usable JavaScript values within our program.

JSON.parse

In our investigation of the JSON Object, I discussed how the JSON Object possesses two methods. On one hand, there is the stringify method, which produces serialized JSON from a datum. And on the other hand, there is a method that is the antithesis of stringify. This method is known as parse. In a nutshell, JSON.parse converts serialized JSON into usable JavaScript values. The method JSON.parse, whose signature can be observed in Listing 6-1, is available from the json2.js library, in addition to browsers that adhere to ECMA 5th edition specifications.

Listing 6-1. Syntax of the JSON.parse Method

```
JSON.parse(text [, reviver]);
```

Until Internet Explorer 7 becomes a faded memory only to be kept alive as a myth when whispered around a campfire as a horror story, it will continue to be wise to include the json2.js library into your projects that work with JSON. Furthermore, json2.js is a fantastic way to gain insight into the inner workings of the method, short of interpreting ECMA specifications.

As outlined in the preceding, JSON.parse can accept two parameters, text and reviver. The name of the parameter text is indicative of the value it expects to receive. The parameter reviver is used similarly to the replacer parameter of stringify, in that it offers the ability for custom logic to be supplied for necessary parsing that would otherwise not be possible by default. As indicated in the method's signature, only the provision of text is required.

You will learn about the optional `reviver` parameter a bit later. First, we will begin an exploration of the `text` parameter. The aptly named parameter `text` implies the JavaScript value, which should be supplied. Of course, this is a string. However, more specifically, this parameter requires serialized JSON. This is a rather important aspect, because any invalid argument will automatically result in a `parse` error, such as that shown in Listing 6-2.

Listing 6-2. Invalid JSON Grammar Throws a Syntax Error

```
var str = JSON.parse( "abc123" );   //SyntaxError: JSON.parse: unexpected character
```

Listing 6-2 throws an error because it was provided a string literal and not serialized JSON. As you may recall from Chapter 4, when the sole value of a string value is serialized, its literal form is captured within an additional pair of quotes. Therefore, `"abc123"` must be escaped and wrapped with an additional set of quotation marks, as demonstrated in Listing 6-3.

Listing 6-3. Valid JSON Grammer Is Successfully Parsed

```
var str = JSON.parse( "\"abc123\"" );   //valid JSON string value
console.log(str)                        //abc123;
console.log(typeof str)                 //string;
```

The JavaScript value of a parsed JSON text is returned to the caller of the method, so that it can be assigned to an identifier, as demonstrated in Listing 6-3. This allows the result of the transformation to be referenced later throughout your program.

While the preceding example was supplied with a simple JSON text, it could have been a composite, such as a collection of key/value pairs or that of an ordered list. When a JSON text represents nested data structures, the transformed JavaScript value will continue to retain each nested element within a data structure commonly referred to as a *tree*. A simple explanation of a data tree can be attributed to a Wikipedia entry, which defines a tree as a nonlinear data structure that consists of a root node and, potentially, many levels of additional nodes that form a hierarchy.[1]

Let's witness this with a more complex serialized structure. Listing 6-4 revisits our serialized `author` object from the previous chapter and renders it into `JSON.parse`. Using Firebug in conjunction with `console.log`, we can easily view the rendered tree structure of our `author` object.

Listing 6-4. Composite Structures Create a Data Tree

```
var JSONtext= '{"name":"Ben","age":36,"pets":[{"name":"Waverly","age":3.5},{"name":"Westley",
"age":4}]}';
var author = JSON.parse( JSONtext );
console.log( author);

/*Firebug Illustrates the parsed Data Tree of our serialized JSON text below
    age      36
    name     "Ben"
▼   pets    [ Object { name="Waverly", age=3.5 },  Object { name="Westley", age=4 } ]
    ► 0        Object { name="Waverly", age=3.5 }
    ► 1        Object { name="Westley", age=4 }
*/
```

---

[1]Wikipedia, "Tree (data structure)," http://en.wikipedia.org/wiki/Tree_%28data_structure%29#Terminology, modified January 2015.

Once a JSON text is converted into that of a data tree, keys, also called members, belonging to any level of node structure are able to be referenced via the appropriate notion (i.e., dot notation/array notation). Listing 6-5 references various members existing on the author object.

Listing 6-5. Members Can Be Accessed with the Appropriate Notation

```
var JSONtext= '{"name":"Ben","age":36,"pets":[{"name":"Waverly","age":3.5},{"name":"Westley",
"age":4}]}';
var author = JSON.parse( JSONtext );
console.log(typeof author)        //object;
console.log(author.name)          // Ben
console.log(author.pets.length)   // 2;
console.log(author.pets[0].name)  // Waverly;
```

The magic of JSON.parse is twofold. The first proponent that allows for the transformation of JSON text into that of a JavaScript value is JSON's use of literals. As we previously discussed, the literal is how JavaScript data types can be "literally" typed within source code.

The second aspect is that of the JavaScript interpreter. It is the role of the interpreter to possess absolute understanding over the JavaScript grammar and determine how to evaluate syntax, declarations, expressions, and statements. This, of course, includes JavaScript literals. It is here that literals are read, along with any other provided source code, evaluated by the interpreter of the JavaScript language and transformed from Unicode characters into JavaScript values. The JavaScript interpreter is safely tucked away and encapsulated within the browser itself. However, the JavaScript language provides us with a not-so-secret door to the interpreter, via the global function eval.

eval

The eval function is a property of the global object and accepts an argument in the form of a string. The string supplied can represent an expression, statement, or both and will be evaluated as JavaScript code (see Listing 6-6).

Listing 6-6. eval Evaluates a String As JavaScript Code

```
eval("alert(\"hello world\")");
```

Albeit a simple example, Listing 6-6 illustrates the use of eval to transform a string into a valid JavaScript program. In this case, our string represents a statement and is evaluated as a statement. If you were to run this program, you would see the dialog prompt appear with the text hello world. While this is a rather innocent program, and one created to be innocuous, you must take great caution with what you supply to eval, as this may not always be the case. Listing 6-7 reveals that eval will also evaluate expressions.

Listing 6-7. eval Returns the Result of an Evaluation

```
var answer = eval("1+5");
console.log(answer) //6;
```

The eval function not only evaluates the string provided, but it can also return the result of an evaluated expression so that it can be assigned to a variable and referenced by your application. Expressions needn't be mere calculations either, as demonstrated in Listing 6-8. If we were to supply eval with a string referencing an object literal, it, too, would be evaluated as an expression and returned as a JavaScript instance that corresponds to the represented object literal.

Listing 6-8. object Literals Can Be Evaluated by the eval Function

```
var array = eval("['Waverly','Westley','Ben']");
console.log(array[1]) //Westley;
```

Because JSON is a subset of JavaScript and possesses its own specification, it is important to always ensure that the supplied text is indeed a sequence of valid JSON grammar. Otherwise, we could be unaware of welcoming malicious code into our program. This will become more apparent when we invite JSON text into our program via Ajax. For this reason, while eval possesses the means to handle the transformation of JSON into JavaScript, you should never use eval directly. Rather, you should always rely on the either the JSON2.js library or the built-in native JSON Object to parse your JSON text.

If you were to open the json2.js library and review the code within the parse function, you would find that the JSON.parse method occurs in four stages.

The first thing the method aims to accomplish, before it supplies the received string to the eval function, is to ensure that all necessary characters are properly escaped, preventing Unicode characters from being interpreted as line terminators, causing syntax errors. For example, Listing 6-9 demonstrates that you cannot evaluate a string possessing a carriage return, as it will be viewed as an unterminated string literal.

Listing 6-9. String Literals Cannot Possess Line Breaks

```
var str="this is a sentence with a new line
... here is my new line";
// SyntaxError: unterminated string literal

// Similarly
eval("\"this is a sentence with a new line \u000a... here is my new line\"");
// SyntaxError: unterminated string literal
```

However, as stated by EMCA-262, section 7.3, line terminator characters that are preceded by an escape sequence are now allowed within a string literal token.[2] By escaping particular Unicode values, a line break can be evaluated within a string literal, as demonstrated in Listing 6-10.

Listing 6-10. String Literals Can Only Possess Line Breaks If They Are Escaped

```
eval("\"this is a sentence with a new line \\u000a... here is my new line\"");  //will succeed
```

The JSON library does not just ensure that Unicode characters are properly escaped before they are evaluated into JavaScript code. It also works to ensure that JSON grammar is strictly adhered to. Because JSON is simply text, its grammar can be overlooked, if it is not created via JSON.stringify or a similar library. Furthermore, because a string can possess any combination of Unicode characters, JavaScript operators could be easily inserted into a JSON text. If these operators were evaluated, they could be detrimental to our application, whether or not they were intended to be malicious. Consider an innocent call that has an impact on our system, as shown in Listing 6-11.

Listing 6-11. Assignments Can Impact Your Existing JavaScript Values

```
var foo=123
eval("var foo = \"abc\"");
console.log(foo); // abc
```

---

[2]ECMA International, *ECMAScript Language Specification*, Standard ECMA-262, Edition 5.1, Section 7.3, www.ecma-international.org/ecma-262/5.1/#sec-7.3, June 2011.

Because JavaScript values can easily be overwritten, as demonstrated in Listing 6-11, it is imperative that only valid JSON text is supplied to eval.

The second stage of the parse method is to ensure the validity of the grammar. With the use of regular expressions, stage two seeks out tokens that do not properly represent valid JSON grammar. It especially seeks out JavaScript tokens that could nefariously cause our application harm. Such tokens represent method invocations, denoted by an open parenthesis (() and close parenthesis ()); object creation, indicated by the keyword new; and left-handed assignments, indicated by the use of the equal (=) operator, which could lead to the mutation of existing values. While these are explicitly searched for, if any tokens are found to be invalid, the text will not be further evaluated. Instead, the parse method will throw a syntax error.

However, should the provided text in fact appear to be a valid JSON, the parser will commence stage three, which is the provision of the sanitized text to the eval function. It is during stage three that the captured literals of each JSON value are reconstructed into their original form. Well, at least as close to their original form as JSON's grammar allows for. Remember: JSON's grammar prohibits a variety of JavaScript values, such as the literal undefined, functions and methods, any nonfinite number, custom objects, and dates. That said, the parse method offers the ability for us to further analyze the produced JavaScript values in a fourth and final stage, so that we can control what JavaScript values are returned for use by our application. If, however, the reviver parameter is not supplied, the produced JavaScript value of the eval function is returned as is.

The final stage of the parse operation occurs only if we supply an argument to the method, in addition to the JSON text we seek to be transformed. The benefit of the optional parameter is that it allows us to provide the necessary logic that determines what JavaScript values are returned to our application, which otherwise would be impossible to achieve by the default behavior.

reviver

The reviver parameter, unlike the replacer parameter of the stringify method, can only be supplied a function. As outlined in Listing 6-12, the reviver function will be provided with two arguments, which will assist our supplied logic in determining how to handle the appropriate JavaScript values for return. The first parameter, k, represents the key or index of the value being analyzed. Complementarily, the v parameter represents the value of said key/index.

Listing 6-12. Signature of reviver Function

```
var reviver = function(k,v);
```

If a reviver function is supplied, the JavaScript value that is returned from the global eval method is "walked" over, or traversed, in an iterative manner. This loop will discover each of the current object's "own" properties and will continue to traverse any and all nested structures it possesses as values. If a value is found to be a composite object, such as array or object, each key that object is in possession of will be iterated over for review. This process continues until all enumerable keys and their values have been addressed. The order in which the properties are uncovered is not indicative of how they are captured within the object literals. Instead, the order is determined by the JavaScript engine.

With each property traversed, the scope of the reviver function supplied is continuously set to the context of each object, whose key and value are supplied as arguments. In other words, each object whose properties are being supplied as arguments will remain the context of the implicit this within the reviver function. Last, it will be imperative for our reviver method to return a value for every invocation; otherwise, the JavaScript value returned will be that of undefined, as shown in Listing 6-13.

Listing 6-13. Members Are Deleted If the Returned Value from `reviver` Is undefined

```
var JSONtext='{"name":"Ben","age":36,"pets":[{"name":"Waverly","age":3.5},{"name":"Westley",
"age":4}]}';
var reviver= function(k,v){};
var author = JSON.parse( JSONtext,reviver);
console.log(author) //undefined
console.log(typeof author) //undefined
```

If the return value from the `reviver` function is found to be undefined, the current key for that value
is deleted from the object. Specifying the supplied v value as the return object will have no impact on the
outcome of the object structure. Therefore, if a value does not require any alterations from the default
behavior, just return the supplied value, v, as shown in Listing 6-14.

Listing 6-14. Returning the Value Supplied to the `reviver` Function Maintains the Original Value

```
var JSONtext='{"name":"Ben","age":36,"pets":[{"name":"Waverly","age":3.5},{"name":"Westley",
"age":4}]}';
var reviver= function(k,v){ return v };
var author = JSON.parse( JSONtext,reviver);
console.log( author );
/* the result as show in firebug below
    age       36
    name      "Ben"
▼ pets        [ Object { name="Waverly", age=3.5 },  Object { name="Westley", age=4 } ]
    ►   0         Object { name="Waverly", age=3.5 }
    ►   1         Object { name="Westley", age=4 }
*/
console.log(typeof author); //object
```

As was stated earlier, a well-defined set of object keys is not only useful for your application to target
appropriate data but can also provide the necessary blueprint to our `reviver` logic for clues leading to how
and when to alter a provided value. The `reviver` function can use these labels as the necessary conditions to
further convert the returned values of the eval, in order to arrive at the JavaScript structures we require for
our application's purposes.

As you should be well aware at this point, JSON grammar does not capture dates as a literal but, instead,
as a string literal in the UTC ISO format. As a string literal, the built-in eval function is unable to handle the
conversion of said string into that of a JavaScript date. However, if we are able to determine that the value
supplied to our `reviver` function is a string of ISO format, we could instantiate a date, supply it with our
ISO-formatted string, and return a valid JavaScript date back to our application. Consider the example
in Listing 6-15.

Listing 6-15. With the `reviver` Function, ISO Date-Formatted Strings Can Be Transformed into date objects

```
var date= new Date("Jan 1 2015");
var stringifiedData = JSON.stringify( date );
console.log( stringifiedData );  // "2015-01-01T05:00:00.000Z"
var dateReviver=function(k,v){
    return new Date(v);
}
var revivedDate = JSON.parse( stringifiedData , dateReviver);
console.log( revivedDate );  //Date {Thu Jan 01 2015 00:00:00 GMT-0500 (EST)}
```

Because the ISO date format is recognized as a standard, JavaScript dates can be initiated with the provision of an ISO-formatted string as an argument. Listing 6-15 shows a program that begins with a known JavaScript date set to January 1, 2015. Upon its conversion to a JSON text, our date is transformed into a string made up of the ISO 8601 grammar. By supplying a reviver function, which possesses the necessary logic, JSON.parse is able to return a date to our application.

For purely illustrative purposes, Listing 6-15 does not have to determine if the value supplied is in fact an ISO-formatted string. This is simply because we know the value being supplied is solely that. However, it will almost always be necessary for a reviver function to possess the necessary conditional logic that controls how and when to treat each supplied value.

That said, we could test any string values supplied to our reviver function against the ISO 8601 grammar. If the string is determined to be a successful match, it can be distinguished from an ordinary string and thus transformed into a date. Consider the example in Listing 6-16.

Listing 6-16. RegExp Can Match ISO-Formatted Strings

```
var book={};
    book.title = "Beginning JSON"
    book.publishDate= new Date("Jan 1 2015");
    book.publisher= "Apress";
    book.topic="JSON Data Interchange Format"

var stringifiedData = JSON.stringify( book );
console.log( stringifiedData );
// ["value held by index 0","2015-01-01T05:00:00.000Z","value held by index 2","value held
by index 3"]

var dateReviver=function(k,v){
    var ISOregExp=/^([\+-]?\d{4}(?!\d{2}\b))((-?)((0[1-9]|1[0-2])(\3([12]\d|0[1-
9]|3[01]))?|W([0-4]\d|5[0-2])(-?[1-7])?|(00[1-9]|0[1-9]\d|[12]\d{2}|3([0-5]\d|6[1-6])))
([T\s](((([01]\d|2[0-3])((:?)[0-5]\d)?|24\:?00)([\.,]\d+(?!:))?)?(\17[0-5]\d([\.,]
\d+)?)?([zZ]|([\+-])([01]\d|2[0-3]):?([0-5]\d)?)?)?)?$/;
    if(typeof v==="string"){
        if(ISOregExp.test(v)){
            return new Date(v);
        }
    }
    return v;
}
var revivedValues = JSON.parse( stringifiedData , dateReviver);
console.log( revivedValues );
/* the result as show in firebug below
▼ publishDate    Date {Thu Jan 01 2015 00:00:00 GMT-0500 (EST)} ,
    publisher    "Apress",
    title        "Beginning JSON",
    topic        "JSON Data Interchange Format"
*/
```

In the preceding example, our application parses a composite structure, which is simply an array. The value of each key is in the form of a string, one of which, however, represents a date. Within the reviver function, we first determine if each value supplied is that of a string, via the operator typeof. If the value is determined to be of the string type, it is further compared against the ISO grammar by way of a regular expression. The variable ISOregExp references the pattern that matches a possible ISO-formatted string.

If the pattern matches the value supplied, we know it is a string representation of a date, and, therefore, we can transform our string into a date. While the preceding example produces the desired effect, a regular expression may not prove most efficient in determining which strings should be converted and which should not.

This is where we can rely on a well-defined identifier. The k value, when supplied as a clearly defined label, as shown in Listing 6-17, can be incredibly useful for coordinating the return of the desired object.

Listing 6-17. Well-Defined Label Identifiers Can Be Used to Establish Which objects Require Added Revival

```
var book={};
    book.title = "Beginning JSON"
    book.publishDate= new Date("Jan 1 2015");
    book.publisher= "Apress";
    book.topic="JSON Data Interchange Format"

var bookAsJSONtext = JSON.stringify(book);
console.log( bookAsJSONtext );
// "{"title":"Beginning JSON",
    "publishDate":"2015-01-01T05:00:00.000Z",
    "publisher":"Apress",
    "topic":"JSON Data Interchange Format"}"

var reviver = function( k , v ){
        console.log( k );

/* logged keys as they were supplied to the reviver function */
// title
// publisher
// date
// publishedInfo
// topic
//(an empty string)

    if( k ==="publishDate"){
        return new Date( v );
    }
    return v;
}

var parsedJSON = JSON.parse( bookAsJSONtext , reviver );
console.log( parsedJSON );

/* the result as show in firebug below
▼ publishDate    Date {Thu Jan 01 2015 00:00:00 GMT-0500 (EST)} ,
    publisher      "Apress",
    title          "Beginning JSON"
    topic          "JSON Data Interchange Format"
*/
```

Listing 6-17 achieves the same results as Listing 6-16; however, it does not rely on a regular expression to seek out ISO-formatted dates. Instead, the reviver logic is programmed to revive only strings whose key explicitly matches publishDate.

Not only do labels offer more possibility when determining whether the value should or should not be converted, their use is also more expedient than the former method. Depending on the browser, the speeds can range from 29% to 49% slower when the determining factor is based on RegExp. The results can be viewed for yourself in the performance test available at http://jsperf.com/regexp-vs-label.

It was briefly mentioned in Chapter 5 that custom classes, when serialized, are captured indistinguishably from the built-in objects of JavaScript. While this is indeed a hindrance, it is not impossible to transform your object into a custom object, by way of the reviver function.

Listing 6-18 makes use of a custom data type labeled Person, which possesses three properties: name, age, and gender. Additionally, our Person data type possesses three methods to read those properties. An instance of Person is instantiated using the new keyword and assigned to the variable p. Once assigned to p, the three properties are supplied with valid values. Using the built-in instanceof operator, we determine whether our instance, p, is of the Person data type, which we soon learn it is. However, once we serialize our p instance, and parse it back into that of a JavaScript object, we soon discover via instanceof that our p instance no longer possesses the Person data type.

Listing 6-18. Custom Classes Are Serialized As an Ordinary object

```
function Person(){
    this.name;
    this.age;
    this.gender;
}
Person.prototype.getName=function(){
    return this.name;
};
Person.prototype.getAge=function(){
    return this.age;
};
Person.prototype.getGender=function(){
    return this.gender;
};

var p=new Person();
    p.name="ben";
    p.age="36";
    p.gender="male";

console.log(p instanceof Person); // true
var serializedPerson=JSON.stringify(p);

var parsedJSON = JSON.parse( serializedPerson );
console.log(parsedJSON instanceof Person); // false;
```

Because the reviver function is invoked after a JSON text is converted back into JavaScript form, the reviver can be used for JavaScript alterations. This means that you can use it as a prepping station for the final object to be returned. What this means for us is that, using the reviver function, we can cleverly apply inheritance back to objects that we know are intended to be of a distinct data type. Let's revisit the preceding code in Listing 6-19, only this time, with the knowledge that our parsed object is intended to become a Person.

Listing 6-19. Reviving an object's Custom Data Type with the reviver Function

```
function Person(){
    this.name;
    this.age;
    this.gender;
};

Person.prototype.getName=function(){
    return this.name;
};
Person.prototype.getAge=function(){
    return this.age;
};
Person.prototype.getGender=function(){
    return this.gender;
};
//instantiate new Person
var p=new Person();
    p.name="ben";
    p.age="36";
    p.gender="male";

//test that p possesses the Person Data Type
console.log(p instanceof Person); // true

var serializedPerson=JSON.stringify(p);

var reviver = function(k,v){
// if the key is an empty string we know its our top level object
    if(k===""){
        //set object's inheritance chain to that of a Person instance
        v.__proto__ = new Person();
    }
    return v;
}

var parsedJSON = JSON.parse( serializedPerson , reviver );

//test that parsedJSON possesses the Person Data Type
console.log(parsedJSON instanceof Person); // true
console.log(parsedJSON.getName()); // "Ben"
```

The __proto__ property used in the preceding example forges the hierarchical relationship between two objects and informs JavaScript where to further look for properties when local values are unable to be found. The __proto__ was originally implemented by Mozilla and has slowly become adopted by other modern browsers. Currently, it is only available in Internet Explorer version 11 and, therefore, shouldn't be used in daily applications. This demonstration is intended for illustrative purposes, to demonstrate succinctly how the reviver function offers you the ability to be as clever as you wish, in order to get the parsed values to conform to your application's requirements.

Summary

JSON.parse is the available mechanism for converting JSON text into a JavaScript value. As part of the JSON global object, it is available in modern browsers as well as older browsers, by way of including the json2.js library into your application. In order to convert the literals captured, json2.js relies on the built-in global eval function to access the JavaScript interpreter. While you learned that using the eval function is highly insecure, the JSON Object seeks out non-matching patterns of the JSON grammar throughout the supplied text, which minimizes the risk of inviting possibly malicious code into your application. If the parse method uncovers any tokens that seek to instantiate, mutate, or operate, a parse error is thrown. In addition, the parse method is exited, preventing the JSON text from being supplied to the eval function.

If the supplied text to the parse method is deemed suitable for eval, the captured literals will be interpreted by the engine and transformed into JavaScript values. However, not all objects, such as dates or custom classes, can be transformed natively. Therefore, parse can take an optional function that can be used to manually alter JavaScript values, as required by your application.

When you design the replacer, toJSON, and reviver functions, using clearly defined label identifiers will allow your application the ability to better orchestrate the revival of serialized data.

Key Points from This Chapter

- JSON.parse throws a parse error if the supplied JSON text is not valid JSON grammar.

- parse occurs in four stages.

- eval is an insecure function.

- Supply only valid JSON to eval.

- A reviver function can return any valid JavaScript value.

- If the reviver function returns the argument supplied for parameter v, the existing member remains unchanged.

- If reviver returns undefined as the new value for a member, said member is deleted.

- reviver manipulates JavaScript values, not JSON grammar.

CHAPTER 7

Persisting JSON: I

In Chapter 5, you learned how JSON.stringify captures the data possessed by an identified JavaScript value. This occurs by reverse engineering the specified target into its literal form, in accordance with the JSON grammar, thus capturing the current state of a model for a particular application as JSON text. You further learned that JSON.parse taps into the innate ability of the JavaScript engine to "parse" the literals that make up a valid JSON text. This revives the state from a previous model for use within the existing session.

To illustrate how to use JSON.parse, each example in Chapter 6 was preceded by the stringify method, in order to provide something to be parsed. Furthermore, this was meant to illustrate the lifecycle of how one method gives rise to the other.

While this is sufficient for the purposes of a demonstration, it will be rare to parse data immediately after it has been serialized by our application. This would result in a very linear and limited use case. These two methods really shine, however, when they are paired with data persistence. It is the persistence of data that enables both methods, stringify and parse, to be used independently of each other. This offers an application many more use-case scenarios. This contrast is illustrated in Figure 7-1.

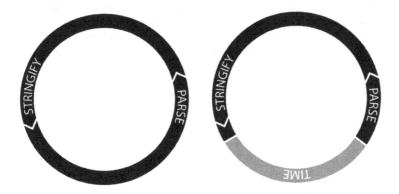

Figure 7-1. *Contrast between use-case scenarios*

Computer science defines the persistence of data as a state that continues to exist after the process from which it was created.[1] Much like the phrase, "you can't step in the same spot of a moving river twice," the process that serializes data will cease to exist the moment the JSON text is produced and the function that ran the process is exited. Therefore, in order to utilize the produced JSON beyond the given process that created it, it must be stored for later retrieval.

---

[1]Wikipedia, "Persistence (computer science)," http://en.wikipedia.org/wiki/Persistence_%28computer_science%29, 2014.

Believe it or not, in the examples in Chapter 5, we were using a slight form of data persistence, according to the aforementioned definition. When the `stringify` method exited, the produced JSON returned by each example was able to continue to be referenced by the application. This is because we had assigned it as the value to a variable, which was often labeled `JSONtext`. Therefore, we managed to persist JSON by definition. However, if we were to navigate away from the application at any point in the course of running the Chapter 5 examples within a browser, the variable `JSONtext` would cease to persist, and the JSON it was assigned would be lost as well.

Because the Internet was founded atop a request-and-response protocol, each request made of a server, regardless of whether it's for `.html`, `.jpg`, `.js`, etc., occurs without consideration of any previous or subsequent requests by the same visitor. This is even if requests made are to the same domain. What is returned from the server is simply the fulfillment of the resource requested. Over the years, many a developer has needed to be able to string together the isolated requests of a common server, in order to facilitate things such as shopping carts for e-commerce. One of the technologies that was forged from this requirement brought forth a technique that we will leverage in order to achieve the persistence of JSON. That technology is the HTTP cookie.

HTTP Cookie

As was previously mentioned, the HTTP/1.1 protocol is incapable of persisting state; therefore, it becomes the duty of the user-agent to manage this undertaking. The HTTP cookie, or cookie for short, was created as a means to string together the actions taken by the user per "isolated" request and provide a convenient way to persist the state of one page into that of another. The cookie is simply a chunk of data that the browser has been notified to retain. Furthermore, the browser will have to supply, per subsequent request, the retained cookie to the server for the domain that set it, thereby providing state to a stateless protocol.

The cookie can be utilized on the client side of an application with JavaScript. Additionally, it is available to the server, supplied within the header of each request made by the browser. The header can be parsed for any cookies and made available to server-side code. Cookies provide both front-end and back-end technologies the ability to collaborate and reflect the captured state, in order to properly handle each page view or request accordingly. The ability to continue to progress the state from one page to another allows each action to no longer be isolated and, instead, occur within the entirety of the user's interaction with a web site.[2]

Like JSON, cookies possess a specification and protocol all their own. By understanding its syntax, we can tap into the persistence of the HTTP cookie and, by extension, persist JSON for later use with an application. The great news is that HTTP cookies are extremely simple, in addition to being recognized by all major browsers dating back to Internet Explorer 3.

Syntax

At its most atomic unit, the cookie is simply a string of ASCII encoded characters composed of one or more attribute-value pairs, separated by a semicolon (`;`) token. Listing 7-1 outlines the syntax for the HTTP cookie.

■ **Note** ASCII is short for "American Standard Code for Information Interchange" and is composed of 128 characters, which are letters from the English alphabet, digits 0–9, basic punctuation, and a few control characters.

---

[2]Wikipedia, "Stateless protocol," `http://en.wikipedia.org/wiki/Stateless_protocol`, 2014.

Listing 7-1. Set-Cookie Syntax as Defined by RFC 6265

```
set-cookie     =     "Set-Cookie:" cookies
cookies        =     1#cookie
cookie         =     NAME "=" VALUE *(";" cookie-av)
NAME           =     attr
VALUE          =     value
cookie-av      =     "expires" "=" value
               |     "max-age" "=" value
               |     "domain" "=" value
               |     "path" "=" value
               |     "secure"
               |     "httponly"
```

Listing 7-1 uses the grammar defined by the HTTP/1.1 specification to outline the syntax of the HTTP cookie. In order to understand the syntax, I would like to direct your focus to the line `cookie = NAME "="  VALUE *(";" cookie-av)`. This line outlines the entire syntax of the cookie. We will dissect this line in two passes. The first half will regard only `cookie = NAME "=" VALUE`. This portion of the syntax outlines the following: "Set some cookie specified by the indicated NAME, to possess the assigned VALUE." A cookie, in short, is nothing more than a key/value pair.

As with all key/value pairs, it will be the purpose of the "key" represented by NAME to both identify as well as provide the means to access an assigned value. VALUE, on the other hand, represents the data or state that's intended to be persisted for the application. To ensure a cookie is stored uniformly among all browsers, it will be imperative that both NAME and VALUE be made up of valid ASCII characters, such as those shown in Listing 7-2.

Listing 7-2. Key/Value Pairs Intended to Be Persisted As a Cookie Must Both Be Valid ASCII Characters

```
"greetings=Hello World!";
"greetingJSON=[\"Hello World!\"]";
```

■ **Note**   Safari as well as Internet Explorer do not correctly handle cookies that contain non-ASCII characters.

While the tokens that make up JSON text are valid ASCII characters, the values held within are not limited to ASCII but, rather, UTF-8. Therefore, if the characters that are represented in your application fall outside of the ASCII range, it will be necessary to encode your UTF-8 characters with Base64 encoding. Two libraries you can use for this purpose are `https://jsbase64.codeplex.com/releases/view/89265` and `https://code.google.com/p/javascriptbase64/`. While both utilize different namespaces, Base64 and B64, they both rely on the same methods to encode and decode. Either of these libraries will be capable of converting your non-ASCII values into ASCII-encoded values. Listing 7-3 demonstrates the use of one of the aforementioned Base64 libraries by converting the characters of our string of UTF-8 characters into those of ASCII, in order to be compliant with the HTTP cookie syntax.

Listing 7-3. UTF-8 Characters Being Converted into ASCII Using a Base64 Library

```
var unicodeValue = "привет мир!";  // Hello World! in Russian;
var asciiString = Base64.encode( JSON.stringify( unicodeValue ) );
console.log(asciiString); // "ItC/0YDQuNCyoLXRgiDQvNC40YAhIg=="
var decodedValue = Base64.decode( asciiString );
console.log( decodedValue );  // "привет мир!"
```

The second half of the line in review, *(";" cookie-av), explains that our cookie can be supplied a sequence of any of the six optional cookie attribute-value pairs, as required by an application. The token that must separate them from their successor in the string is the semicolon (;). While it is not necessary to supply whitespace characters between the semicolon and the attribute value, it will aid to keep your code clean and legible. The possible cookie-av values are listed in Listing 7-1 as "expires", "max-age", "domain", "path", "secure", and "httponly". Each attribute value defines a specific scope to the defined cookie.

expires

The expires attribute is quite literally the "key," pun intended, to the duration over the persistence of the specified cookie. Should the expires attribute be specified, its value counterpart will inform the browser of the date and time it is no longer necessary to further store said cookie. The value supplied is required to be in UTC Greenwich Mean Time format. Being that UTC GMT is a standard, we can achieve this value with ease, by way of the built-in methods of the Date object as demonstrated in Listing 7-4.

Listing 7-4. toUTCString Produces a UTC Greenwich Mean Time Value

```
var date= new Date("Jan 1 2015 12:00 AM");
var UTCdate= date.toUTCString() ;
console.log( UTCdate );  // "Thu, 01 Jan 2015 06:00:00 GMT"
```

Listing 7-4 initiates a date instance with the supplied string of January 1, 2015. Furthermore, the time is set to exactly 12 AM. Utilizing date's built-in method, toUTCString, the date and time it represents is translated into its GMT equivalent and then returned to the caller of the method. When we log that value, we can clearly note that the date has been converted, as it is signified by the appended abbreviation **GMT**. If you were to run the code from Listing 7-4, you might receive a different value. That is because the JavaScript Date Object correlates to your location and time zone. Nevertheless, the date and time that you specify will be equal to the difference in time zone between your location and Greenwich.

If we were to assign the date from Listing 7-4 to our author cookie in Listing 7-5, the cookie would be available until exactly Thursday, 12:00 AM January 1, 2015, or Thursday, 01 Jan 2015 06:00:00 Greenwich Mean Time.

Listing 7-5. Appending Date to the Key/Value Pair to Provide an Expiration

```
var date= new Date("Jan 1 2015 12:00 AM");
"author=test; expires="+ date.toUTCString();
```

If the value supplied to the expires attribute occurs in the past, the cookie is immediately purged from memory. On the other hand, if the expires attribute is omitted, then the cookie will be discarded the moment the session has ended. Essentially, the browser would continue to persist the cookie only as long as the session remained open.

It used to be that the moment you exited the browser, all sessions were immediately closed. Today, however, it's worth noting that sessions may persist well after the browser is exited. This is due to the specific features that vendors have incorporated into their browsers, such as restoring previously viewed pages/tabs if the browser crashes. Additionally, they provide us the ability to restore pages/tabs from History. Therefore, session cookies may continue to persist in memory longer than expected.

As we will be looking to persist our JSON indefinitely, we will almost always supply an expires attribute value to our cookies.

max-age

The max-age attribute, like the expires attribute, specifies how long a cookie should persist. The difference between the two is that max-age specifies the life span of the cookie in seconds. While the max-age attribute is defined by the original specification and continues to exist today, it is not an attribute that is acknowledged by Internet Explorer 6 through 8. That said, it will be wise to favor the expires attribute and ignore max-age.

domain

The domain attribute explicitly defines the domain(s) to which the cookie is to be made available. However, the domain specified must somehow possess a relationship to the origin setting the cookie. In other words, if www.sandboxed.guru is setting a cookie, it cannot supply apress.com as the domain. This would prove to be a huge security concern, if it were possible to set cookies for other domains.

It is the responsibility of the browser to make available, to both JavaScript and the server, all cookies whose supplied domain attribute matches that of the domain of the visited URL. To ensure that the domains match, the browser will compare the two. This comparison can be illustrated with a regular expression (see Listing 7-6).

Listing 7-6. Using a Regular Expression to Demonstrate Matching Origins

```
var regExp=(/www.sandboxed.guru$/i).test('www.sandboxed.guru');   //true
```

Listing 7-6 defines a pattern that matches against the tail end of a host domain. The pattern www.sandboxed.guru represents the cookie's assigned domain attribute. The $ token further specifies that the pattern explicitly ends with .guru. This is necessary to prevent the cookies of sandboxed.guru from being available to another domain that might just so happen to possess our origin within its subdomain. This would be quite the security risk. Note the difference between the URLs sandboxed.guru and guru.com. They are two entirely different domains. Now consider what might occur if guru.com were to use the following subdomain: sandboxed.guru.com (see Listing 7-7).

Listing 7-7. Matching URLs are Determined Through the Top Level Domain (.com)

```
(/sandboxed.guru/i).test('sandboxed.guru.com');   //true
(/sandboxed.guru$/i).test('sandboxed.guru.com'); //false
```

Listing 7-7 demonstrates that without specifying the $ to force a tail-end match, two completely different properties could potentially be considered a match.

■ **Note**   To prevent possible matches that could exist within subdomains, browsers explicitly check that a match must end with the appropriate top-level domain.

The i simply informs the pattern to remain case-insensitive during the match. If the domain attribute and the server domain are determined to be a match, then for each HTTP request, any and all cookies will be sent to the server and made available to the JavaScript application of each page.

The domain attribute is optional, but for security purposes, one must be set. By default, the domain attribute will be set to the absolute origin that the cookie is set from. This can be slightly limiting if you have subdomains that require visibility of these cookies, or vice versa. Consider a domain attribute that is defaulted to `www.sandboxed.guru` for a particular cookie. That cookie will never be available to `sandboxed.guru` because of the preceding `www`. Similarly, if the `domain` attribute is defaulted to `sandboxed.guru`, that cookie will not be visible to `json.sandboxed.guru`.

However, by assigning the `domain` attribute value, we have the ability to broaden the scope of our cookies. For instance, if we specify a `domain` attribute as the top-level domain, preceded by the `.` token (`.sandboxed.guru`), the `domain` attribute would match not only a top-level domain (`sandboxed.guru`) but any and all subdomains as well (`json.sandboxed.guru`). This is demonstrated in Table 7-1.

Table 7-1. *Illustrating Which Origins Are Considered Matches Against the Value Possessed by the domain Attribute*

`domain` **Attribute**	**Origin**	**Match**
`www.sandboxed.guru`	`sandboxed.guru`	`false`
`sandboxed.guru`	`www.sandboxed.guru`	`false`
`.sandboxed.guru`	`sandboxed.guru`	`true`
`.sandboxed.guru`	`www.sandboxed.guru`	`true`
`.sandboxed.guru`	`json.sandboxed.guru`	`true`

It is not necessary to apply the `.` token. As long as we explicitly specify a hostname for the `domain` attribute, the `.` token will automatically be prepended to all non-fully-qualified domains by the user agent.

path

While the `domain` attribute specifies to which domain(s) a set cookie is scoped, the `path` attribute further enforces to which subdirectories a cookie is available. If a `path` attribute is not explicitly specified, the value is defaulted to the current directory that set the cookie. Furthermore, every subdirectory of the defaulted directory will be provided access. However, explicitly defining the `path` attribute allows us to narrow or broaden the scope of the cookie to that of a particular directory and all of its subdirectories. Listing 7-8 demonstrates how cookies can further scope a cookie to that of a particular URL for any domain that is deemed a potential match.

Listing 7-8. Demonstrating Path Scoping with Cookies Set from `http://json.sandboxed.guru/chapter7/ficticious.html`

```
"cookieDefault=test; domain=.sandboxed.guru";
  http://json.sandboxed.guru/chapter7/          //cookieDefault is provided for this request
  http://json.sandboxed.guru/chapter7/css/      //cookieDefault is provided for this request
  https://www.sandboxed.guru/                    //cookieDefault is NOT provided for this request
  http://json.sandboxed.guru/chapter3/js/       //cookieDefault is NOT provided for this request
  https://json.sandboxed.guru/chapter3/img/     //cookieDefault is NOT provided for this request

"cookieA=test; domain=.sandboxed.guru; path=/";
  http://json.sandboxed.guru/chapter7/          //cookieA is provided for this request
  https://www.sandboxed.guru/                    //cookieA is provided for this request
  http://json.sandboxed.guru/chapter3/js/       //cookieA is provided for this request
  https://json.sandboxed.guru/chapter3/img/     //cookieA is provided for this request
```

```
"cookieB=test; domain=.sandboxed.guru; path=chapter3/js/";
  http://json.sandboxed.guru/chapter7/      //cookieB is NOT provided for this request
  http://json.sandboxed.guru/               //cookieB is NOT provided for this request
  https://json.sandboxed.guru/chapter3/js/  //cookieB is provided for this request
  https://json.sandboxed.guru/chapter3/     //cookieB is NOT provided for this request
```

▪ **Note** Cookies that are scoped to a particular domain and/or path are able to be used indistinguishably by HTTP and HTTPS protocols.

secure

The secure attribute is slightly misleading, as it does not provide security. Rather, this attribute, which does not require being assigned a variable, informs the browser to send the cookie to the server only if the connection over which it is to be sent is a secure connection, such as HTTPS. Transmitting data over a secure transport reduces the ability for any network hijackers to view the contents being transported. This helps to ensure that the cookie remains concealed from possible snoopers. While this flag ensures that a cookie's value remains hidden from an attacker, it does not prevent the cookie from being overwritten or even deleted by an attacker.

httponly

The httponly attribute, when specified, limits the availability of the cookie to the server and the server alone. This means the cookie will not be available to the client side, thereby preventing client-side JavaScript from referencing, deleting, or updating the cookie. This httponly flag, when used in conjunction with the secure flag, helps to reduce cross-site scripting from exploiting the cookie. As this chapter is focused on the persistence of JSON data from a client-side perspective, we will be avoiding this attribute.

▪ **Note** Cookies set with the httponly flag can only be set by the server.

When specifying any of the preceding attribute-value pairs, there is no particular order in which they must be specified. Furthermore, each is case-insensitive and can appear in lowercase or uppercase form.

document.cookie

A cookie can be created by a server, server-side code, HTML meta tags, and even JavaScript. In this chapter, we will solely be focused on the creation and the retrieval of cookies by way of the JavaScript language. Up until now, we have been equating a particular syntax of string as the representative for a cookie. The reality is that it is not a cookie until we supply it to our document.

The Document Object Model, or DOM for short, can be referenced via the document object in JavaScript. This document object possesses a variety of interfaces that allows us to manipulate HTML elements and more. One interface on which we will be focusing is the appropriately named document. cookie interface. The cookie attribute of the document object is responsible for supplying the browser with a provided string of name/value pairs, enabling the persistence of said key/value pairs. Additionally, this property acts as the interface for their retrieval from the document. Listing 7-9 uses document.cookie to create our first cookie.

Listing 7-9. Supplying Our First Key/Value Pair to `document.cookie` in Order to Become a Cookie

```
document.cookie= "ourFirstCookie=abc123";
```

While it appears in Listing 7-9 that we are assigning a string to the cookie property, in actuality we are providing a string as the argument to a setter method. A setter method is a method that is used to control changes to a variable.[3] Behind the scenes, the document receives the value being assigned and treats it as an argument to an internal method, which immediately sets the assignment as the value to be stored within an internal collection. This collection, which has come to be referred to as the cookie jar, is stored in a file that is available only to the browser that stores it. Because each browser sets cookies within its cookie jar, cookies are only available to the browser that is used at the time they are set.

As we are not truly assigning a value to the `document.cookie` property, we can add any number of name/value pairs to `document.cookie`, without fear that we will overwrite what we had previously set as a cookie, as seen in Listing 7-10.

Listing 7-10. Subsequent Assignments to `document.cookie`

```
document.cookie= "ourFirstCookie=abc123";
document.cookie= "ourSecondCookie=doeRayMe";
document.cookie= "ourThirdCookie=faSoLaTeaDoe";
```

As I stated earlier, the name/value pairs are not being overridden with each new assignment. All name/value pairs assigned to `document.cookie` are not held as the value of cookie but, rather, stored safely within the cookie jar. The cookie jar is simply a resource located on the file system of the user's computer, which is why cookies have the ability to persist.

In order to view all cookies on your machine, follow the outlined steps for the modern browser of your choice.

For Chrome:

1. Open Chrome.

2. Navigate your browser to `chrome://settings/cookies`.

3. Click any site to view all cookies for that particular site.

For Firefox:

1. Open Firefox.

2. From the Firefox menu, select Preferences.

3. Click the Privacy tab.

4. Click the linked words "remove individual cookies."

5. Click any site to view all cookies for that particular site.

---

[3]Wikipedia, "Mutator method," `http://en.wikipedia.org/wiki/Mutator_method`, 2014.

For Safari:

1.   From the Safari menu, select Preferences.

2.   In the preferences window, select Privacy.

3.   In the Privacy window, click Details. (Unfortunately, with Safari, you can only see what sites have set cookies. You won't be able to view full details.)

For Internet Explorer:

1.   Open Internet Explorer.

2.   From the Tools menu (the gear icon), select Internet Options.

3.   On the General tab, within the section "Browser History," select Settings.

4.   From the Settings panel, click "View objects" or "View Files."

If you only care to view the cookies that are available to the sites you are currently viewing, this can easily be achieved by way of the developer console. Utilizing the developer's tools provided by a modern browser, we can easily witness the cookies we have created thus far. Figure 7-2 displays the stored cookies of Listing 7-10, by way of the developer tools provided by Chrome Version 35.0.1916.114.

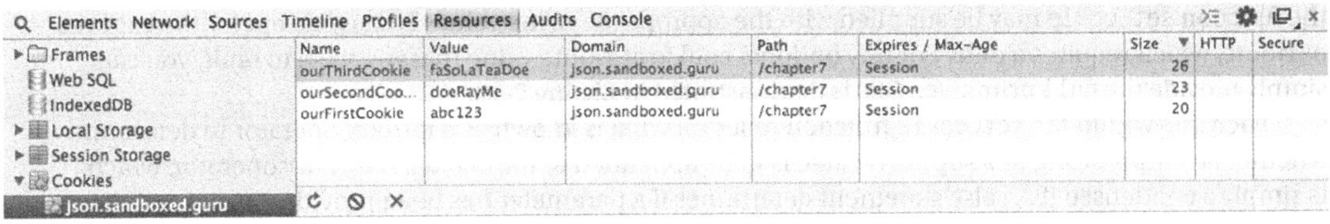

Figure 7-2. *Chrome's Developer Tools Console displays the cookies for the currently visited URL* `json.sandboxed.guru/chapter7/`

As you can note from the Name column in Figure 7-2, each cookie has, in fact, been stored rather than overwritten. Furthermore, you can see what values are set for each optional `cookie-av`, as follows:

```
Domain: json.sandboxed.guru
Path: /chapter7
Expires: Session
```

As you may recall, Listing 7-10 merely supplied the name/value pair and did not append any optional cookie attribute values. However, the `domain`, `path`, and `expires` attributes are required of the cookie. Therefore, the values supplied, as shown in Figure 7-2, have been set to their defaulted values.

As discussed earlier, both the `domain` and `path` attribute values are defaulted to the respective aspects of the URL from which a cookie is set. The `domain` attribute, which is set to `json.sandboxed.guru`, clearly identifies the domain name from which the application ran. Furthermore, the path set to `/chapter7` is a reflection of the directory from which the resource set the preceding cookies.

▣ **Note**   The preceding results reflect the cookies set from the following URL:
`http://json.sandboxed.guru/chapter7/7-7.html`.

Last, the expires attribute is defaulted to a session, which means that the moment the session ends, the browser is no longer required to store the cookie further. In order to provide a level of control over the cookie attribute values, we must append them as required by the syntax of the HTTP cookie. This can be done easily by devising a function to handle this, as portrayed in Listing 7-11.

Listing 7-11. The setCookie Function Simplifies the Creation of HTTP Cookie Values

```
function setCookie(name, value, expires, path, domain, secure, httpOnly) {
                document.cookie = name + "=" + value
                //if expires is not null append the specified GMT date
                + ((expires)? "; expires=" + expires.toUTCString() : "")
                //if path is not null append the specified path
                + ((path) ? "; path=" + path : "")
                //if domain is not null append the specified domain
                + ((domain) ? "; domain=" + domain : "")
                //if secure is not null provide the secure Flag to the cookie
                + ((secure) ? "; secure" : "");
};
```

The function setCookie within Listing 7-11 provides us with a simple means to create a cookie, by supplying the necessary arguments for each cookie-av parameter. For each value that you wish to override, the function setCookie may be supplied with the appropriate string value. That is, except for the expires attribute, which requires a date. For any optional cookie attribute value that you wish to omit, you can simply provide the null primitive. This is demonstrated in Listing 7-12.

Each line within the setCookie function relies on what is known as a tertiary operator to determine whether an empty string or a supplied value is to be appended to the cookie. A tertiary operator, which is simply a condensed if . . . else statement determines if a parameter has been provided an argument to append. If the parameter has not been supplied an argument, an empty string is assigned as the value for the specified cookie attribute.

■ **Note** It is the responsibility of the user-agent to set values for any attribute value that is not valid. Attributes that possess empty strings will be replaced with a default value.

Listing 7-12. The Function setCookie Has Been Created to Help in the Provision of Cookie Attribute Values

```
setCookie("ourFourthCookie",                    //name
        "That would bring us back to Doe",  //value
        new Date("Jan 1 2016 12:00 AM"),    //expires
        "/",                                //path
        null);                              //secure
```

Listing 7-12 utilizes the setCookie function to create a cookie that will persist until January 1, 2016. The attribute's values can be viewed within the cookie jar, as demonstrated within the Developer Tools Console, as shown in Figure 7-3.

	Name	▲ Value	Domain	Path	Expires / Max-Age	Size	HTTP	Secure
▶ ☐ Frames	ourFourthCookie	That would bring us back to Doe	json.sandboxed.guru	/	Fri, 01 Jan 2016 05:00:00 GMT	46		
☷ Web SQL								
☷ IndexedDB								
▶ ▦ Local Storage								
▶ ▦ Session Storage								
▼ ▦ Cookies								
▦ json.sandboxed.guru								

Figure 7-3. *Developer Tools Console displaying the configured cookie attribute values for the currently viewed URL*

While document.cookie is the entry point to the method that controls the storage of cookies, it can also be used to obtain the many name/value pairs that have been stored, provided their domain attribute matches the domain from which they are being requested. In order to read from the cookie jar, we simply reference the cookie property of the document, without providing it an assignment, as demonstrated in Listing 7-13.

Listing 7-13. Retrieving All Persisted Cookies for the Scoped Origin and Path via document.cookie

```
console.log(document.cookie); // "ourFourthCookie=That would bring us back to Doe"
```

The code within Listing 7-13 simply logs out the returned value from document.cookie and sends it to the console for inspection. What is outputted is the name/value pair that has continued to persist. This is assuming you are running this code prior to January 1, 2016. Otherwise, because the expires attribute would be explicitly set to a date that occurred in the past, it would be removed from memory, and nothing would appear.

▦ **Note**   Running the preceding code after January 1, 2016,12:00 AM would inform the browser that it no longer is required to store the cookie.

What you may recognize immediately is that the product returned from document remains unaltered from what we initially supplied in Listing 7-12. Unfortunately, document neither separates the supplied key from its assigned value for ease of use, nor does the document possess a method that can separate them for us. Therefore, in order to extract the value from the string returned, we will have to separate the value from the key ourselves. Listing 7-14 accomplishes this with simple string manipulation.

Listing 7-14. Separating the Value from the Supplied Key from a Singularly Returned Cookie

```
1  var returnedCookie = "ourFourthCookie=That would bring us back to Doe";
2  //15 characters in is the = sign
3  var seperatorIndex = returnedCookie.indexOf("=");
4
5  //extract the first 15 characters
6  var cookieName  = returnedCookie.substring(0,seperatorIndex);
7
8  //extract all characters after the '=' 15th character
9  var cookieValue = returnedCookie.substring(seperatorIndex+1, returnedCookie.length);
10
11 console.log(cookieName);  //"ourFourthCookie"
12 console.log(cookieValue); //"That would bring us back to Doe"
```

Listing 7-14 begins by searching for the first occurrence of the equal (=) token (**line 3**), as that is the token that separates the key from its value. Once this index is made known, we can consider everything up to that index the "key" and everything beyond it the "value." Utilizing the implicit method of the String Object, we can extract a sequence of characters within a numeric range. We begin with the range of characters from 0 up to the 15th character being the = token for Name (**line 6**). The next set of characters, which begins at the 16th character, ranges through the remaining characters of the string, thus successfully extracting the value.

You may also notice that the string returned does not supply us with any of the attribute-value pairs that it was initially assigned. This is strictly due to the fact that the cookie-av values are intended to be utilized by the browser alone. It is the browser's job to ensure that cookies are being supplied to the necessary domain, path, and over the proper transport protocol. Our application merely requires informing the browser, at the moment the cookie is set, how it is necessary to handle the storage and access to the cookie.

While Listing 7-14 outputted only one cookie, this will not always be the case. In the event that numerous cookies are stored and requested from that of a matching origin/path, each persistently stored cookie will be concatonated and returned by the document. Each name/value pair is separated from another by way of the semicolon (;) token, as demonstrated in Listing 7-15.

Listing 7-15. Multiple Cookies Are Concatenated and Delimited by a Semicolon (;)

```
setCookie("ourFourthCookie",
        "That would bring us back to Doe",
        new Date("Jan 1 2016 12:00 AM"),"/",null,null);

setCookie("ourFifthCookie",
        "Doe a dear a female dear",
        new Date("Jan 1 2016 12:00 AM"),"/",null,null);

console.log(document.cookie);
//"ourFifthCookie=Doe a dear a female dear; ourFourthCookie=That would bring us back to Doe"
```

By identifying the tokens of the grammar that make up the cookie syntax, we can separate the name/value pairs from one another. Additionally, we can separate the value from the specified name. This can be achieved by searching the provided string for the semicolon (;) and equal sign (=) tokens.

Listing 7-16. Extracting the Value from a Specified Key Among Many

```
 1 function getCookie(name) {
 2     var regExp = new RegExp(name + "=[^\;]*", "mgi");
 3     var matchingValue = (document.cookie).match(regExp);
 4     console.log( matchingValue )    // "ourFourthCookie=That would bring us back to Doe"
 5     for(var key in matchingValue){
 6         var replacedValue=matchingValue[key].replace(name+"=","");
 7         matchingValue[key]=replacedValue;
 8     }
 9     return matchingValue;
10 };
11 getCookie("ourFourthCookie");   // ["That would bring us back to Doe"]
```

The function getCookie within Listing 7-16 utilizes a regular expression to seek out any name/value pairs from the string returned by document.cookie. The pattern name+"=[^\;]*", as highlighted on **line 2**, defines a pattern to match all sequences of characters within a string that is found to possess a specified name immediately followed by the = token. From there, any valid ASCII character is considered to be a match, as long as that character is not a semicolon (;) token. Should the string returned by the document.cookie possess any sequences of characters that match this pattern, they are captured, respectively, within an array and returned for reference (**line 3**).

92

At this point, if a match has been made, what will be indexed within the returned array are the name/value pairs that match the cookie name supplied to the method. If we were to log out the results found within the array at this point, we should view the following: "ourFourthCookie=That would bring us back to Doe" (**line 4**). In order to separate the value from Name and the equal sign, we iterate over all matched occurrences and replace the found name and = token with those of an empty string (**line 6**), thereby exposing the value. The value is then reassigned back to the key to which it is referenced within the matchingValue array (**line 7**). Last, the getCookie function returns the array of all found values (**line 9**).

Thus far, you have learned how to successfully write and store persistent values by way of HTTP cookies. Utilizing our new functions, setCookie and getCookie, let's revisit the Person object from the previous chapter and store its serialized JSON text within a cookie (see Listing 7-17).

Listing 7-17. Pairing the JSON Object and the Cookie to Store objects

```
1  function Person() {
2        this.name;
3        this.age;
4        this.gender;
5  };
6  Person.prototype.getName = function() {
7        return this.name;
8  };
9  Person.prototype.getAge = function() {
10       return this.age;
11 };
12 Person.prototype.getGender = function() {
13       return this.gender;
14 };
15
16 //instantiate new Person
17 var p = new Person();
18       p.name = "ben";
19       p.age = "36";
20       p.gender = "male";
21
22 var serializedPerson = JSON.stringify(p);
23 setCookie("person", serializedPerson, new Date("Jan 1 2016"),"/","sandboxed.guru",null);
24 console.log( getCookie( "person" )); "{"name":"ben","age":"36","gender":"male"}"
```

Running the preceding code within a browser will create a cookie, as previously, only this time, the cookie created possesses JSON as the supplied value. Also as before, by opening up the developer consoles provided by modern browsers, we can view all stored cookies within the cookie jar for the current origin.

As you can clearly see from Figure 7-4, our person cookie, like the others, has been added to the cookie jar. It will remain available to all JavaScript code from within any directory of the scoped domain sandboxed.guru, as well as any and all subdomains.

Name	Value	Domain	Path	Expires / Max-Age	Size	HTTP	Secure
ourFifthCookie	Doe a dear a female dear	json.sandboxed.guru	/	Fri, 01 Jan 2016 05:00:00 GMT	38		
ourFourthCookie	That would bring us back to Doe	json.sandboxed.guru	/	Fri, 01 Jan 2016 05:00:00 GMT	46		
person	{"name":"ben","age":"36","gender":"male"}	.sandboxed.guru	/	Fri, 01 Jan 2016 05:00:00 GMT	47		

Figure 7-4. *Developer console exhibiting the persistence of our person cookie and its JSON value*

To further illustrate this point, simply navigate to `http://json.sandboxed.guru/chapter7/cookie-test.html` and create your own `person` cookie to store. After you submit your cookie to the document, either refresh the page to find the `person` column populated or navigate to `http://sandboxed.guru/cookie-test.html` to find that this top-level domain has access to your new `person` cookie. Now hit Delete, to remove the persisted cookie, and generate another, this time with different data. Once more, visit the subdomain `http://json.sandboxed.guru/chapter7/cookie-test.html`, and you will see that new cookie pre-populated.

For all of its benefits, the cookie does come with a few limitations. Sadly, the cookie can only store a maximum amount of bytes. In fact, it can only store roughly 4KB, which would be roughly 4,000 ASCII characters. While 4,000 characters is a lot, it can add up quickly, depending on what you are storing. Furthermore, Base64 characters can require up to three times more bytes per character than ASCII.

You learned that `document.cookie` does not provide any information beyond the stored name/value pair. This is problematic, because there is no way to truly know how many bytes are available to us. Another issue that cookies face is that they are scoped to the browser, which means that the preserved state is only available to the specific browser that preserves it. Last, because the cookie was originally crafted to help maintain a visitation between a server and a browser, cookies are automatically sent with every request made to the server that possesses the allowed origin by the cookie. The issue here is that the more cookies that are used, each occupying x number of bytes is sent to the server with every single request. Essentially, unless your server is utilizing the cookie, you are needlessly transmitting 4KB for each cookie stored for every request.

While the cookie has its advantages, it is also archaic. It was just a matter of time before another front-end technology came along. That tool is HTML 5's Web Storage.

Web Storage

HTML5 introduced the concept of Web Storage to pick up where the cookie had left off. While Web Storage may be considered to be the HTTP cookie successor, it would simply be a matter of the context in which you can make that statement. A better way to view Web Storage is simply to look at it as cookies' counterpart. Its creation is not necessarily to replace the cookie. The cookie itself serves a very important purpose, which is to maintain the session between a browser and a server. This is something that Web Storage does not intend to replace, because it exists to meet the growing needs of the times in a way that the cookie is simply incapable of fulfilling, when it comes to the persistence of client-side data.[4]

It strives to reduce the overhead of HTTP requests and offers an incredibly large amount of storage per origin. In fact, the allowed capacity ranges about 5MB. Similar to its predecessor, the Web Storage API enables state to be stored via JavaScript, either indefinitely or solely for the duration of a session. Much like the cookie, Web Storage concerns itself with the persistence of name/value pairs. Because each value supplied to the storage object must be in string form, it can quickly become cumbersome to deal with a plethora of string values, thereby making JSON data the ideal candidate.

Web Storage is accessible to JavaScript, by way of Window Object and can be accessed as `Window.localStorage` and `Window.sessionStorage`. Because the window object is global and can always be reached from within any scope, each storage object can be referenced without the explicit reference of the window object, shortening each reference to `localStorage` and `sessionStorage`.

---

[4]W3C, W3C Recommendation, "Web Storage," `http://www.w3.org/TR/webstorage/#introduction`, July 30, 2013.

Both forms of the aforementioned storage objects, whether they be local or session, allow for the storage of state through a similar API. However, as you may have already surmised, the difference between the two regards the contrast among the durations for which the state of data is retained. The sessionStorage, as the name implies, allows data to persist only as long as the session exists. Whereas the data stored via localStorage will persist indefinitely, either until the state is deleted by the application or user, by way of the browser's interface. Unlike the cookie, all data stored within localStorage will not be set to expire.

Web Storage Interface

Web Storage allows for the storing of data, the retrieval of data, and the removal of data. The means by which we will be working with data and the storage object is via the Web Storage API. As Table 7-2 outlines, there are six members that make up the Web Storage API, and each provides a specific need for working with data persistence.

Table 7-2. *Six Members of the Web Storage API*

Members	Parameter	Return
setItem	string (key), string (value)	void
getItem	string (key)	string (value)
removeItem	string (key)	void
clear		void
key	Number (index)	string (value)
length		Number

Unlike the singular interface of the HTTP cookie, which is used to store, retrieve, and delete data, Web Storage possesses an API to make working with the persistence of data all the more practical. Furthermore, regardless of the storage object you intend to use, whether it's local or session, the API remains uniform.

setItem

The Storage Object method setItem possesses the signature of Listing 7-18 and is the method that we will use to persist data. As was mentioned previously, much like the HTTP cookie, Web Storage persists data in the form of name/value pairs. However, while the cookie itself did not distinguish the name from the value it retained, Web Storage does. Therefore, setItem does not merely accept a singular string but, rather, requires two strings to be provided. The first string represents the name of the key, and the second string will represent the value to be held.

Listing 7-18. Signature of the setItem Method

```
setItem( key , value )
```

When a value is set, it will occur without providing a response back to the invoker of the method. However, if a value is unable to be set, either because the user has disabled the storage or because the maximum capacity for storage has been reached, an Error will be thrown. It's as they say, "no news is good news." In other words, if an error does not occur on setItem, you can rest assured the data has been set successfully.

Because a runtime error can cause your script to come to a halt, it will be imperative to wrap your call to setItem with a try/catch block. Then, you can catch the error and handle exceptions gracefully.

Listing 7-19. Storing Our First Item

```
localStorage.setItem("ourFirstItem,"abc123");
```

As with the key/value pairs of a JavaScript object, each key must possess a unique label. If you were to store a value with the name of a key that currently exists, that value would effectively replace the previously stored value.

Listing 7-20. Replacing the Value Possessed by the ourFirstItem Key

```
localStorage.setItem("ourFirstItem","abc123");
localStorage.setItem("ourFirstItem","sunday Monday happy-days");
```

At this point in time, if we were to retrieve the value set for ourFirstItem, we would witness that the previous value of "abc123" had been replaced with the theme song from the television sitcom *Happy Days*.

■ **Tip** Because an error will be thrown if the user has disabled Web Storage, it would be wise to wrap every call to the Storage Object API within a try/catch block.

---

getItem

The Storage Object method getItem (see Listing 7-21) is the counterpart to the setItem method. It, like our getCookie method from Listing 7-16, allows us to retrieve the persisted state that corresponds to the key provided to the method (see Listing 7-22).

Listing 7-21. Signature of getItem

```
getItem( key )
```

Listing 7-22. Obtaining a Value for a Specified Key

```
console.log( localStorage.getItem( "ourFirstItem" ) );   //sunday Monday happy-days
console.log( localStorage.getItem( "ourSecondItem" ) );   //null
```

The key is the only expected parameter, as indicated in Listing 7-22, and will return the corresponding state for the supplied key. If, however, the name of the key supplied does not exist on the Storage Object, a value of null will be returned.

removeItem

The Storage Object method removeItem is the sole means of expiring the persistence of an individual key/value pair. Its signature is similar to that of getItem, in that it accepts one parameter, as shown in Listing 7-23. This parameter is the key that pertains to the data that you no longer wish to persist (see Listing 7-24).

Listing 7-23. Signature of removeItem

```
removeItem( key )
```

Listing 7-24. Utilizing `removeItem` to Expire a Persisted State

```
console.log( localStorage.getItem( "ourFirstItem" ));     //sunday Monday happy-days
         localStorage.removeItem( "ourFirstItem" );
console.log( localStorage.getItem( "ourFirstItem" ));     //null
```

clear

As indicated in Listing 7-25, the method `clear` does not require any parameters. This is because this method is simply used to instantly purge each and every key/value pair retained by the targeted Storage Object.

Listing 7-25. Signature of the `clear` Method

```
clear( )
```

key

The Storage Object method key is used to obtain the identities of all stored keys that possess accompanying data retained by the given Storage Object. As the signature outlined in Listing 7-26 demonstrates, the method can be provided with that of an index, which will return in kind with the member at the supplied index. If a value does not exist for the provided index, the method will return a value of `null`.

Listing 7-26. Signature of the key Method

```
key( index )
```

length

As it will not be beneficial to supply indexes that are beyond the boundaries of stored keys, the Storage Object provides us with access to the length of all values stored by the Storage Object in question. This total can be obtained via the `length` property. The `length` property, when used in conjunction with a loop, as demonstrated in Listing 7-27, provides us with the ability to remain within the boundaries of the values stored.

Listing 7-27. Obtaining the Stored Keys from a Storage Object Is Simple with a Loop

```
var maxIndex= localStorage.length;
for(var i=0; i<maxIndex; i++){
     var foundKey = localStorage.key( i );
}
```

Reusing the key/value pair used by our first cookie, we will demonstrate the ease of the Web Storage API.

Listing 7-28. Utilizing Web Storage to Persist the Value Supplied to Our `Person` Instance

```
1 function setItem( key , value ){
2    try{
3         localStorage.setItem( key , value );
4    }catch(e){
5         //WebStorage is either disabled or has exceeded the Storage Capacity
6    }
7 }
```

```
 8 function getItem( key ){
 9    var storageValue;
10    try{
11        storageValue= localStorage.getItem( key );
12    }catch(e){
13        //WebStorage is disabled
14    }
15    return storageValue;
16 }
17
18  function Person() {
19        this.name;
20        this.age;
21        this.gender;
22  };
23  Person.prototype.getName = function() {
24        return this.name;
25  };
26  Person.prototype.getAge = function() {
27        return this.age;
28  };
29  Person.prototype.getGender = function() {
30        return this.gender;
31  };
32
33  //instantiate new Person
34  var p = new Person();
35      p.name = "ben";
36      p.age = "36";
37      p.gender = "male";
38
39  var serializedPerson = JSON.stringify(p);
40  setItem( "person" , serializedPerson );
41  console.log( getItem( "person" )); // "{"name":"ben","age":"36","gender":"male"}" ||
    "undefined"
```

Listing 7-28 revisits our person example from Listing 7-17 to point out how the Web Storage API and cookie interface vary. The examples similarly use their component to store and retrieve the same value. However, the use of the API provided by Web Storage simplifies things greatly. Unlike in our cookie example, Web Storage requires less work for setting—and especially retrieving—data. **Line 41** of Listing 7-28 simply requests the data of the supplied key and logs it for inspection to the developer console. The reason why the value returned may be either what is stored or (signified by the || operator) "undefined", is due to the fact that Web Storage may be disabled, which will prevent the variable storageValue (**line 9**) from being set. Unlike its cookie counterpart, getItem handles the management of key/value pairs for us, so that we don't have to manipulate the returned string. Could you imagine performing a JavaScript search over 5MB worth of ASCII characters? The application would become nonresponsive.

What you may have also noticed is that we never specified a domain or path at any point in time during our review of Web Storage. This is because, unlike the cookie, the Storage Object strictly adheres to the same-origin policy, meaning that resources can only be shared/accessed from the same document origin, if the two share the same protocol, hostname, and port. You will learn more about the same-origin policy in Chapter 9.

Summary

The HTTP cookie and Web Storage are extremely useful client-side tools for storing and persisting JSON data. They can be utilized to retain the state of a user's engagement with a web site, web app, or even a game. As cookies and Web Storage are stored on the user's browser, each visitor can potentially possess different information, which can further add to the benefit of local persistence. Such benefit would be personalization/optimization. However, for all their benefits, the cookie and Web Storage are not without their limitations.

The first and foremost concern surrounds security. As both the cookie and a Storage Object can be set and retrieved with JavaScript, it's best practice to store information that is not particularly sensitive. While it may not be understood by the average visitor of your site how data is being utilized between your application and their browser, those who are seeking to exploit these technologies do understand. As this data is accessible to JavaScript, by utilizing the same techniques covered in this chapter, a user or a site hijacker can manipulate or alter persisted state at any point in time, for malicious or benign intent. This, of course, will vary, based on the data as well as the nature of the application that makes use of it.

As I previously indicated, the HTTP cookie and Web Storage are scoped to a visitor's browser. Data that may have been set to persist, whether by cookie or Storage Object, is dependent on the browser the visitor previously used to interact/view your application. This means the persistence of state has the potential to vary from one browser to the other, each time a user visits your application. This inconsistency may prove to be problematic, depending on your application's needs. Last, as the data that is being retained will persist on the visitor's file system and not the server's, it can easily be removed by the visitor at any point he or she chooses, through the interface provided by the browser.

These aforementioned issues can be avoided when used in conjunction with a server-side database, which will be the topic of discussion in Chapter 12. In the next chapter, I will discuss how to transmit JSON to and from our applications via JavaScript.

Key Points from This Chapter

- Data persistence is the continued existence of state after the process that created it.

- HTTP/1.1 is a stateless protocol.

- Cookies and Web Storage are used to retain state.

- Cookies are sent with every HTTP/1.1 request.

- Session data will cease to exist after the session exits.

- Sessions do not necessarily end when a browser is closed.

- Cookies are exchanged via HTTP and HTTPS, unless flagged as secure.

- Cookies can only store 4KB worth of ASCII characters.

- Cookies can be shared among subdomains.

- Web Storage can store 5MB of data.

- Each origin possesses its own Storage Object.

- Web Storage strictly adheres to a same-origin policy.

CHAPTER 8

■ ■ ■

Data Interchange

Thus far, you have been learning how to work with JSON data that has been stringified, parsed, persisted, and retrieved—all from within the scope of a running application. However, as JSON is a data-interchange format, it is capable of being transmitted across the Internet, which offers our applications much more possibility than we have currently been allowing them.

With the use of data interchange, we can send JSON across the Internet into a database that is owned/controlled by us. The visitor cannot as easily delete data this way, as it could be with Web Storage and the HTTP cookie. Furthermore, the ability to transmit data allows our application the ability not only to push out JSON but also to load it into our applications. In other words, not only can we load into our application the data that we've stored, but we can also tap into the data that others are willing to share as well. This may be data that is available to the general public free of charge or by a paid service. Consider the vast array of social sites out there that offer to the public free of charge the data that they capture. Twitter, Facebook, and Instagram are prime examples of social properties that are willing to offer aspects of their data via an API. Because of the many positive attributes that JSON possesses, it is the favored data format of nearly every social API.

In upcoming discussions, you will learn how to load JSON into our application, transmit JSON from our application, and persist JSON into a database over which we have control. Then, we will look at how to incorporate the data from the API of the social property Twitter. However, before we jump into those topics, it will be of great benefit to understand the communication that takes place under the hood of our browser during the request for a resource and the response from a server, as well as the underlying technologies that we will utilize to enable both.

Hypertext Transfer Protocol

The Hypertext Transfer Protocol, or simply HTTP, is the underlying mechanism responsible for our daily interactions with the Internet. It is used in conjunction with many underlying networks of protocols, in order to facilitate the appropriate request/response between a client and a server. Typically, the client utilized in the request/response exchange is that of a web browser, such as Chrome, Firefox, Internet Explorer, or Safari. However, it can also be that of another server. Regardless of whether the client is a browser or a server, the request/response can only take place upon the initiation of a request. Furthermore, a response can only be provided from a web server.

Anytime a resource is requested from a server, whether it's a document, an image, a style sheet, etc., a request must be initiated.

HTTP-Request

It is the role of the request to outline the specifics that detail the required resource from the server. It will be these details that help to ensure that the server provides the appropriate response. A request can be thought of as your order at a restaurant. When you provide a waiter with your order, you are outlining what you are expecting from the kitchen. Additionally, it may include your preferences of how you would like it to be cooked or served. In the preceding analogy, the HTTP protocol is the waiter, the order is the HTTP request, and the food provided represents the HTTP response.

The HTTP request consists of three general components, each with a particular use for detailing what resource is required from a server. These three components can be viewed in Table 8-1.

Table 8-1. *Structure of the HTTP Request*

	Parts	Required
1	Request Line	Yes
2	Headers	No
3	Entity Body	No

Request Line

The first component, known as the request line, is absolutely mandatory for any request. It alone is responsible for the type of request, the resource of the request, and, last, which version of the HTTP protocol the client is making use of. The request line itself is composed of three parts, separated from one another by whitespace. These three components are Method, Request-URI, and HTTP-Version.

Method represents the action to be performed on the specified resource and can be one of the following: GET, POST, HEAD, PUT, LINK, UNLINK, DELETE, OPTIONS, and TRACE. For the purposes of this chapter, I will only discuss the first two.

The method GET is used to inform the server that it possesses a resource that we wish to obtain. GET is most commonly used when navigating to a particular URL in a browser, whereas the POST method is used to inform the server that you are providing data along with your request. The POST method is commonly used with HTML forms. The response that is supplied upon a form's submission often reflects content that accounts for the form submission.

Because the GET method does not concern itself with any alterations to a server, it is commonly referred to as a *safe method*. The POST method, on the other hand, is referred to as an *unsafe method*, as it concerns working with data.

The URI of the request line simply identifies the resource, which the request method applies. The specified URI may be that of a static resource, such as a CSS file, or that of a dynamic script whose content is produced at the moment of a request.

Last, the request line must indicate the HTTP-Version utilized by the client. Since 1999, the Request-Version of browsers has been HTTP/1.1. Examples of a request line are shown in Listing 8-1.

Listing 8-1. Syntactic Structure of a Request Line

```
GET   http://json.sandboxed.guru/chapter8/css/style.css    HTTP/1.1
GET   http://json.sandboxed.guru/chapter8/img/physics.jpg  HTTP/1.1
POST  http://json.sandboxed.guru/chapter8/post.php         HTTP/1.1
```

Headers

The second component of the request concerns the manner by which the request is able to provide supplemental meta-information. The meta-information is supplied within the request in the form of a header, whereas a header, at its most atomic unit, is simply a key/value pair separated by the colon (:) and made up of ASCII characters. The server can utilize this information in order to best determine how to respond to the request.

The HTTP protocol has formalized a plethora of headers that can be utilized to relay a variety of detail to the server. These headers fall under one of three categories: general headers, request headers, and entity headers.

General Headers

The first category of header is that of the general headers. The headers that apply to this category identify general information pertaining to the request. Such general information may regard the date of the request, whether or not to cache the request, etc. The following are general headers:

- Cache-Control

- Connection

- Date

- Pragma

- Trailer

- Transfer-Encoding

- Upgrade

- Via

- Warning

Request Headers

The second category of headers is that of the request headers. These headers can be supplied with the request to provide the server with preferential information that will assist in the request. Additionally, they outline the configurations of the client making the request. Such headers may reveal information about the user-agent making the request or the preferred data type that the response should provide. By utilizing the headers within this category, we can potentially influence the response from the server. For this reason, the request headers are the most commonly configured headers.

One very useful header is the Accept header. It can be used to inform the server as to what MIME type or data type the client can properly handle. This can often be set to a particular MIME type, such as application/json, or text/plain. It can even be set to */*, which informs the server that the client can accept all MIME types. The response provided by the server is expected to reflect one of the MIME types the client can handle. The following are request headers:

- Accept

- Accept-Charset

- Accept-Encoding

- Accept-Language

- Authorization

- Expect

- From

- Host

- If-Match

- If-Modified-Since

- If-None-Match

- If-Range

- If-Unmodified-Since

- Max-Forwards

- Proxy-Authorization

- Range

- Referer

- TE

- User-Agent

At this point, feel free to navigate the browser of your choice to the following URL: `http://json.sandboxed.guru/chapter8/headers.php`. The content that is displayed is the response to that of an HTTP request. Ironically, the content displayed presents the HTTP request for the requested URI. Here, you can view the combination of general headers and the request headers submitted with the request. Generally speaking, as we navigate the Internet, the browser supplies the various headers with each request on our behalf. Therefore, some of the request headers supplied possess values that reflect those configured within our browser settings. Because each browser may vary in its values supplied to the reflected headers, your results may not reflect mine, shown in Listing 8-2.

Listing 8-2. The Composition of an HTTP GET Request

```
GET /chapter8/headers.php HTTP/1.1
Host: json.sandboxed.guru
Cache-Control: max-age=0
Connection: close
X-Insight: activate
Cookie: person={"age":"36","name":"ben","gender":"male"}
Dnt: 1
Accept-Encoding: gzip, deflate
Accept-Language: en-us,en;q=0.7,fr;q=0.3
Accept: text/html,application/xhtml+xml,application/xml;q=0.9,*/*;q=0.8
User-Agent: Mozilla/5.0 (Macintosh; Intel Mac OS X 10.9; rv:30.0) Gecko/20100101 Firefox/
30.0 FirePHP/0.7.4
```

■ **Note** The Referer header is the result of a spelling mistake that was not caught before it was incorporated within the HTTP specification.

As you can clearly see, the first line, the request line, details the method to apply to the indicated URI of /chapter8/headers.php. While the URI is that of a dynamic page, the request line states: GET the resource provided by headers.php. That resource, of course, generates its content upon receipt of the HTTP request, in order to reveal the headers as your browser configures them.

While this information will only be present for the particular URI utilizing our developer console, we will be able to view any and all HTTP requests and their responses for any resource. This can be accomplished by profiling the network activity from within the developer's console of your favorite modern browser. Feel free to refresh the page once you have your developer console open and the network tab in view. Figure 8-1 displays the HTTP request and its headers for the request URI http://json.sandboxed.guru/chapter8/headers.php.

Figure 8-1. *The request headers exhibited by the Chrome developer console*

Entity Headers

The third category of headers is that of the entity headers. These headers are used to supply meta-information regarding any data that is being sent to the server along with the request. The provision of data that accompanies a request is always tied to the unsafe HTTP methods, such as PUT and POST. Safe methods, on the other hand, will never possess an entity body. However, when data is supplied, it will be these headers that describe the data type being sent, the character encoding it possesses, and the amount of bytes of data being transferred. The following are entity headers:

- Allow
- Content-Encoding
- Content-Languages
- Content-Length
- Content-Location
- Content-MD5
- Content-Range

- Content-Type

- Expires

- Last-Modified

Entity Body

The final component of the request is the entity body. While the entity headers carry the meta-information, the entity body is strictly the nomenclature for the data being sent to the server. The syntax of the entity can reflect that of HTML, XML, or even JSON. However, if the Content-Type entity header is not supplied, the server, being the receiving party of the request, will have to guess the appropriate MIME type of the data provided.

I will now review the request of an unsafe method, so that you can observe a request that is in possession of an entity body. Feel free to navigate your browser to the following URL: http://json.sandboxed.guru/chapter8/post.php. By filling out the two form fields and clicking submit, the form post will automatically trigger an HTTP request that will supply the filled-in fields as data. The response that will be outputted to the screen will reflect the captured headers of the POST request. Listing 8-3 reveals the HTTP request and the entity it possesses. Feel free to utilize your developer's console, to compare the request with the results shown below.

Listing 8-3. The Composition of an HTTP POST Request

```
POST /chapter8/headers.php HTTP/1.1
Host: json.sandboxed.guru
Cache-Control: max-age=0
Connection: close
X-Insight: activate
Referer: http://json.sandboxed.guru/chapter8/post.php
Dnt: 1
Accept-Encoding: gzip, deflate
Accept-Language: en-us,en;q=0.7,fr;q=0.3
Accept: text/html,application/xhtml+xml,application/xml;q=0.9,*/*;q=0.8
User-Agent: Mozilla/5.0 (Macintosh; Intel Mac OS X 10.9; rv:30.0) Gecko/20100101
Firefox/30.0 FirePHP/0.7.4
Content-Length: 37
Content-Type: application/x-www-form-urlencoded

fname=ben&lname=smith&mySubmit=submit
```

As you can see from Listing 8-3, an empty line following the other two request components separates the entity body. Furthermore, the two supplied entity headers, Content-Length and Content-Type, provide the server with an understanding of what is being supplied, relieving the server from having to guess how to properly parse the data.

HTTP Response

For every HTTP request there is an HTTP response. Additionally, the structural composition of the HTTP response, as displayed in Table 8-2, is identical to that of the HTTP request with one major exception: the request line is replaced with a status line.

Table 8-2. Structure of the HTTP Response

	Parts	Required
1	Status Line	Yes
2	Headers	No
3	Entity Body	No

Status Line

The first component of the HTTP response is the status line, which details the result of the request. The composition of the status line is composed of three parts: the version of the HTTP protocol utilized by the server, a numeric status code, and an associated textual phrase that describes the status of the request. Each component is separated from the other with whitespace.

The HTTP version simply reflects the version of the HTTP protocol used by the server.

The status code represents a three-digit number that reflects the status of the request. It is the duty of the status code to inform the client whether the request was understood, if it resulted in an error, and/or if the client must take further action. There are five categories of statuses, and each three-digit status code is a member of an appropriate status class.

The status classes, as illustrated in Table 8-3, are divided into groups of hundreds, meaning that the indicated classes can possess 100 different unique status codes. While this is not currently the case, by providing each class with ample padding, additional statuses can be incorporated in the future.

Table 8-3. Response Status Classes of the HTTP-Request

Status Class	Reason Phrase
100–199	This class of status code indicates a provisional response, consisting only of the status line and optional headers.
200–299	This class of status code indicates that the client's request was successfully received, understood, and accepted.
300–399	This class of status code indicates that further action needs to be taken by the user-agent, in order to fulfill the request.
400–499	This class of status code is intended for cases in which the client seems to have erred.
500–599	This class of status code indicates cases in which the server is aware that it has erred or is incapable of performing the request.

The most common classes that will be used by the average user will be among the following: 200's, 400's, and 500's. These represent the response messages from the server that will help to indicate if the resource requested has been satisfied or if there were errors along the way. The most common status codes encountered by front-end developers are the following: 200, 204, 404, and 500.

200 OK: The server has successfully recognized the request.

204 No Content: The server has successfully recognized the request; however, there is no new entity body to return.

404 Page Not Found: The indicated resource is unable to be located by the server.

500 Internal Server Error: The server has encountered an issue preventing the request from being fulfilled.

The textual phrase of the status line is utilized, so that it can be easily read and interpreted by humans. Each phrase details the meaning of its associated status code.

■ **Note** You can read more on the existing status codes here: `http://www.w3.org/Protocols/rfc2616/rfc2616-sec10.html`.

Headers

The second component of the response concerns the mechanism by which the response is able to provide the client with supporting meta-information. As with requests, response headers are grouped into three categories: general headers, request headers, and entity headers.

General Headers

The first category of headers is the general headers. The headers that apply to this category identify general information. Such general information may regard the date of the response or whether the connection should remain open or closed. The following are general headers:

- Cache-Control
- Connection
- Date
- Pragma
- Trailer
- Transfer-Encoding
- Upgrade
- Via
- Warning

Response Headers

The second category of headers is the response headers. These headers provide the client of the request with information pertaining to the configurations of the server, as well as the requested URI. For example, the server can provide response headers to inform the request of what HTTP methods are accepted, as well as whether authorization is required in order to access the specified URI. These headers can even inform the request whether it should occur at a later point in time. The following are response headers:

- Accept-Ranges
- Age
- ETag
- Location
- Proxy-Authentication

- Retry-After
- Server
- Vary
- WWW-Authenticate

Entity Headers

The third category of headers is the entity headers. These headers are used to supply meta-information regarding the data being sent along with the response. As with entity headers for a request, the most beneficial entity headers for a response will be those that describe the MIME type of the entity provided, so that it may be parsed/read properly. This is achieved via the Content-Type header. The configured value of the Content-Type will often reflect a MIME type that was indicated as the value of the Accept header within the request. The following are entity headers:

- Allow
- Content-Encoding
- Content-Languages
- Content-Length
- Content-Location
- Content-MD5
- Content-Range
- Content-Type
- Expires
- Last-Modified

Entity Body

The final component of the response is that of the entity body. Whereas entity headers outline the meta-information, the entity body is the data provided by the server.

Let's now revisit our earlier HTTP request from Figure 8-1, only this time, let's focus on the response captured in Figure 8-2. Figure 8-2 reveals the response that is returned by the server for the following URL: `http://json.sandboxed.guru/chapter8/headers.php`. The first thing to note is the status line located below the response headers heading. It begins by revealing the HTTP version and is immediately followed by the status of the request.

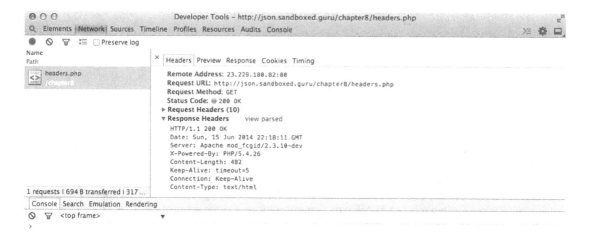

Figure 8-2. *The response headers exhibited by the Chrome developer console*

In this particular case, the response is successfully fulfilled, as indicated by the status code of 200. Furthermore, from the textual phrase that follows the status code, we can read that the messaging is that of OK. Below the status line, we are able to observe a variety of headers, which belong to the general headers and entity headers categories. I want to draw your attention to the final header in the listing. This particular entity header is configured to define the MIME type of the entity body being returned. This enables the browser to parse it accordingly and display it upon its arrival. In this particular case, the data being provided is HTML and, therefore, possesses the Content-Type of text/HTML.

The actual data that is returned can be viewed in the response tab, which is none other than the markup that is being presented upon arrival of the URL.

If the preceding content is new to you, don't worry, for you are not alone. In fact, typically, only those who are server-side developers know the preceding information. This is because they generally write the code to analyze the request headers and, in turn, configure the appropriate response. Typically, HTTP requests are made behind the scenes and handled by the browser, allowing front-end developers like us to remain ignorant of the communications taking place. However, in the upcoming section, I will discuss the technique that enables us to initiate and configure our own HTTP requests, allowing us to send and receive JSON via JavaScript.

Ajax

Ajax itself is not a technology but, rather, a term coined by Jesse James Garrett in 2005. Ajax stands for *Asynchronous JavaScript and XML* (a.k.a. Ajax) and has become synonymous with modern-day front-end development, and for great reason. It offers the ability to initiate HTTP-Requests such as GET and POST on demand and without having to navigate away from the current web page, as shown in Figure 8-3.

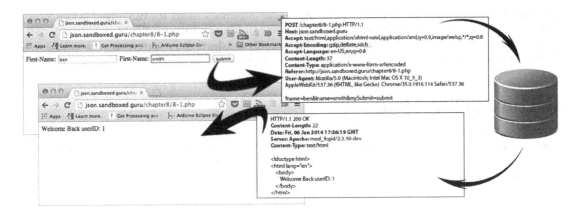

Figure 8-3. *The full life cycle of an HTTP GET request*

Figure 8-3 demonstrates the process by which data is integrated into a web page when solely handled by the server. The demo begins with a user landing on a web page and being invited to sign in to the site experience via a simple form. Upon clicking submit, the browser initiates a new request to the server, in order to retrieve the appropriate response that reflects the data that has been provided by the user. The headers within that request detail the necessary information for the server to respond accordingly. Once the server receives the request, it fetches the resource being requested, retrieves some information from the database, and inserts it within the content to be returned, thereby revealing an updated page for the visited URL: `json.sandboxed.guru/chapter8/8-1.php`.

The terms *Asynchronous JavaScript* and *XML* refer to the various web technologies that are used to incorporate the exchange of data between the current web page and a server in the background. You might be thinking that if the *x* in *Ajax* stands for XML, and this is a book on the use of JSON, why then should we care about Ajax? While the *x* does stand for *XML*, the request/response initiated via Ajax continues to remain bound to the rules of the HTTP protocol. Therefore, the server can return any and all valid data types, such as HTML, Text, XML, JSON, etc. We, of course, will be working with JSON. The *x* in *Ajax* came to be simply because the original XMLHttpRequest only supported XML parsing.[1]

The XMLHttpRequest object provides the interface by which JavaScript can initiate an HTTP-Request directly from within a running application, enabling communication with a server. This allows for data to be pushed out or consumed. Furthermore, as the *A* in *Ajax* suggests, this communication occurs asynchronously, implying non-blocking. This allows the executing application and the user to continue, without requiring either to stop what they're doing, until the request has been fulfilled by the server. The HTTP request occurs outside of the process used to run our JavaScript application. More specifically, it occurs in a separate process that is used only by the browser. When the server has fulfilled the request, the browser will alert our application to its availability, by notifying our application via an event. By listening in on this event, we can obtain the response from the server to parse and use, as our application requires.

The XMLHttpRequest object, which is the ECMAScript HTTP API,[2] originated as a proprietary feature within Internet Explorer 5, as a part of the Active X framework. Its practicality and implications became immediately recognized and were quickly implemented by competing browsers. Anticipating the possible

---

[1]MDN: Mozilla Developer Network, "HTML in XMLHttpRequest," `https://developer.mozilla.org/en-US/docs/Web/API/XMLHttpRequest/HTML_in_XMLHttpRequest`, May 26, 2014.
[2]World Wide Consortium (W3C), "XMLHttpRequest," `www.w3.org/TR/2012/WD-XMLHttpRequest-20121206/#introduction`, December 6, 2012.

variations and problems that could soon arise among vendor implementations, the W3C urged to formalize the standard of the syntax, which can be read at the following URL: www.w3.org/TR/2014/ WD-XMLHttpRequest-20140130/. This standard outlines the API that developers can leverage to invoke an HTTP request that will facilitate the invocation of an HTTP request.

XMLHttpRequest Interface

The HTTP API, as exposed by the XMLHttpRequest object, consists of a variety of methods, event handlers, properties, and states, all of which provide our JavaScript application the ability to successfully facilitate an HTTP request, in addition to obtaining the response from a server. For this reason, each method, property, handler, and state will be integral in a particular aspect of the request or the response.

Global Aspects

The sole global method of the XMLHttpRequest interface is that of the constructor (see Table 8-4), which, when invoked, will return to our application a new instance of the XMLHttpRequest object. It will be through the interface inherited by this object that we will initiate and manage our requests. Furthermore, by instantiating multiple instance of the XMLHttpRequest object, we can manage simultaneous requests.

Table 8-4. XMLHttpRequest Constructor

Method/Property	Parameter	Returned Value
constructor	N/A	XMLHttpRequest (**object**)

Listing 8-4 demonstrates the instantiation of an XMLHttpRequest object and assigns the instance to a variable labeled xhr. It will be fairly common to see xhr as the reference, as this is simply the acronym for the **X**ML**H**ttp**R**equest object.

Listing 8-4. Creating an Instance of the XMLHttpRequest Object

```
var xhr = new XMLHttpRequest();
```

Whether you are working with one xhr or many, as the HTTP request occurs asynchronously, it is necessary for our application to be notified of any change in state, for the duration of the request. Such notifications may be whether the response has been fulfilled or the connection has timed out. The XMLHttpRequest Level 2 standard outlines the event handlers possessed by each xhr instance, so that we may remain aware of the status of the request. These event handlers can be viewed in Table 8-5.

Table 8-5. *The xhr Event Handlers for Monitoring the Progress of the HTTP Request*

Event Handlers	Event Handler Event Type
onloadstart *	loadstart *
onprogress	progress
onload	load
onloadend *	loadended *
onerror	error
ontimeout	timeout
onabort *	abort *
onreadystatechange	readystatechange

▪ **Note** The progress events that do not appear with an asterisk (*)beside them are implemented by all modern browsers, in addition to Internet Explorer 8. However, those beside an asterisk require IE 10 or greater.

The event handlers in Table 8-5 will alert our application to a variety of notifications pertaining to the state of the request. Furthermore, they can be utilized in one of two possible implementations.

The first is that we can remain object-oriented and register the event of the state to which we choose to listen. For each event to which we listen, we can assign a particular function to be triggered upon notification, such as that in Listing 8-5. As different browsers implement various ways to register an event, it is necessary to make use of a cross-browser solution, as I have on line 11.

Listing 8-5. The Registration for Event Listeners Belonging to the xhr object for Each Notification of State

```
1  var xhr = new XMLHttpRequest();
2  addListener(xhr, 'loadstart', function() { alert("load-start"); });
3  addListener(xhr, 'progress', function() { alert("progress"); });
4  addListener(xhr, 'load', function() {  alert("load"); });
5  addListener(xhr, 'loadended', function() {  alert("loadended"); });
6  addListener(xhr, 'timeout', function() {  alert("timeout");});
7  addListener(xhr, 'abort', function() {  alert("abort"); });
8  addListener(xhr, 'readystatechange', function() { alert("readystatechange");});
9
10 //cross browser addListener
11 function addListener(elem, eventName, handler) {
12      if (elem) {
13          elem.addEventListener(eventName, handler, false);
14      } else if (elem.attachEvent) {
15          elem.attachEvent('on' + eventName, handler);
16      } else {
17          elem['on' + eventName] = handler;
18      }
19 }
```

The alternative to being notified of a change in a particular state is to assign a function as the callback to the event handler, which exists as a property of the object itself. This manner of implementation is demonstrated in Listing 8-6.

Listing 8-6. Assigning Callback Functions to Each of the xhr Status Event Handlers

```
1    var xhr = new XMLHttpRequest();
2        xhr.onloadstart        = function() {  alert("onloadstart");  };
3        xhr.onprogress         = function() {  alert("onprogress");  };
4        xhr.onload             = function() {  alert("onload");  };
5        xhr.onloadend          = function() {  alert("onloadend");  };
6        xhr.ontimeout          = function() {  alert("ontimeout");  };
7        xhr.onabort            = function() {  alert("onabort");  };
8        xhr.onreadystatechange = function() {  alert("onreadystatechange");  };
```

Whether the implementation you choose to be made aware, regarding state notifications of the HTTP request, reflects that of Listing 8-5 or that of Listing 8-6, both will produce the equivalent results. The result produced is the invocation of the corresponding function that has been assigned as the receiver of a particular notification, when that event is dispatched.

There are eight progress notifications in total that will inform an application as to the particular state of the HTTP request. These notifications are the following: loadstart, progress, error, load, timeout, abort, loadend, and onreadystatechange.

The loadstart event is dispatched the moment the HTTP request begins. This is not to be confused with the moment communication occurs between the client and the server. As the loadstart event reflects the start of a request, it should be expected to be dispatched a total of one time for each request initiated.

The progress event is dispatched the moment the HTTP connection is established and the request/response is effectively relaying data. During the course of the transmission, the progress event will continue to fire until there is no further data to transmit. This, however, does not always indicate that a successful request has been fulfilled.

The error event will be dispatched exactly once, or not at all, during the course of each HTTP request initiated by the xhr object. Should the request result in an error, the error event will immediately be dispatched. This event is useful for being informed that the request was unsuccessful.

The load event will be dispatched exactly once, or not at all, during the course of each HTTP request initiated by the xhr object. Should the request be successfully fulfilled, the load event will be immediately dispatched. This event is useful for being informed that the request has been completed. It should be mentioned that just because a load is considered completed by the xhr object does not necessarily mean that the request was successfully satisfied. Therefore, it will be imperative to provide your callback method with the logic to determine the status code, in order to ensure that it was truly successful. The status code, in addition to the status text, can be obtained by the status and statusText properties of the xhr. I will discuss these two properties a bit later in the chapter.

The timeout event will be dispatched exactly once, or not at all, during the course of each HTTP request initiated by the xhr object. Should the duration of the request be determined to have surpassed a particular interval, the connection will have been deemed to be timed out, notifying our application of the matter.

The abort event is dispatched exactly once, or not at all, during the course of each HTTP request initiated by the xhr object. Should the request at any time be aborted, the abort event will be immediately dispatched.

The loadend event is dispatched exactly once during the course of each HTTP request initiated by the xhr object. The loadend notification is dispatched the moment the HTTP request is no longer active in its attempt to fulfill a request. This event is dispatched after the following possible notifications: error, abort, load, and timeout.

The onreadystatechange is the original, and at one time the only, event handler of the XMLHttpRequest implemented by earlier browsers. This event is used to notify a supplied function of the progress of the initiated HTTP request. The onreadystatechange event is dispatched multiple times during the course of each HTTP request initiated by the xhr instance. In fact, the event is dispatched each time the readyState property of the xhr instance is assigned a new state. The possible states that can be assigned to the readyState property are those outlined in Table 8-6.

Table 8-6. *The Possible States of the xhr object and Numeric Representation*

States	Numeric Representation
UNSENT	0
OPENED	1
HEADERS_RECEIVED	2
LOADING	3
DONE	4

The states outlined in Table 8-6 are assigned to that of the readyState property that exists on each xhr instance. The assigned state reflects the progress of the HTTP request itself. There are five possible states that can be assigned to the readyState property, and each infers the given state of the request.

The state UNSENT is the default state of the readyState property. This state is used to inform our application that the xhr object, while instantiated, is not yet initialized. The readyState property during this state returns a value of 0.

The state OPENED replaces the UNSENT state the moment the request method, open, has been invoked, initializing our xhr instance. The readyState property during this state returns a value of 1.

The state HEADERS_RECEIVED is assigned as the value of the readyState property upon receiving the headers that accompany the response that will ultimately be received from a server. The readyState property during this state returns a value of 2.

The state LOADING is assigned as the value of the readyState property as the transmission of data pertaining to the response entity body is received. The readyState property during this state returns a value of 3.

The state DONE is assigned as the value of the readyState property upon the conclusion of the HTTP request. This state reflects only the closure of the request. As with the load event, the done state does not identify if the request resulted in an error, a time-out, or a successful fulfillment of a request. Therefore, it will be imperative to determine the statusCode when determining how to process the request. The readyState property during this state returns a value of 4. Listing 8-7 demonstrates an event handler that monitors all states of the readyState property.

Listing 8-7. Determining the State of the xhr object for Each Change in State

```
1  var xhr = new XMLHttpRequest();
2      xhr.onreadystatechange = handlStateChange;
3
4  function handleStateChange() {
5      if (xhr.readyState === 0) {
6              alert("XHR is now instantiated");
7      } else if (xhr.readyState === 1) {
8              alert("XHR is now Initialized");
9      } else if (xhr.readyState === 2) {
10             alert("Headers are now Available");
```

```
11        } else if (xhr.readyState === 3) {
12              alert("Receiving Data");
13        } else if (xhr.readyState === 4) {
14              alert("HTTP Request ended");
15        }
```

As an older implementation, the onreadystatechange does not offer an application as accurate a notification system as the other seven progress events. Furthermore, the processing that is required by our JavaScript to determine the state of the HTTP request, if extensive, has the ability to block the thread, thereby delaying the events from being triggered.

The Request Aspect

The methods and properties that are outlined within this section make up the facade that enables one to correctly configure the metadata of the HTTP request. (See Table 8-7.)

Table 8-7. *The Request Methods of the* xhr *object*

Method	Parameters	Returned Value
open	String (method), String (URI), Boolean (async), String (user), String (password)	N/A
setRequestHeader	String (field), String (value)	N/A
send	String (entity body)	N/A
abort	N/A	N/A

open

The open method, whose signature can be viewed in Listing 8-8, acts as the starting point that will be used to configure the HTTP request.

Listing 8-8. The Signature of the open Method of the xhr object

```
open( HTTP-Method, request-URI [, async [, user [, password]]]);
```

As revealed by Listing 8-8, the open method accepts five arguments. Three are optional, and two are required.

The first parameter, HTTP-Method, indicates to the server what method it requires to be performed on the specified request URI. A resource may be the target of a "safe" or "unsafe" method. As discussed in the earlier sections of the chapter, the two types of methods this chapter will focus on are GET and POST.

The second parameter, request-URI, identifies the target of our request. The argument supplied to the request-URI can be specified either as a relative URL or, alternatively, an absolute URL. As the XMLHttpRequest object is subject to the same-origin policy, the URI supplied must possess the same origin as the application configuring the request. If, however, the URL provided is that of another host outside of the current origin, the server of the URL being targeted must allow for cross-origin resource sharing. I will discuss cross-origin resource sharing in the next chapter.

■ **Note**   The XMLHttpRequest object is subject to the same-origin policy.

The required parameters will be appended together, along with the HTTP protocol version, which is typically 1.1, to form the very first line of the request, which is the request line, as shown in Listing 8-9.

Listing 8-9. A GET Request for the URI xFile.php via the HTTP/1.1 Protocol

```
GET /xFile.php HTTP/1.1
```

The third parameter of the open method does not supply metadata to the request but, rather, indicates if the request will occur asynchronously or synchronously. When this parameter is left undefined, it defaults to true, thereby processing the HTTP request in another thread.

The final two optional parameters, user and password, are used to supply credentials that may be required of a resource whose access requires basic authentication. These values will add to the metadata of the request only if the server responds with a 401 Unauthorized status code.

setRequestHeader

The next method, setRequestHeader, offers our application the opportunity to specify particular headers that will complement the request by providing supplemental information. These can be any of the recognized standard HTTP/1.1 attribute-value fields. As indicated by the signature of the setRequestHeader defined in Listing 8-10, the field and value are to be supplied as individual strings. Behind the scenes, the xhr object will append them together, separated by a colon (:) token. Furthermore, any number of request headers can be supplied to the request in question.

Listing 8-10. Signature of the setRequestHeader Method of the xhr object

```
setRequestHeader( field , value );
```

Via setRequestHeader, our application can supply any attribute value that aids in the fulfillment of the response from the server. Such headers, as illustrated in Listing 8-11, are the Accept headers, which outline the preferred media types that our application recognizes. As the content we will be requesting most commonly from the server will be that of JSON, we will be using the **application/json** media type.

Additionally, if the HTTP-Method is specified to be that of an "unsafe" method, we can assign the Content-Type as a request header, to outline the encoding and MIME type of the supplied entity body provided with the request. I will discuss how to append an entity body in the **send** method later in this section.

The headers supplied can also represent custom attribute values, which can be useful for supporting custom requests. It's common practice to precede all custom headers with an X.

Listing 8-11. The Provision of the Accept Header and a Custom Header via the setRequestHeader Method

```
setRequestHeader( "Accept" , "application/json" );      //requesting JSON as the response
setRequestHeader( "X-Custom-Attribute" , "Hello-World" );  //custom header
```

For the most part, all standard HTTP/1.1 headers can be supplied. However, there are a few particular headers that cannot be overridden, due to security measures as well as maintaining the integrity of data.[3] These values are listed in Table 8-8. If your application attempts to supply values for any of the listed headers in Table 8-8, they will be overridden to their default values.

---

[3]A. van Kesteren et al., "XMLHttpRequest," dvcs.w3.org/hg/xhr/raw-file/tip/Overview.html, May 2014.

Table 8-8. *The Assorted HTTP Headers That Cannot Be Set Programmatically via JavaScript*

Accept-Charset	Cookie	Keep-Alive	Trailer
Accept-Encoding	Cookie2	Origin	Transfer-Encoding
Access-Control-Request-Headers	Date	Referer	Via
Access-Control-Request-Method	DNT	Upgrade	
Connection	Expect	User-Agent	
Content-Length	Host	TE	

send

The send method of the xhr object is what prompts the submission of the request. As indicated by its signature in Listing 8-12, the send method can be invoked with an argument supplied. This argument represents the entity body of the request and is typically used if the request method is specified as one of the "unsafe" methods, such as POST.

Listing 8-12. The Signature of the send Method of the xhr object

```
send ( data );
```

The data supplied can consist of nearly anything; however, it must be supplied in the form of a string. Data can be as simple as a word or a series of key/value pairs strung together to resemble a form post, or even that of JSON text. Listing 8-13, Listing 8-14 and Listing 8-15 demonstrate three different Content-Types being submitted via a form post.

Listing 8-13. Data Sent As the Entity Body of the Request with the Content-Type Defaulted to text/plain

```
var xhr =  new XMLHttpRequest();
    xhr.open("POST", "http://json.sandboxed.guru/chapter8/xss-post.php");
    xhr.send( "fname=ben&lname=smith" );
    //content-type will be defaulted to text/plain; charset=UTF-8.
```

Listing 8-14. Data Sent As the Entity Body of the Request with the Content-Type Specified As x-www-form-urlencoded

```
<form action="8-1.php" method="post" onsubmit="return formSubmit();">
    First-Name:<input name="fname" type="text" size="25" />
    Last-Name:<input name="lname" type="text" size="25" />
</form>
<script>
function formSubmit(){
    var xhr =  new XMLHttpRequest();
        xhr.open("POST", "http://json.sandboxed.guru/chapter8/xss-post.php");
        xhr.setRequestHeader("Content-Type", "application/x-www-form-urlencoded");
        xhr.send( "fname=ben&lname=smith&mySubmit=submit" ) ;
    return false;
}
</script>
```

Listing 8-15. Data Sent As the Entity Body of the Request with the Content-Type Specified As JSON

```
var person={name:"ben", gender:"male"};
var xhr = new XMLHttpRequest();
    xhr.open("POST", "http://json.sandboxed.guru/chapter8/xss-post.php");
    xhr.setRequestHeader("Content-Type", "application/json");
    xhr.send( JSON.stringify( person ) );
```

Whatever the supplied data, if you do not define the MIME type of the data by way of the Content-Type header, the type for the data provided will be defaulted to **text/plain; charset=UTF-8**, as in Listing 8-13. At this point, if you were to run the preceding listings (8-13 through 8-15) from your local machine, the request would fail. This is due to the fact that xhr strictly adheres to the same-origin policy. Requests can only be to a server if the request is initiated from the same origin. There is a way around this, which I will discuss further in the next chapter. In the meantime, feel free to run these listings and monitor the HTTP request via the developer console. Each listing can be viewed at the following URLs:

```
http://json.sandboxed.guru/chapter8/8-12.html
```

```
http://json.sandboxed.guru/chapter8/8-13.html
```

```
http://json.sandboxed.guru/chapter8/8-14.html
```

■ **Note** If you have been following along with the supplied URLs and have yet to clear your cookies, you may have witnessed some of the cookies from the previous chapter sent within the above requests.

abort

The final method of the request, abort, informs the HTTP request to discontinue/cancel the request. This method effectively closes any connection that has been made to a server or prevents one from occurring if a connection has not yet been made.

In addition to methods, the xhr object provides a few attributes that can help us with configuring our request. These properties can be found in Table 8-9.

Table 8-9. The Request Attributes of the xhr object

Properties	Returned Value
Timeout	Number (duration)
withCredentials *	Boolean (credentials)
upload *	XMLHttpRequestUpload (object)

■ **Note** The request properties that are not distinguished by an asterisk (*) are implemented by all modern browsers, in addition to Internet Explorer 8. Those marked by an asterisk require IE 10 or greater.

timeout

The timeout property can be set in milliseconds to that of any duration. The value supplied will be the maximum allotted time for a request to complete. If a request surpasses the provided time, the time-out event is dispatched to notify our application.

withCredentials

The withCredentials property can be set to that of either true or false. The value supplied is used to inform the server that credentials have been supplied with a cross-origin resource request.

upload

The upload property, when read, provides our application with a reference to an XMLHttpRequestUpload object. This object provides our application with the ability to monitor the transmission progress for the entity body of a supplied request. This will be useful for any entity body that contains an excessive amount of data, such as when allowing users to post various file attachments, such as images, or media.

At this point in time, you should possess the necessary understanding of the various methods and properties possessed by the xhr object that will allow for devising and configuring an HTTP request from a JavaScript application. The xhr provides us the vehicle we can leverage to transmit JSON to and from our application.

EXERCISE 8-1. AJAX FORM POST

With this newfound knowledge, you should be able to convert the HTML `<form>` element of the following code into an Ajax call.

```
<body>
    <div class="content">
        <form action="http://json.sandboxed.guru/chapter8/exercise.php"
            method="post" onsubmit="return ajax();">
            First-Name:<input name="fname" type="text" size="25" />
            Last-Name: <input name="lname" type="text" size="25" />
            <input name="mySubmit" type="submit" value="submit" />
        </form>
    </div>
    <script>
        function ajax() {
            //... insert HTTP Request here
        }
    </script>
</body>
```

As we will be controlling the request via JavaScript, and because our favored Content-Type is JSON, make sure that the data of the entity body is provided as JSON. You can compare your answer to that of the preceding code.

Normally, the XMLHttpRequest object is incapable of making successful requests to servers that do not possess the same origin as the document from which the request it initiated. However, I have employed a technique, which you will learn about in Chapter 9, that will allow your xhr instances to successfully make requests to the following request URI: http://json.sandboxed.guru/chapter8/exercise.php.

Unfortunately, if you are authoring your code using Internet Explorer 8 or 9 to make requests against varying origins, you cannot utilize the XMLHttpRequest object. Instead, you must initialize the XDomainRequest object. Furthermore, while the XMLHttpRequest enables you to specify the Content-Type via the setRequestHeader, the XDomainRequest does not possess this capability.

The Response Aspect

While the xhr object enables us to configure the request, it will serve no purpose without the understanding of how to extract the response provided. Therefore, the xhr object also incorporates various methods and properties that are concerned solely with working with the response provided by the server.

As you learned earlier in the chapter, both the HTTP request and the response of said request are broken into three components. These represent the request-line/status-line, headers, and the payload. While both the headers and the payload are used in collaboration to arrive at a parsed response, they are obtained separately via the xhr interface. The methods listed in Table 8-10 reflect the three methods of the xhr interface that are utilized for working with the headers of the HTTP response, which will ultimately inform our application of any details pertaining to the response.

Table 8-10. *Response Methods of the xhr object*

Method	Parameters	Returned Value
getAllResponseHeaders	N/A	String (value)
getResponseHeader	String (key)	String (value)
overrideMimeType	String (Content-Type)	N/A

getAllResponseHeaders

The getAllResponseHeaders method of the xhr interface is used to return the various headers that have been configured by the server to accompany the supplied response. When invoked, xhr returns a string of all headers of the response as key/value pairs, each of which remains separated from another by a carriage return and new line control characters. These control characters are represented by the following Unicode values respectively: \u000D and \u000A. Furthermore, each key/value pair is separated from another via the colon (:) token.

Knowing the syntax of the value returned, we can parse the string and simply extract each header into an array, with the help of some minor string manipulation, as revealed in Listing 8-16.

Listing 8-16. Extracting All Values That Are Configured to the Provided Response Headers

```
    ...truncated code
5 //when the xhr load event is triggerd parse all headers
6 xhr.onload = parseHeaders;
7
8 //parseHeaders will manipulate the string
9 function parseHeaders() {
10     var headers = new Object();
```

```
11      var responseHeaders = (this.getAllResponseHeaders());
12      //match sequences of characters that preceded control characters into an array
13      var headerArray = (responseHeaders.match(/[^\u000D\u000A].*/gi));
14      for (var i = 0; i < headerArray.length; i++) {
15          var akeyValuePair = headerArray[i];
16          var colonIndex = akeyValuePair.indexOf(":");
17          var headerKey  = akeyValuePair.substring(0, colonIndex);
18          var headerValue = akeyValuePair.substring(colonIndex + 1);
19          headerValue = (headerValue.charAt(0) == " ") ? headerValue(1) : headerValue;
20          headers[headerKey] = headerValue;
21      }
22 }
```

Listing 8-16 demonstrates how all headers can be extracted with a simple function labeled parseHeaders. Once the xhr load event notification is dispatched, parseHeaders is invoked (**line 6**). Once the parseHeaders function runs, we initialize an object, which will be used to retain any and all found headers and their values.

As parseHeaders is invoked by xhr, references to this remain implicitly set to the context of the xhr object. Therefore, referencing this enables our function to invoke the getAllResponseHeaders method, obtaining the string of all header-value pairs (**line 11**). The returned string is assigned as the value to the variable labeled responseHeaders.

Utilizing a regular expression, we can extract any sequence of characters that precede the two control characters, thereby separating one header-value pair from another. All found matches are then appended to an array in the order they are encountered. Once the entire string has been compared against the pattern, an array is returned, containing all matches respectively. In order to manipulate these matches further, we assign the array as the value to variable headerArray (**line 13**). From there, we iterate over each indexed value, so that we can separate the key from its value. Knowing that a colon (:) token is used to separate the two, we can determine the location of said token (**line 16**), allowing us to extract everything up to the token (**line 17**) and everything after the token (**line 18**). The two substrings, respectively, reflect the header and its value. While the HTTP protocol states that headers and values are separated via the colon (:) token, they are also separated by an additional space. Therefore, if the first character of the substring that represents our value is that of a space, it is effectively removed (**line 19**). From there, we apply each key and its correlating value to the headers object.

While it may not be immediately apparent why you would have to analyze all supplied headers, it will simply come down to the use case. The getAllResponseHeaders is essential when your actions rely on the metadata of the response. Such a use case would be when you pair an HTTP request with that of the request method HEAD, which is used to solely fetch header information from a server.

getResponseHeader

The getResponseHeader method, whose signature can be viewed in Listing 8-17, can be utilized to obtain the value for the specified response header, as configured by the server. The key supplied can be either uppercase or lowercase, but the format of the argument must be that of a string.

Listing 8-17. The Signature of the getResponseHeader Method of the xhr object

```
getResponseHeader( key );
```

If the key supplied is not a configured header among those possessed by the response, the value returned will be that of null. Much like getAllResponseHeaders, being able to analyze the meta-information supplied within the response can be vital in coordinating how you display, update, or even utilize the data provided.

As was explained earlier, the *X* in *Ajax* represents XML, because, at the time, XML was the only data type outside of plain/text able to be parsed by the xhr object. While many browsers have been making great strides to offer a variety of natively returned data types, ranging from plain text to JSON, Internet Explorer 8 and 9 continue to provide us only with the original two flavors. This makes for a particularly strong case as to why one would require the use of getResponseHeaders. If the data type supplied from the server is not in fact XML, with the use of the getResponseHeaders method, one is able to obtain the correct Content-Type of the supplied entity body and correctly parse the string per the syntax of said data format, as demonstrated in Listing 8-18.

Listing 8-18. HTTP POST to exercise.php with Configured Content-Type and Accept Headers

```
 1 var xhr = new XMLHttpRequest();
 2 xhr.open("POST", "http://json.sandboxed.guru/chapter8/exercise.php");
 3 xhr.setRequestHeader("Content-Type", "application/json");
 4 xhr.setRequestHeader("Accept", "application/json");
 5 xhr.onreadystatechange = changeInState;
 6 xhr.send('{"fname":"ben","lname":"smith"}');
 7
 8 function changeInState() {
 9     var data;
10     if (this.readyState === 4 && this.status === 200) {
11     var mime = this.getResponseHeader("content-type").toLowerCase();
12         if (mime.indexOf('json'))) {
13             data = JSON.parse(this.responseText);
14         } else if (mime.indexOf('xml'))) {
15             data = this.responseXML;
16         }
17     }
18 }
```

Listing 8-18 leverages our earlier exercise to help demonstrate the benefit of the getResponseHeader method. Thus far, I have not discussed what data type the earlier exercise returns as the response entity. I also have not yet discussed any of the properties that enable you to read the obtained request. Unless you looked at the headers provided by the response via the developer console, you may not have known whether the entity body returned was that of XML, HTML, plain text, or JSON. Odds are you cleverly deduced it was JSON, as you realized the context of this book. However, the point is that you may not have known for certain. Therefore, rather than assuming, it's best to account for the varying possibilities, so that you are able to work with the supplied data accordingly.

Listing 8-18 begins with the initialization of our xhr object and supplies it with the necessary HTTP-Method and request-URI **(line 2)**. As our request method is specified as POST and will be supplying data to the server, we continue to configure the Content-Type of the provided data **(line 3)**, informing the server how to parse it correctly. As this book concerns working with JSON, we inform the server that our application accepts the Content-Type of application/json **(line 4)**. In order to monitor the state of the request, the changeInState function is assigned as the callback **(line 5)**. While I chose to make use of the onreadystatechange to monitor the state of the request, I could have just as easily used the onload event handler. However, as the event handlers are only available in Internet Explorer 8, I wanted to demonstrate how to achieve the results of the onload notification, for those who must continue to work with older browsers.

Last, we use the send method of the xhr object to invoke the HTTP request and, in doing so, provide it with the necessary JSON data to POST **(line 6)**.

The function changeInState **(line 8)** supplied as the callback to the onreadystatechange is not only used to determine the change in state but also the Content-Type, if the request is successful **(line 11)**. If you relied on the onload event handler, you would not have to determine the state, as the event suggests it's done. However, because the onreadystatechange is triggered each time the readyState property of the xhr object is updated, it's imperative to query the status of the request.

In order to distinguish among the five various states of the xhr object, it is necessary to determine the value of the readyState property. If the readyState value is 4, we know the current state of the xhr object is DONE. However, in order to determine if the response has successfully provided us with an entity body, the status code is also analyzed (**line 10**). If the status code is found to be 200, which signifies that a response is successful, we can begin to determine how to parse the data of the response.

We begin by utilizing the getResponseHeader to obtain the lowercase value of the specified Content-Type for the response, as configured by the server (**line 11**). Once we have obtained the value, we determine if it matches the JSON MIME type (**line 12**) or that of XML (**line 14**). Depending on the outcome of the determined type, the appropriate value is assigned to the data variable. If the Content-Type is found to be that of XML, the value is obtained via the responseXML property of the xhr object (**line 15**). However, should it be determined that the response has been provided in the JSON data format, we must obtain the raw string from the responseText and supply it to the native JSON Object to be parsed (**line 13**). I will discuss the responseXML and responseText properties in the next section.

overrideMimeType

The overrideMimeType method enables our application to override the configured Content-Type of the response body when obtained. FireFox, Chrome, and Safari have implemented this method, which was added in the XMLHttpRequest Level 2 draft standard. However, at the time of this writing, it is currently unavailable in Internet Explorer 11.

Obtaining the Response

The variety of properties of the xhr object listed in Table 8-11 provides us with the necessary means to obtain the provided response of the HTTP request. It will be with the help of these attributes that we will come full circle in our ability to initiate a request and, ultimately, obtain the response of that request.

Table 8-11. *The Response Properties of the xhr object*

Properties	Access type	Returned Value
readyState	Read	Integer (state)
status	Read	Integer (HTTP status Code)
statusText	Read	string (HTTP status)
responseXML	Read	XML (value)
responseText	Read	string (value)
responseType	Read/Write	XMLHttpRequestResponseType (object)
response	Read	* (value)

readyState

The readyState property of the xhr object exhibits the current state of the HTTP request. Throughout the asynchronous process of the HTTP request, the readyState attribute will be updated regularly to reflect the status of the request. The values for which it can be assigned are the integers discussed previously in Table 8-6.

> ■ **Note** As the states reflected are rather broad, the readyState property will often be paired with other properties, such as the status or statusText properties, in order to arrive at the necessary outcome.

status

The status property of the xhr object supplies an application with the ability to obtain the HTTP status code of the response. Currently, there are five classes for the status codes. These classes are those outlined earlier in the chapter in Table 8-3.

Listing 8-18 relied on both the readyState and the status property to determine if the load had completed successfully. As shown on **line 10**, if(this.readyState === 4 && this.status === 200), we determined via the readyState if the xhr request had ended, in addition to determining whether the status of the response is that of 200. A status code of 200 indicates that the request has been acknowledged.

statusText

statusText, like the status, is yet another property of the xhr object that is concerned with providing us the appropriate status regarding the fulfillment of the response. Each status code is accompanied by a textual phrase that provides additional information regarding the status. Via statusText, the description that accompanies the status code can be obtained and read by our application.

Using our 200 status code as an example, it is accompanied with the textual phrase OK. This is very helpful when obtaining descriptive issues that can be relayed back to the user, or even a developer, during the course of debugging.

> ■ **Note** The textual phrase that accompanies the status code is intended more for debugging than for controlling the flow of an application.

responseXML

responseXML is the attribute of the xhr object that enables an application to obtain an XML response provided by the server. As the data supplied within the response will not always be configured as one of the XML Content-Types, application/xml or text/xml, the responseXML attribute will not always provide a value. In the case of a server providing a response with the Content-Type that is not indicative of XML, a value of null will be returned when read from our application.

It should be made known that responseXML is not solely for an XML document. Due to the resemblance, the responseXML attribute can also be used to retrieve HTML documents identified by the text/html Content-Type.

responseText

responseText is a property of the xhr object that provides our applications with the ability to obtain the raw text of the entity body, as provided by the response. While responseXML may often possess a value of null, responseText will always possess a value.

Because the `responseText` attribute provides our application with the raw entity body received as a string, we must obtain the value of the Content-Type header. The configured Content-Type header will give us insight as to the syntax required for parsing the string. Once this is obtained, we can parse the string into the intended format, as demonstrated on line 13 of Listing 8-18.

responseType

The `responseType` property of the `xhr` object is concerned with the parsing of data types natively, beyond that of mere XML. As has been previously stated, the `xhr` object has the ability to parse a response as XML data. However, as XML is not today's data interchange standard, and has not been for quite some time, much of the parsing that occurs is forced to take place on the client side. Unfortunately, this puts the onus on the application to parse a string. Essentially, this increases the odds of blocking the single thread of the JavaScript engine. By allowing the browser to parse the request, the JavaScript thread is less likely to become blocked.

The `responseType` property has been added to the XMLHttpRequest Level 2 draft standard in an attempt to offload the parsing from the client side for five particular Content-Types. These are the following: `arraybuffer`, `blob`, `document`, `text`, and `json`. This is great news for JSON because, as you may recall, `JSON.parse` is a blocking method. In order to offload the parsing of our response entity to the process handling the request, we must configure the `responseType` before we invoke the `send` method. Any one of five aforementioned data types can be assigned as the value for the `responseType` attribute.

By configuring our request with a `responseType` attribute, we are able to inform the `xhr` process to parse the entity body against the indicated syntax. In Listing 8-19, I've indicated that the syntax is that of JSON.

Listing 8-19. HTTP Request Configured to Parse JSON

```
1 var xhr = new XMLHttpRequest();
2 xhr.open("POST", "http://json.sandboxed.guru/chapter8/exercise.php");
3 xhr.setRequestHeader("Content-Type", "application/json");
4 xhr.setRequestHeader("Accept", "application/json");
5 xhr.onreadystatechange = changeInState;
6 xhr.responseType = "json";
7 xhr.send('{"fname":"ben","lname":"smith"}');
```

response

The `response` property of the `xhr` object, like `responseXML` and `responseText`, provides our application with a way to obtain the entity body of the fulfilled request. However, the major difference is that the value `read` will be parsed, that is, if we have configured the HTTP request with `responseType`. Otherwise, the value returned is an empty string.

Listing 8-20 revisits the previous listing and configures the request to utilize the `responseType` of JSON (**line 6**). As the parsing will now occur within a separate process from our application, we no longer need to parse the JSON ourselves. Therefore, we can replace line 14 with that of the `response` attribute, which should now hold a JavaScript object.

Listing 8-20. HTTP Request Obtaining the Parsed JSON from the xhr Response Property

```
1 var xhr = new XMLHttpRequest();
2     xhr.open("POST", "http://json.sandboxed.guru/chapter8/exercise.php");
3     xhr.setRequestHeader("Content-Type", "application/json");
4     xhr.setRequestHeader("Accept", "application/json");
5     xhr.onreadystatechange = changeInState;
```

```
6      xhr.responseType = "json";
7      xhr.send('{"fname":"ben","lname":"smith"}');
8
9  function changeInState() {
10     var data;
11     if (this.readyState === 4 && this.status === 200) {
12     var mime = this.getResponseHeader("content-type").toLowerCase();
13         if (mime.indexOf('json'))) {
14             data = this.response;
15         } else if (mime.indexOf('xml'))) {
16             data = this.responseXML;
17         }
18     }
19 }
```

While the responseType and response properties have been implemented in most browsers, Internet Explorer continues to remain behind the times. XMLHttpRequest Level 2 methods and attributes are only available in IE 10 or greater.

The preceding examples relied on the provision of dynamic data from a database on my server. However, Ajax does not necessarily have to work with dynamic data. In fact, Ajax is fantastic at loading static files as well. Listing 8-21 exposes the content body of a file labeled images.json, which reveals the following JSON within.

Listing 8-21. JSON Content Within /data/imagesA.json

```
{
    "images": [
            {
                "title": "Image One",
                "url": "img/AndroidDevelopment.jpg"
            }, {
                "title": "Image Two",
                "url": "img/php.jpg"
            }, {
                "title": "Image Three",
                "url": "img/Rails.jpg"
            }, {
                "title": "Image Three",
                "url": "img/Android.jpg"
            }
    ]
}
```

Listing 8-21 reveals an object that possesses a singular member labeled "images". Images, as a key, reference the value of an ordered list, where each index of said ordered list references an object. These objects represent the necessary details pertaining to various images that will be added dynamically to our page. The key url reflects the location from which the image is supplied, while the title is used to populate the alt tag of the dynamically inserted image. Listing 8-22 reveleals the code that will load, parse and insert data/imagesA.json into an HTML document.

Listing 8-22. The Body of an HTML File That Utilizes Ajax to Load the JSON Document data/imagesA.json

```
1  <body>
2  <input type="submit" value="load images"  onclick="loadImages('data/imagesA.json')"/>
3    <script>
4    function loadImages(url) {
5        var body = document.getElementsByTagName("body")[0];
6        var xhr = (window.XDomainRequest) ? new XDomainRequest() : new XMLHttpRequest();
7          xhr.open("GET", url);
8          xhr.onload = function() {
9            var data = JSON.parse(this.responseText);
10           var list = data.images;
11           for (var i = 0; i < list.length; i++) {
12               var image = list[i];
13               var listItem = document.createElement("li");
14               var img = document.createElement("img");
15                 img.src = image.url;
16                 img.alt = image.title;
17               listItem.appendChild(img);
18               body.appendChild(listItem);
19           }
20         };
21         xhr.onerror = function() {
22           alert( this.status  + " " + this.statusText);
23         };
24       xhr.send();
25    };
26    </script>
27 </body>
```

Listing 8-22 demonstrates the use of Ajax to load the static file from Listing 8-21, populating a variety of images within the page. The document reveals nothing but a submit button within the page (**line 2**). This button, when clicked, will trigger the JavaScript code that will both load the image.json file and dynamically insert each found image into the body of our page. This will allow users to load our image set at a time of their choosing, rather than adding to the initial file size of the web page. When the button is clicked, the function loadImages (**line 4**) initiates the HTTP request. Because only modern browses and later versions of Internet Explorer possess the XMLHttpRequest object, we must first determine what object must be instantiated, to make the proper request. We do so by determining whether the window object possesses the XDomainRequest object (**line 6**). If the XDomainRequest object is available, we use our tertiary operator as a condensed if/else block, to instantiate an XDomainRequest instance. If, however, the evaluation to determine whether the XDomainRequest is available fails, our code will instantiate the more modern XMLHttpRequest. Once our xhr object is instantiated, we configure it with the appropriate request method and URL (**line 7**).

Because we are working with static content, rather than making a POST request, we will rely on the GET HTTP-Method to obtain the provided URI. Using the onload and onerror event handlers of the xhr object, we will monitor the state of the request. If the request is successful, the onload event handler will initiate the body of code that will obtain the request body from responseText. Knowing that the content provided within is JSON, we will obtain the plain/text from responsetText and parse it utilizing the JSON Object (**line 9**). Once we obtain our data tree, we can reference the ordered list of images via the images key (**line 10**). From there, using a for loop, we iterate over each and every index possessed by our ordered list (**line 11**). By regarding each image object individually, we can obtain the values held within to construct the necessary markup that will be used to present our images.

In order to have our images display as a vertical list, we create a list item for each image. By using the `document.createElement` method, we are able to create HTML elements simply by providing the method with a string representing the tag we wish to create. In this case, as we wish to create a list item, we supply the `document.createElement` method with the string `li` and retrain the reference to the `HTMLobject` returned (**line 13**); Next we create another `HTMLobject` (**line 14**), only this time it will be an element that represents the `img` tag. Using the reference to the image, we supply its attributes `src` and `alt` with the details that were extracted from the image objects (**line 15** and **line 16**). Next, we use the `appendChild` method to append the image as a child of our list item (**line 17**). Additionally, we add the list item as a child of the body of the page, so that it will be visible to the document (**line 18**). This process is repeated until all images have been account for.

If the request fails, our application will alert us to the status code and the status description of the failure (**line 22**). Last, we invoke the request to begin by calling the `send` method on the instantiated `xhr` object (**line 24**). The preceding code should result as shown in Figure 8-4.

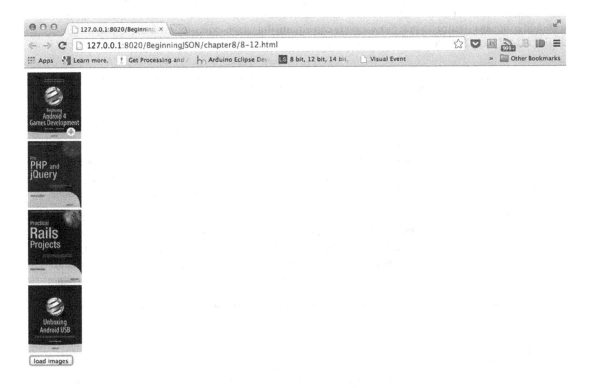

Figure 8-4. *Use of Ajax to load and display images*

It should be mentioned that the object that enables HTTP requests are strictly for making requests from a web server. Therefore, attempting to load files via Ajax locally will not work, unless they are run from a web server. Many web editors, such as WebStorm, Aptana, and VisualStudio, will run your local code within a temporary server, in which case, you would have no trouble following along with the provided source code.

Despite earlier discussions surrounding Content-Type and how the server should always configure it, you may have recognized that we did not have to configure the Content-Type, even though we were being provided JSON. Yet, if by some chance you were to have inspected the response header of Listing 8-22 with the developer console, you would have witnessed that the Content-Type of the response read "application/json," as indicated in Figure 8-5.

▼ **Response Headers**　　view parsed

```
HTTP/1.1 200 OK
Date: Sat, 14 Jun 2014 17:38:17 GMT
Server: HttpComponents/4.1.3
Content-Length: 270
Content-Type: application/json
Connection: keep-alive
```

Figure 8-5. *The response header for* `imagesA.json` *exhibits the configured Content-Type as* `application/json`

As was mentioned in the history of JSON in Chapter 4, Douglas Crockford's formalization of JSON included the registered Internet media type `application/json`, in addition to the file extension `.json`. While a file extension doesn't explicitly define the encoding of the content contained within, servers are able to infer Content-Types for commonly recognized file extensions. As JSON is the preferred interchange format, it should come as no surprise that most servers can equate the `.json` extension with the Content-Type of `application/json`. Therefore, the response is configured with the inferred Content-Type: `application/json`.

EXERCISE 8-2. LOAD MORE IMAGES

If you haven't done so already, click the "load images" button from the previous listing two more times and take note of what's occurring. With each click, a new `xhr` object is instantiated, initiating a new HTTP request. Providing the request is being fulfilled, the page should now display duplicates of the images loaded. As it serves little use to display duplicate content, rewrite the code from Listing 8-22, so that each subsequent request will load a new JSON file containing no more than four different images.

You will find more images within the `img` folder that accompanies the source code for this chapter. (You can find the code samples for this chapter in the Source Code/Download area of the Apress web site [`www.apress.com`]). Reference these images within two more static JSON documents to be loaded in and displayed via Ajax. Feel free to duplicate the `images.json` file located within the data folder and simply replace the titles and URLs. Or, you can devise the JSON with the assistance of one of the editors discussed in Chapter 4.

Summary

This chapter covered the essentials of the Hypertext Transfer Protocol (HTTP), which is necessary to comprehend when working with the interchange of data. By applying this knowledge, combined with the built-in objects that enable HTTP requests via JavaScript, we have been able to send, as well as receive, JSON in the background of our applications. Furthermore, using the techniques that make up Ajax, we were able to incorporate data without the need for full-page refreshes.

Ajax has surely broadened the scope of possibility for modern-day front-end development. Conversely, its popularity has also resulted in an increase of security concerns. As browsers continue to improve measures to thwart malicious behavior, the ease of data interchange across origins has often been a difficult task to circumvent. In the upcoming chapters, you will not only learn how to overcome these issues from a server-side implementation, you will also set up a local server, so that you can employ these techniques.

Key Points from This Chapter

- A request/response possesses three components.
- A request is initiated by a client.
- A response can only be provided from a web server.
- The GET method is a safe method.
- The POST method is an unsafe method.
- The request URI identifies the resource that the request method applies.
- The current HTTP version is 1.1.
- General headers pertain to general information.
- Request headers communicate preferential information.
- Entity headers supply informative information regarding the supplied entity body.
- General headers and entity headers can be configured by both client and server.
- Response status codes are used to indicate the status of the request.
- The Content-Type header regards the MIME type of an entity.
- The Accept header is used to inform the server of the data types it can work with.
- The XMLHttpRequest Object enables HTTP requests from JavaScript.
- The XMLHttpRequest Object is available in all modern browsers as well as IE 8.
- XMLHttpRequest cannot be used for cross-origin requests in IE 8/9.
- XDomainRequest can be used for cross-origin requests in IE 8/9.
- XDomainRequest lacks the setRequestHeader method.
- XMLHttpRequest and XDomainRequest expose event handlers to notify of state.
- The .json extension is recognized by servers and will default the Content-Type to application/json.
- Custom headers begin with an *X*.
- Status code 200 represents a successful request.
- Prior to IE 10, XMLHttpRequest could only parse XML/HTML documents.

CHAPTER 9

■ ■ ■

X-Origin Resources

The browser's inclusion of the XMLHttpRequest object offers front-end developers a means of interchanging data simply, with the use of JavaScript. Prior to Ajax becoming a highly recognized term, the exchange of data was primarily made possible through a series of full-page requests. Only through front-end hacks could data appear to be loaded-in dynamically. Therefore, when it became possible to make HTTP requests from within JavaScript, it instantly became a hot topic.

Such a prevalence of network access has much cause for concern, however. As Ajax became regular practice, web sites were becoming more and more exposed to the possible injection of malicious code. Needless to say, this is a serious matter for sites transmitting data, let alone sensitive data such as credit cards, bank accounts, or even personally identifiable information. In order to reduce web sites' being exposed to malicious requests, the XMLHttpRequest restricts network access only to resources that can be considered trusted. However, therein lies part of the problem: How do you define what resources are considered trustworthy?

The policy that prevents data from being usable from varying origins is the same-origin policy (or SOP). This chapter will discuss the impact of the SOP when regarding the interchange of resources between two varying origins. Additionally within this chapter, I will discuss the techniques that can be used to combat said limitations.

Same-Origin Policy

The same-origin policy (SOP) has been in effect since the introduction of JavaScript and continues to remain an important aspect of web security. The SOP is the security model commonly adhered to by all user-agents. While the policy has been revisited many times since its genesis (largely in an ad hoc fashion), today, the SOP governs a variety of front-end securities, such as matters surrounding DOM access, cookies, Web Storage, and network access. The SOP even applies to web plug-ins, such as Flash, Java, and Silverlight. While the latter list is not complete, it's certainly more than enough to demonstrate how the SOP can be a major obstacle for modern-day web development.

In the previous chapter, I presented you with an exercise that required the use of an HTTP request that would POST data to the specified resource exercise.php, residing at the address http://json.sandboxed. guru/chapter8/. Upon a successful reception of the request, the server would respond in kind with an entity body, which could be used by any application. However, you may recall that I mentioned that this is behavior not typically allowed by the user-agent. In that particular example, I employed a technique for that particular resource that enables an Ajax request to be successful. Ordinarily, the user-agent wouldn't allow the request to succeed, as the origin from which your request initiated did not reflect the same origin as the resource.

Generally speaking, the SOP restricts which network messages one origin can send to another. The purpose of this policy is to prevent a resource such as a JavaScript application from origin-A from obtaining the resources provided by origin-B, as the intent may be malicious. This policy is, of course, enforced by the user-agents that are being used to make such network requests.

■ **Note**   Due to legacy purposes, SOP policies vary to the degree by which they are enforced between the various web technologies.

At this point in time, I'd like for you to attempt to load another static file from my server. Only this time, I have not employed the same techniques as the exercise in Chapter 8.

EXERCISE 9-1. XHR AND SOP

Open your preferred browser and navigate to `http://sandboxed.guru/xss-exercise.html`. Next, open the developer tools provided by your browser and ensure that the console tab is in view. Using the free-form field within the console, construct an HTTP request that makes use of the GET method to enact on the following resource: `http://json.sandboxed.guru/chapter9/data/images.json`.

Be sure to use the log method of the console, `console.log( string );`, to print to the console the raw text of the response (responseText), in order to witness the returned data once the load is complete. Last, be sure to log out an error message if the onerror event handler is dispatched, should anything go wrong with our request.

If you are using Internet Explorer 8 or 9, it will be essential to instantiate the XDomainRequest over the XMLHttpRequest object, as we will be making a cross-origin request. A convenient way of determining whether your script must instantiate the XDomainRequest object over the XMLHttpRequest object for cross-origin requests is to test whether the browser executing the request possesses a particular attribute that belongs to the XMLHttpRequest Level 2 interface. This attribute is particular to cross-origin requests and exists in modern browsers as well as Internet Explorer 10 and up. The attribute is the withCredentials attribute. Utilizing the JavaScript in operator, we can test whether or not the withCredentials attribute exists on an XMLHttpRequest instance. If the attribute does not exist, we must instantiate an XDomainRequest instance. This technique eases our efforts to determine if the browser should rely on XDomainRequest, or not, for these types of requests. If you were to incorporate this conditional logic along with the necessary code required by the exercise, your code should resemble that of Listing 9-1.

Listing 9-1. Determining Whether to Use the XDomainRequest or the XMLHttpRequest Level 2 Interface for a Cross-Origin Request

```
1 var xhr= new XMLHttpRequest();
2   if(!"withCredentials" in xhr){
3     xhr= new XDomainRequest();
4   }
5     xhr.open("GET","http://json.sandboxed.guru/chapter9/data/images.json");
6     xhr.onload=function(){
7         console.log(this.responseText);
8     };
```

```
9      xhr.onerror=function(){
10         console.error( "Error Occurred" );
11     }
12     xhr.send();
```

Listing 9-1 begins by creating an instance of the XMLHttpRequest and assigns the instance as the reference to a variable labeled xhr (**line 1**). Utilizing the in operator, along with the instance held by xhr, we can determine if the withCredentials attribute is exposed by the object (**line 2**). If the value returned by the expression is false, the instance is incapable of fulfilling cross-origin requests; therefore, we replace the existing xhr reference with an instance of the XDomainRequest (**line 3**).

Once you have coded the request within the console of the developer's tools, such as in Figure 9-1, execute the code and observe the result.

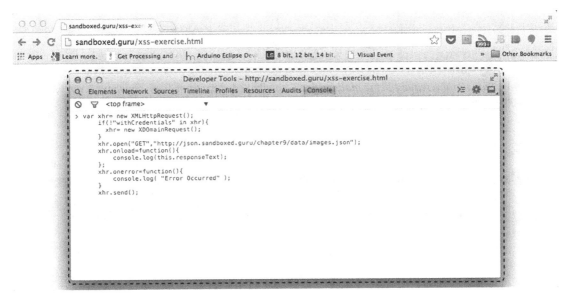

Figure 9-1. Cross-origin request being made to json.sandboxed.guru from sandboxed.guru

Next navigate your browser to http://json.sandboxed.guru/chapter9/xss-exercise.html; run the preceding code once more; and observe the results.

If you followed along with the exercise, you should have witnessed the alert box containing the raw JSON data during the execution of the latter request, as seen in Figure 9-2. However, while executing the same request from the initial origin, sandboxed.guru, the alert box was not presented. Instead, messaging was output to the console, alerting us to the fact that the request cannot occur (see Figure 9-3).

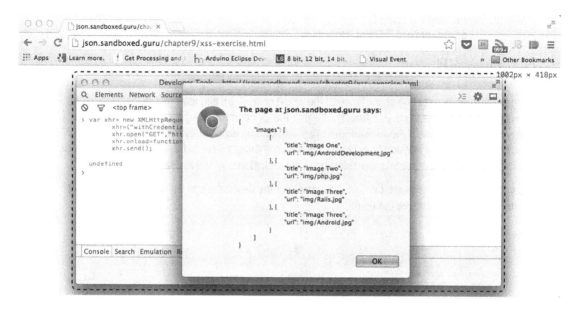

Figure 9-2. *Same-origin request being made to* json.sandboxed.guru *from* json.sandboxed.guru, *resulting in response*

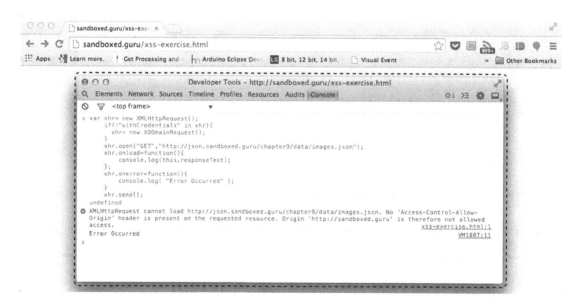

Figure 9-3. *Chrome developer tools indicating that the request is not allowed access*

As shown in Figure 9-3, Chrome's developer console reveals the following error messaging:

XMLHttpRequest cannot load http://json.sandboxed.guru/chapter9/data/images.json. No 'Access-Control-Allow-Origin' header is present on the requested resource. Origin 'http://sandboxed.guru' is therefore not allowed access.

From the preceding message, we can ascertain that the request cannot be completed, because the response for the resource `exercise.php` is not configured to possess the Access-Control-Allow-Origin header. Depending on the browser used to make the request, you will most assuredly receive a different message. For example, Firefox, as shown in Figure 9-4, sends the following error messaging:

Cross-Origin Request Blocked: The Same Origin Policy disallows reading the remote resource at http://json.sandboxed.guru/chapter9/data/images.json. This can be fixed by moving the resource to the same domain or enabling CORS.

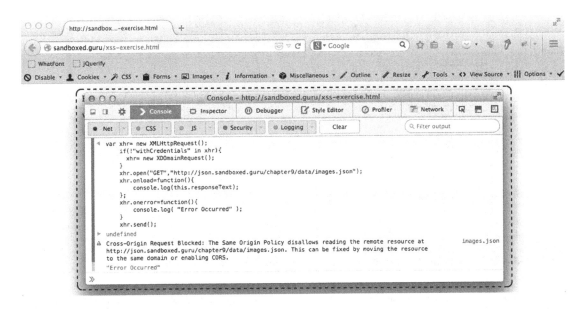

Figure 9-4. *Firefox alert stating that the request is not allowed access*

Unfortunately, Internet Explorer's implementation of the `XDomainRequest` will not alert us to any error messaging, other than the one provided by us to be output upon a possible dispatch of the `onerror` notification. On the other hand, if you were using Internet Explorer 10 or greater, as those versions implement a vast majority of the XMLHttpRequest Level 2 standardization, they would inform you of the failed incident. Furthermore, the error message reveals that incorporating Cross-Origin Resource Sharing (CORS), similar to Chrome and Firefox, can resolve the problem. Before I begin to discuss CORS, I will continue to discuss our findings further.

Depending on the browser you are using to make the request, you may not witness any HTTP response headers from within the network panel of the developer console. This, unfortunately, might lead you to believe that the request is prevented from even taking place. While the response may not appear in the network tab of the developer toolbar, I can assure you that the request has, in fact, been submitted to the requested resource. However, being that the request is not considered trusted or authorized, the user-agent shields us from being able to witness a response from the server.

If you were to make the same request with the popular Firebug add-on for Firefox, you would continue to receive the same error message as with the other browsers. Yet, upon navigating to the network panel, you would be able to see a series of response headers for the request. Furthermore, the Content-Length entity header, as configured by the response, suggests there is an entity body of precisely 270 bytes, and that the MIME type of the data, as configured by the Content-Type header, is that of application/json. Last, the status line reveals that the request was understood as it is configured, with the status code 200 and the text phrase of OK (see Figure 9-5). These aspects should demonstrate unquestionably that the request is being received. However, if you were to view the Response tab from within the navigation view, you will find the data to be missing.

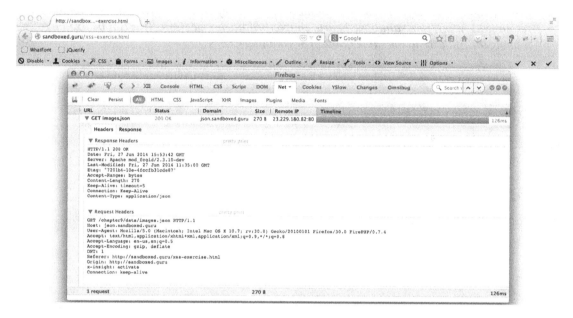

Figure 9-5. *Firebug developer tool revealing the response status line as successful*

Based on the outcome of the earlier exercise, it should be evident that resources are limited in their ability to be requested from varying origins, regardless of whether the two origins involved are owned by the same individual. It should be evident that a domain and its subdomain are not considered trusted by default and, therefore, cannot make resource requests of one another. Resource requests are inherently trusted only from resources that have the same origin. This is why the subsequent request of our exercise alerted us to JSON data, while the former attempt did not.

In short, the following resource http://json.sandboxed.guru/chapter9/data/images.json is available only to another resource that has the same origin, i.e., http://json.sandboxed.guru. While these two URLs are considered to have the same origin, it is for reasons that may not be as obvious as you might think. Origins aren't considered to be of the same origin solely because they possess the same hostname. Specifically, a resource is considered authorized to obtain/retrieve content from another resource only if the two resources possess the exact same scheme, domain, and port.

I hope that Listing 9-2 looks familiar, as this is the general schema for a web URL. If you are thrown by the :port/ component, that is okay, as it's not always required to incorporate the port into a URL. However, that does not detract from the fact that it's always accounted for behind the scenes.

Listing 9-2. Syntax of an HTTP URL

```
scheme://domain:port/path/?key=value
```

> **Scheme**: The scheme, sometimes referred to as the protocol, defines how an indicated resource will be obtained. There are a variety of protocols that can be specified, such as ftp, http, and even https. Typically, the scheme that is used when viewing web sites will be that of http. However, it can also be that of https, where the *s* means that the transmission occurs securely. This is commonly used when you log in to a site such as a bank or web mail.

> **Domain**: As you may have guessed, the domain is the human-friendly means of referring to a specific destination. However, this domain name itself is actually converted behind the scenes to a static IP address.

> **Port**: The port number is an optional endpoint that can be used to specify a specific application running on a common IP address. When a port is not defined, it falls back to the default port for the supplied scheme. *In the case of an HTTP scheme the default port is **80**. In the case of HTTPS, the default port is **443**.*

These three distinct aspects of the HTTP-URL scheme are used by the user-agent to determine whether it must enforce the SOP. Table 9-1 demonstrates which requests will be considered authorized and which won't.

Table 9-1. *The Same-Origin Policy in Effect, Demonstrating Whether a Source Origin Is Authorized to a Request*

Request Origin	Resource Origin	Allowed	Reason
http://json.sandboxed.guru/a.html	http://json.sandboxed.guru/b.php	True	
http://json.sandboxed.guru/a.html	http://json.sandboxed.guru/chapter8/b.php	True	
http://json.sandboxed.guru/a.html	https://json.sandboxed.guru/b.php	False	Scheme
http://json.sandboxed.guru/a.html	http://json.sandboxed.guru:81/b.php	False	Port
http://json.sandboxed.guru/a.html	http://json.sandboxed.guru:80/b.php	True	
http://json.sandboxed.guru/a.html	http://sandboxed.guru/b.php	False	Domain

To further prevent any script from forging the request, certain headers are unable to be defined via the setRequestHeader method of the XMLHttpRequest object. Instead, they are explicitly defined by the user-agent. Any attempt to provide a value for these headers via the setRequestHeader will be overridden by the user-agent. These headers are the following:

- Host
- Origin
- Referer
- Via

The requests made by browsers work on our behalf, hence the term *user-agent.*[1] It is they who enforce the SOP, to ensure that our daily Internet interactions remain as safe as possible. The SOP is an extremely important concept to understand, which is why this chapter is important to a subject that looks to network access to exchange JSON data. The fact that the user-agent acts on our behalf is an important concept for a front-end developer to grasp. The reason, as you will soon see, is because the power to bypass the limitations of the SOP lies on the back-end side of programming, rather than the front end. Unfortunately, not all back-end developers are aware of these SOP requirements, simply because server-side programing does not involve a user-agent that governs HTTP requests. To put it plainly, they don't have to deal with these issues. As the adage goes "there's more than one way to skin a cat," and there is an exuberant amount of server-side languages. In this chapter, all back-end programming will be demonstrated with the use of the highly popular PHP language. However, the programming language could just as easily be Java, .NET, etc.

If you are a Chrome user, such as myself, there is a fantastic HTTP request plug-in that I use to conveniently test web services. This plug-in is known as Postman and can be obtained from the browser via the extensions URL `https://chrome.google.com/webstore/search/postman%20rest%20client`. Alternatively, the browser extension can be obtained from the developer's web site: `www.getpostman.com/`. Once the extension is installed, navigate to the following URL: `chrome://apps/`, within your Chrome browser, and launch Postman by clicking the visible shortcut. Upon launch of the application, you should witness an interface that is not unlike that shown in Figure 9-6.

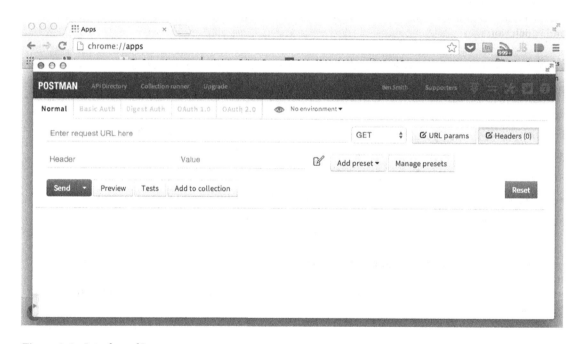

Figure 9-6. *Interface of Postman*

---

[1]What's My User Agent, "What's a User Agent String," `www.whatsmyuseragent.com/WhatsAUserAgent`, 2015.

Figure 9-6 reveals the interface of the Postman HTTP request builder. As an extension to the browser, Postman doesn't rely on the XMLHttpRequest or XDomainRequest objects to fulfill network requests. Therefore, any request from Postman occurs unencumbered by the SOP. Utilizing the applications interface, we will re-create the request from our earlier exercise, to obtain the following resource: http://json.sandboxed.guru/chapter9/data/images.json.

Within the form field that states "Enter request URL here," supply the aforementioned URL. To the right-hand side of this field, you can witness a combo-box. This input field represents the request method. By giving focus to this field, we are able to select the necessary method to enact on the supplied resource. Fortunately for us, GET is the default selection, so we will leave that as is. To the right of the combo-box is the button labeled "Headers," which, when clicked, will reveal a pair of input fields below the URL field of the request. Utilizing the Header and Value fields, respectively, we can configure specific headers of the request. Figure 9-7 illustrates the provision of two familiar headers, Accept-Language and Accept.

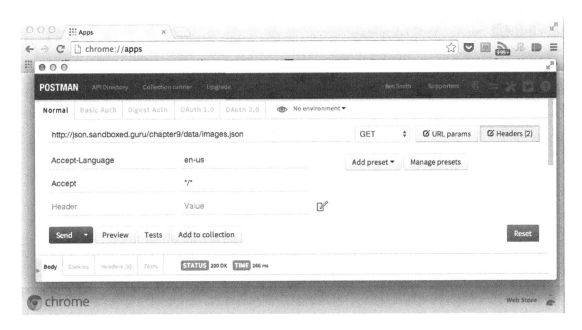

Figure 9-7. *Configuring a GET request with Postman*

At this point, locate the Send button at the lower left of the screen, to initiate the request. Upon sending the request, depending on your Internet connection, you should be provided with a status line of 200, revealing that the request was successful. Following the status, you should see the JSON content for the requested resource. The results should reflect those captured in Figure 9-8.

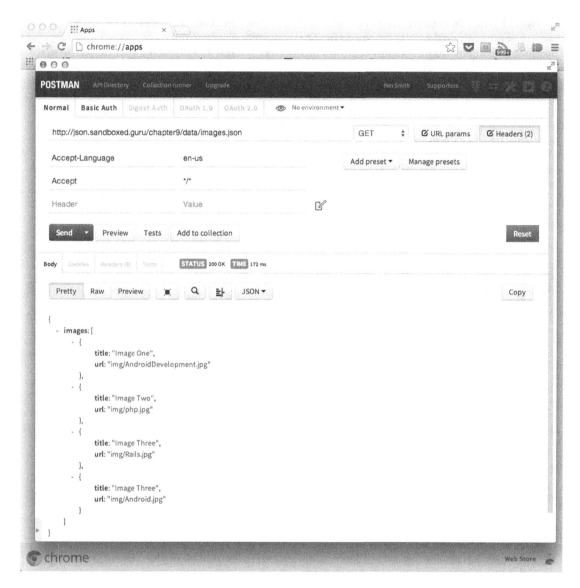

Figure 9-8. *A successful response is provided*

Circumventing Same-Origin Policy

As has been revealed, the browser limits the network access occurring between two varying origins, in order to enforce the same-origin policy. However, as the SOP has been adjusted in an ad hoc fashion over time, a couple of loopholes do exist, which we will leverage, in order to facilitate cross-origin requests.

CORS

The first technique that I will discuss, which sidesteps the same-origin policy (SOP), is that of CORS. CORS, as mentioned previously, is an acronym that stands for Cross-Origin Resource Sharing. CORS, which is the W3C-approved technique to handle cross-origin requests, does not eliminate the SOP. It elaborates upon the model in a way that enables servers to opt in to requests that may not be trusted, thus, informing the user-agent that it should not prevent the response from being obtained from Ajax requests of varying origins. The CORS specification defines how a server, as well as a user-agent, is to coordinate the authorization of a request by a web application from a varying origin.

The overview of how CORS works is simple. For every Ajax request, the user-agent is notified that a request is to be initiated via the send method of the xhr object. As a result of this invocation, the request begins. However, during the request, the user-agent and the server communicate via the inclusion of special HTTP headers, in order to determine if the request should be facilitated.

In our earlier exercise, we received notice from the browser that our request was unable to be carried out, due to the fact that the received response lacked the Access-Control-Allow-Origin header. Access to our origin was refused. The fact that the response did not possess a particular response header was all it took to inform the user-agent that the provided data was not intended for the origin that initiated the request. Therefore, whether or not the server successfully received the request was moot, as the user-agent denied our application access.

Access-Control-Allow-Origin is just one header among a handful that is defined by the CORS specification. In fact, there are fewer than ten in total. Three are configured by the user-agent to accompany the request, and six can be configured by the server to accompany the response. However, not all nine must be used to coordinate the authorization of an HTTP-Request. In fact, most of the time, a maximum of four headers will be exchanged. However, for the purposes of this chapter, we will consider two:

- Access-Control-Allow-Origin

- Origin

What determines which of the nine CORS headers are necessary to authorize the request depends on whether the request is deemed "simple" or requiring "preflight." What distinguishes a request as being the former or the latter ultimately boils down to the request method chosen to enact on the indicated resource, in addition to the configured request headers.

A simple request, as defined by the specification, is one that identifies GET, POST, or HEAD as its request method. Additionally, a simple request cannot specify headers that are not among those white-listed. Those headers are the following:

- Accept

- Accept-Language

- Content-Language

- Content-Type

While you may initially find the preceding headers reasonable for GET requests, I think you will find them rather limiting for POST, after you realize that Content-Type can only be configured as application/x-www-form-urlencoded, multipart/form-data, or text/plain. What this means is that when a POST request is accompanied by an entity body whose Content-Type is configured as application/json, a preflight request must occur prior to the actual request.

A preflight request is simply an initial HTTP request submitted by the user-agent to the requested server, using the OPTIONS request method to obtain the necessary server information and configured headers that might suggest the Ajax request is authorized. In other words, before attempting to make a request that is not considered simple, and, therefore, may be considered malicious, the user-agent determines if the remote server indicates any interest in receiving such a request. As indicated earlier, this is accomplished via the OPTIONS method, which simply informs the remote server to provide a list of all acceptable headers and methods that can accompany a request to the indicated resource. If the response is not configured to handle the headers/methods as they are explicitly outlined by the user-agent, the actual request will be canceled.

I will discuss how to configure a server's response to accommodate preflight requests in more detail in Chapter 11. In the meantime, feel free to review the CORS headers required of preflight requests, in Table 9-2.

For every "simple" cross-origin request, the user-agent, in addition to configuring any default headers, must configure a header that is essential to the CORS specification. This header, which is simply labeled "Origin," indicates, as its configured value, the source origin of the request. On receiving the request, the server can use the configured value possessed by the Origin header to configure the fulfillment of the request. As briefly discussed, an origin is considered authorized by a user-agent if, and only if, the fulfillment of the request possesses the Access-Control-Allow-Origin header and is configured to indicate as trusted the origin that initiated the request. If the Access-Control-Allow-Origin header is not present, access to the response will not be permitted. However, if the header is present, the user-agent will determine via an algorithm whether the configured value matches the source origin. This algorithm makes up Section 7.2 of the CORS specification, Resource Sharing Check.

Resource Sharing Check

The configured headers provided by the server are merely the mechanism by which to communicate with the user-agent. They do not guarantee that a source origin can bypass the same-origin policy (SOP). As the user agent governs the SOP, it is the user-agent's responsibility to determine whether the source origin and the value accompanying the Access-Control-Allow-Origin header meet the authorization requirements. The user-agent accomplishes this via the following steps of an algorithm:[2]

1. If the response includes zero or more than one Access-Control-Allow-Origin header value, return fail and terminate this algorithm.

2. If the Access-Control-Allow-Origin header value is the * character and the omit credentials flag is set, return pass and terminate this algorithm.

3. If the value of Access-Control-Allow-Origin is not a case-sensitive match for the value of the Origin header as defined by its specification, return fail and terminate this algorithm.

4. If the omit credentials flag is unset and the response includes zero or more than one Access-Control-Allow-Credentials header value, return fail and terminate this algorithm.

5. If the omit credentials flag is unset and the Access-Control-Allow-Credentials header value is not a case-sensitive match for true, return fail and terminate this algorithm.

6. Return pass.

---

[2]World Wide Consortium (W3C), "Cross-Origin Resource Sharing," www.w3.org/TR/cors/#resource-sharing-check, January 16, 2014.

In short, the value of the Access-Control-Allow-Origin header, as configured by the server, must satisfy all origins via the provision of the wild card token * or be provided as a case-sensitive match for the indicated origin, as supplied within the request. On the other hand, if the resource-sharing check determines that authorization should not be allowed, we are provided with the aforementioned network error indicating that the origin lacks sufficient authorization. As the SOP specifies trust per URI,[3] the preceding outlined steps occur for each requested cross-origin resource. Listing 9-3 demonstrates how a resource can grant proper authorization to all source origins, utilizing PHP.

Listing 9-3. Authorizing All Source Origins per the Current Resource

```
1 <?php
2 header('Access-Control-Allow-Origin: *');
3 $headers=getallheaders();
4 $origin =$headers["Origin"];
3 echo '{"message":"congratulations '.$origin .', your origin has been successfully
authorized by your
        user-agent"}';
4 ?>
```

The most minimal configuration required on the server's behalf, as demonstrated in the preceding listing, is to configure the Access-Control-Allow-Origin header with the value of the wild-card * token. With the preceding Access-Control-Allow-Origin header in place, any simple request made via XMLHttpRequest or XDomainRequest and occurring from any origin will be provided the appropriate authorization. If you were to run the following code from Listing 9-4, the source origin of your request would be entitled access to the JSON provided.

Listing 9-4. A GET Request Being Made of cors.php

```
1 <script>
2 var xhr= new XMLHttpRequest();
3   if(!"withCredentials" in xhr){
4     xhr= new XDomainRequest();
5   }
6   xhr.open("GET", "http://json.sandboxed.guru/chapter9/cors.php");
7   xhr.onload = function() {
8       alert(this.responseText);
9   };
10  xhr.send();
11 </script>
```

No matter the source origin of the request, executing the request from the preceding listing will result in an alert box prominently appearing to inform the user that the source origin of the request has been granted authorization to the JSON response, as revealed in Figure 9-9.

---

[3] Adam Barth, Internet Engineering Task Force (IETF), "The Web Origin Concept," www.ietf.org/rfc/rfc6454.txt, 2011.

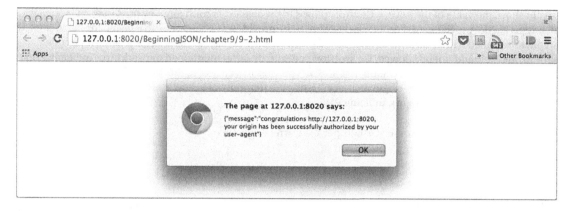

Figure 9-9. *Successful attempt at Cross Origin Resource Sharing*

As you can clearly witness from the URL in Figure 9-9, our local request, signified by the IP address `127.0.0.1`, is able to receive access to the JSON body provided by the resource, whose origin is `http://json.sandboxed.guru`. By reviewing the headers of the request, as captured by the developer's console, we can witness the inclusion of the Origin and Access-Control-Allow-Origin headers used to coordinate the source origin's authorization, as shown in Figure 9-10.

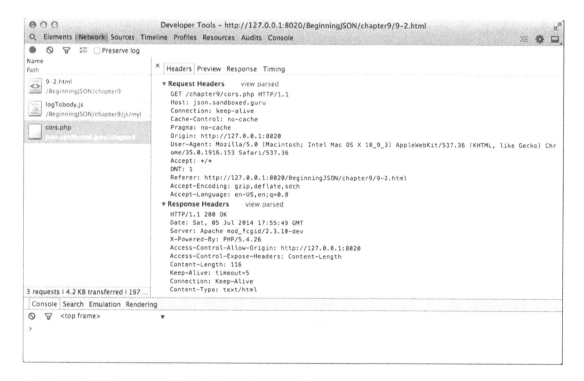

Figure 9-10. *CORS response exhibiting the configuration of the Options and Access-Control-Allow-Origin headers*

With the use of the two aforementioned CORS headers, we can successfully bypass the SOP and successfully enable cross-origin requests. However, this does not entitle a cross-origin request to be treated similarly to that of an SOP. Although the server has authorized the request, the user-agent continues to refrain from providing information that may reduce the security of either the client or response. For this reason, cookies, basic-authorization, and custom headers are prevented from reaching their destination, unless otherwise coordinated between the user-agent and server via two more headers. Furthermore, the user-agent will limit the application's exposure to any headers provided by the server that are not considered to be among the following six white-listed simple response headers:

- Cache-Control

- Content-Language

- Content-Type

- Expires

- Last-Modified

- Pragma

To further broaden the scope of the authorization, to enable these aspects as required by your application, the server must coordinate with the user-agent by configuring any necessary header as supplied by the CORS specification. Following are two tables that outline the various CORS headers, as utilized by the two request categories simple and preflight.

The headers in Table 9-2 are concerned with all aspects of simple requests.

Table 9-2. *CORS Simple Headers*

Header	Role	Configured by
Origin	Indicates where the cross-origin request originates	User-Agent
Access-Control-Allow-Origin	Indicates whether a resource can be shared by returning the value configured for the Origin request header, *, or null	Server
Access-Control-Allow-Credentials	Indicates whether the response to the request can be exposed when the omit credentials flag is unused	Server
Access-Control-Expose-Headers	Indicates which headers are safe to expose to the API XMLHttpRequest object via the getResponseHeaders method	Server

The headers within Table 9-3 are concerned with the more complex requests, which require an initial request, in order to determine if the server acknowledges the configured aspects of the request that are not recognized as simple. If the server indicates that it is willing to handle said aspects, only then will the actual request be sent to the server. If, however, the server does not indicate that it can handle those aspects, the user-agent will cancel the request altogether, once again resulting in the same network error indicating insufficient authorization.

Table 9-3. *CORS Preflight Headers*

Header	Role	Configured by
Access-Control-Request-Headers	Indicates which headers will be used in the actual request	User-Agent
Access-Control-Request-Method	Indicates which method will be used in the actual request	User-Agent
Access-Control-Allow-Methods	Indicates which methods can be used during the request for a targeted resource	Server
Access-Control-Allow-Headers	Indicates which header field names can be used during the request of the targeted resource	Server
Access-Control-Max-Age	Indicates how long the results of a preflight request can be cached	Server

Although CORS is the official W3C technique to abide by when working with cross-origin requests, the CORS headers can only be used by the user-agent that conforms to the algorithms of the CORS specification. This is to say that only those browsers that implement the XMLHttpRequest Level 2 specification can fully support CORS. As you learned in Chapter 8, modern browsers, in addition to Internet Explorer 10 and greater, support the XMLHttpRequest Level 2 specification. For this reason, this chapter will continue to outline two other techniques that enable cross-origin requests.

The Proxy

While the same-origin policy (SOP) is enforced by the browser, I did recently discuss that the SOP is not at all a component of the HTTP protocol. Rather, it's a security model that is strictly adhered to by the browsers of which we make use. As demonstrated by our earlier use of Postman, when we use tools that do not rely on the browser, we are able to make requests indiscriminately. This is because the foundations of the HTTP protocol rely on the ability for any server to fulfill a request. However, it is up to the targeted server to determine whether or not that request should be allowed.

As the name suggests, the concept of a server proxy is to forward an authorized request to a local server to a remote server. (Remember: An authorized request comes from the same origin.) The process begins with an HTTP request being made to a same-origin web server. From there, either the same request, or a new request, is provided to a remote server by the local web server, unhindered by the user-agent. Provided the request is successful, the response is returned up the chain from the remote server to the local server that made the request and back to the client who invoked the request, our Ajax call. The forwarding of requests can be observed from the diagram in Figure 9-11.

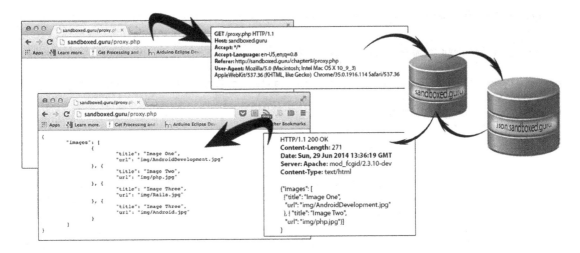

Figure 9-11. *Proxy diagram from* `sandboxed.guru` *to* `json.sandboxed.guru` *and back*

Because the communications that take place via the user-agent remain between the same origin, all proxy requests are considered trusted and, therefore, authorized to view the response. We will begin with a review of the xhr code, as seen in Listing 9-5.

Listing 9-5. HTTP Request to the Authorized /proxy.php Resource

```
1 var xhr= new XMLHttpRequest();
2    xhr.open("GET","http://sandboxed.guru/proxy.php");
3    xhr.onload=function(){
4        console.log(this.responseText);
5    };
6    xhr.onerror=function(){
7        console.log( "Error Occurred" );
8    }
9    xhr.send();
```

Listing 9-5 should not appear new, as we have been using the same code from both the previous chapter as well as this chapter. Ultimately, we initiate a GET request to http://sanboxed.guru/proxy.php. The only thing to point out is that Listing 9-5 does not make use of the XDomainRequest. This is strictly because the XDomainRequest is only required in Internet Explorer versions 8 and 9, to make requests to varying origins. However, as the proxy technique utilizes a server program that runs on the same server from which the request will occur, we can utilize the XMLHttpRequest from IE 8+. This will provide us with more control over the request as well. Remember: The XDomainRequest object does not possess the setRequestHeader, whereas the XMLHttpRequest object does.

Upon the submission of the request, the target of the request, local resource /proxy.php, whose code can be observed in Listing 9-6, will be executed.

Listing 9-6. PHP Server-Side Proxy Implementation

```php
1 <?php
2 if ($_SERVER['REQUEST_METHOD'] === 'GET') {
3     $ch = curl_init();
4     curl_setopt($ch, CURLOPT_URL,'http://json.sandboxed.guru/chapter9/data/images.json');
5     curl_setopt($ch, CURLOPT_RETURNTRANSFER, false);
6     $output = curl_exec($ch);
7     curl_close($ch);
8 }
9 ?>
```

Listing 9-6 demonstrates the minimal PHP code required to create a request using a library known as cURL, which is simply a command-line utility that enables the interchange of data. Let's walk through the preceding code to understand what is taking place.

The script begins by ensuring that the request method to be enacted on proxy.php is a GET (**line 1**). This is necessary to ensure that extraneous use of the proxy is prevented from occurring from requests other than GET requests.

Once we have determined that the request method is in fact GET, we proceed with initializing our cURL object (**line 3**). The cURL object, when initialized, returns an instance, which is stored on a variable labeled $ch. As with the xhr object, we configure our instance of the cURL object with the necessary headers and values to initiate the request. Our first line provides the URL of our resource, http://json.sandboxed.guru/chapter9/data/images.json (**line 4**). The next configuration is used to obtain the response as a string, rather than outputting the response directly (**line 5**). In this particular case, we set the value to false, as we will have no need to further modify the response from the remote server. The next line (**line 6**) executes the request. Once the response is obtained, we close the cURL resource (**line 7**).

It should be noted that the use of cURL is code blocking, and, therefore, the response awaited by our xhr object continues, until either the connection times out or a response is finally provided. However, once the cURL request is provided a response from the remote server, the response provided is sent back to the client request, which was prompted by Ajax, whereby either the onload or onerror event handler will be triggered.

While the preceding code successfully demonstrates how a proxy can be used to successfully bypass the SOP, the proxy is rather limited. As the indicated resource on line 4 of Listing 9-6 is hard-coded, we would require multiple proxies, if there were multiple files that our application required. While this can get quite cumbersome, we can eliminate that issue with relative ease, either by appending a query string parameter to the end of our resource or by providing the URI as a value belonging to a custom header.

In order to make this something that can be witnessed from a browser, in addition to an Ajax request, the code that follows (Listing 9-7) makes use of the former option (the query string parameter).

Listing 9-7. An xhr object Whose Target Resource Possesses a Query String Parameter Indicating the URI for the Proxy to Obtain

```javascript
1 var xhr= new XMLHttpRequest();
2     xhr.open("GET","http://sandboxed.guru/proxy.php?uri=images.json");
3     xhr.onload=function(){
4         console.log(this.responseText);
5     };
6     xhr.onerror=function(){
7         console.log( "Error Occurred" );
8     }
9     xhr.send();
```

Listing 9-7 remains unchanged from that of Listing 9-5, with the minor appendage to the indicated resource (**line 2**). We have supplied the resource with a key/value pair, which, when supplied in a URL, is a query string parameter. In this case, the key is that of **uri**, and its value represents the desired resource to be obtained by our proxy. Our proxy must then be modified slightly to anticipate the use of a query string value. These changes that account for the new query string parameter are outlined in bold in Listing 9-8.

Listing 9-8. PHP Code Accounting for the Added `jsonp` URL Parameter

```php
1  <?php
2  if (strtolower($_SERVER['REQUEST_METHOD']) === 'get') {
3      $uri = (isset($_GET[uri]));
4      if ($uri) {
5          $uri = htmlentities($_GET[uri]);
6          $ch = curl_init();
7          curl_setopt($ch, CURLOPT_URL, 'http://json.sandboxed.guru/chapter9/data/' . $uri);
8          curl_setopt($ch, CURLOPT_RETURNTRANSFER, false);
9          $output = curl_exec($ch);
10         curl_close($ch);
11     } else {
12         header('HTTP/1.1 400 Bad Request');
13         echo 'Append ?uri=xxxx to the target resource where xxxx is the value of the URI on
                    json.sandboxed.guru/chapter9/data/xxxx';
14     }
15 }
16 ?>
```

Listing 9-8 revisits our proxy from Listing 9-6, with the new query string parameter being taken into account. We begin by determining if the **uri** key has been provided with the request and assign the returned Boolean value produced by the evaluation onto a variable labeled $uri (**line 3**). From there, we determine what block of code should be executed, depending on whether the $uri value is set (**line 4**). If the $uri variable is evaluated to be true, we continue to execute the code block that initiates the proxy. At this point, we have only determined if the **uri** parameter has been provided with the request. Now, we must obtain the value that it possesses. Repurposing the $uri variable, we reassign it with the obtained value held by the key (**line 5**). The period (.) token, in PHP, is used to concatenate strings, thereby joining the URL with the dynamic resource. Being that our Ajax request provided the **uri** as images.json, line 7 will result in the final URL of http://json.sandboxed.guru/chapter9/data/images.json. While this is precisely the same URL we previously targeted, the required resource is specified dynamically and, therefore, can request a variety of resources stored within the preceding path.

Should the **uri** parameter not be present for the provided request, the proxy will not be triggered to provide a response from the remote source. Instead, the request will be fulfilled with that of a response from our proxy server. As the request is not properly formed, the server configures the status line to possess a status code of 400 (**line 12**). It further specifies the textual phrase that accompanies the status code, which is Bad Request. This status code is utilized to inform the client that he/she should not continue to repeat the request without further modification. Last, in order to further clarify how to correct the request, we output a message stating that a query string must be provided (**line 13**).

At this point, feel free to navigate your browser to http://sandboxed.guru/proxy.php to see the results of the proxy for yourself. Upon reception of the provided messaging, append the uri parameter to the URL, whose value can be any of the following resources: images.json, string.json, or script.json.

JSONP

The final technique that enables us to interchange JSON between two varying origins is that of JSON with padding. JSON with padding, or JSONP, as Bob Ippolito coined it in 2005, regards a particular technique in which a client can obtain JSON simply by leveraging the HTML <script> element.

The same-origin policy (SOP) does not govern the requests of externally referenced content via specific HTML tags. Such tags are those of <img>, <style>, <iframe>, and <script>. As you may recall from your past experiences in web development, script tags are able to embed externally referenced JavaScript files, regardless of whether the requesting origin matches the origin of the targeted resource. Such an example that may be familiar is shown in Listing 9-9.

Listing 9-9. Script Tag Targeting the Externally Hosted jQuery Script from a CDN

```
<script src="//code.jquery.com/jquery-1.11.0.min.js"></script>
```

Listing 9-9 utilizes the script tag to retrieve the jQuery library from the jQuery CDN, regardless of the origin of the request. Furthermore, once the resource is obtained, the external script gains total access to our document, and vice versa, making this ideal transport for JSON. Unfortunately, as you will shortly see, not all JSON values can be properly parsed when obtained via the HTML <script> element.

Listing 9-10 demonstrates grammatically valid JSON, as the content of an indicated resource located at the URL http://json.sandboxed.guru/chapter8/data/imagesA.json.

Listing 9-10. JSON Content Within imagesA.json

```
{
    "images": [
            {
                "title": "Image One",
                "url": "img/AndroidDevelopment.jpg"
            }, {
                "title": "Image Two",
                "url": "img/php.jpg"
            }, {
                "title": "Image Three",
                "url": "img/Rails.jpg"
            }, {
                "title": "Image Three",
                "url": "img/TSQL.jpg"
            }
    ]
}
```

As with our earlier jQuery inclusion, we should be able to load imagesA.json into an application as an external reference, via the script tag, as shown in Listing 9-11.

Listing 9-11. Script Tag Referencing imagesA.json

```
<script src="http://json.sandboxed.guru/chapter8/data/imagesA.json"></script>
```

Unfortunately, if we were to incorporate the code from Listing 9-11 into an HTML document and view that document in a browser, we would arrive at the following syntax error, as shown in Figure 9-12.

Figure 9-12. *Loading* /data/imagesA.json *via the* <script> *tag results in a syntax error*

The preceding error is not the result of our HTML Document loading a JSON document as an external reference but, rather, how the script engine evaluates JavaScript. Consider the more succinct JSON example being supplied to the eval function in Listing 9-12. When the following JSON is provided to the JavaScript engine, it, too, results in an error.

Listing 9-12. Supplying a JSON Collection to the Script Engine via eval

```
eval( '{ "test":"abc" }' );  //fails
```

This error occurs for no other reason than the fact that the provided content is not considered syntactically valid JavaScript. However, as explained earlier, the error is not due to the fact that we are supplying JSON. As you should recall, JSON is a subset of JavaScript. The issue simply lies in the fact that the engine favors the evaluation of statements, rather than those of expressions. According to Section 12.4, Expression Statements, of the ECMA-262 standardization:

> *An **ExpressionStatement cannot start with an opening curly brace** because that might make it ambiguous with a Block.*

While this can be viewed as a setback, it is certainly not a roadblock. We simply require a way to coax the parser into seeing the provided script as an expression. Fortunately, JavaScript provides us with the operator that can manage this. That operator, of course, is the grouping operator signified by the open and closed parenthetical (( )) tokens.

■ **Note** Only the initial ({ }) braces cause the parser to throw a syntax error. No other object literal suffers the same fate.

By wrapping our script with the grouping operator, we can inform the parser to handle the evaluation in the context of an expression. It is the padding of the parentheses for which the phrase *JSON with padding* refers.

By padding our object literal within the grouping operator, as seen in Listing 9-13, the script engine no longer alerts us to a syntax error. However, having crossed one hurdle, we find ourselves facing yet another.

Listing 9-13. Wrapping JSON with the Grouping Operator

```
eval( '( { "test":"abc" } )' );  //Successfully parsed
```

Once the script engine properly parses the provided JSONP, we find ourselves without a means of obtaining the parsed data. However, this can be easily overcome using the JSONP model. By preceding our JSONP with a function name, that function will be invoked upon the script's evaluation, essentially acting as an event handler. Furthermore, the evaluated object literal, wrapped within parentheses, will be parsed into a valid JavaScript object and provide as the argument the indicated function, allowing our function to obtain the parsed JSON. The structural composition of JSONP is **CALLBACK_IDENTIFIER(JSONtext);**. Listing 9-14 is an example of this.

Listing 9-14. Example of the JSONP Model

```
someMethod({ "test" : "abc" });
```

As you might expect, this requires our HTML document to be in possession of a function whose identifier is equal to that of the function name prepended to our JSONP, lest the parser throw a `ReferenceError`, as indicated in Figure 9-13.

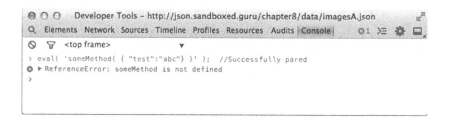

Figure 9-13. *Reference error, can't find* someMethod

In Listing 9-15, the object literal, padded by the parentheses on both sides, is properly recognized by the engine as an expression and, therefore, parsed into a proper JavaScript object. From there, the evaluation is provided to the indicated function as the argument. Upon the invocation of someMethods, the statement(s) within the body of the function are able to reference the parsed data (**line 3**). In this case, the statement simply logs out the test key, resulting in abc being sent to the developer console.

Listing 9-15. Invocation of the Method Evaluated, and the Provision of a JSON Argument

```
1 eval( 'someMethod( ({ "test" : "abc" }) )' );
2 function someMethod(data){
3     console.log(data.test);  //abc;
4 }
```

It is the function name that forges the contract between the provider of the JSONP and the client that seeks to make use of it. This is an important fact, because if the name is defined statically, it reduces the interoperability among applications. Therefore, to keep the method name from conflicting with any application, the JSONP model requires that the resource allow the client of the request to define the name of the function that will precede the JSONP.

The manner by which the client informs the server to the preferred callback is quite simple. The client appends a jsonp query string parameter to the targeted URL and assigns its value the name of the function to invoke (see Listing 9-16).

Listing 9-16. JSONP Request

```
1 <script>
2    var test=function(data){
3        //do something with data here.
4    }
5 </script>
6 <script src='http://json.sandboxed.guru/chapter9/data/jsonp.php?jsonp=test'></script>
```

Listing 9-16 declares a function, which will operate on a supplied piece of data and assigns it to the variable test (**line 1**), where it can be referenced later. Next, utilizing the script tag (**line 6**), we make a request to our JSONP resource and append to it the jsonp parameter, whose value is that of the preferred function to invoke upon the evaluation of the received script.

Now, while Listing 9-16 accounts for the front end, the resource must account for the supplied parameter. Once again, any server-side language can manage this easily enough. I, however, will demonstrate the code as it appears in PHP (see Listing 9-17).

Listing 9-17. Fulfillment of JSON or JSONP, Pending the Provision of the jsonp Parameter

```
1 <?php
2 header('Content-Type: application/javascript');
3 $callback = (isset($_GET["jsonp"])) ? $_GET["jsonp"] : "";
4 $JSONtext = '{
      "images": [
          {
              "title": "Image One",
              "url": "img/AndroidDevelopment.jpg"
          }, {
              "title": "Image Two",
              "url": "img/php.jpg"
          }, {
              "title": "Image Three",
              "url": "img/Rails.jpg"
          }, {
              "title": "Image Three",
              "url": "img/Android.jpg"
          }
      ]
  }'
5 echo $callback . '(' .$JSONtext. ');';
6 ?>
```

Listing 9-17 reveals the PHP code for the requested URI: `http://json.sandboxed.guru/chapter9/data/jsonp.php`. For the most part, the content within can be recognized as the `imagesA.json` from Listing 9-10. However, the lines that appear in bold have been added to serve JSONP. The script begins by properly indicating the header of the response. As the body of the response is no longer JSON, but rather JavaScript, we must ensure that clients treat the body as JavaScript. Therefore, we set the Content-Type to `application/javascript` (**line 2**). Next, utilizing the parameters of the URL, we determine if the key labeled `jsonp` has been provided. If it has indeed been set, we assign its value to a variable labeled **$callback**. If the `jsonp` parameter is not present with the GET request, we assign an empty string to said variable (**line 3**). Next, to keep the code clean for review, I assign the intended JSON text to a variable labeled **$JSONtext** (**line 4**). This value will later be padded with parentheses and a possible callback identifier. Last, using PHP's concatenation operator `.`, we join the provided callback with that of our padded JSON and output the final representation as the response of the request (**line 5**).

While Listing 9-16 demonstrates the implementation of a `<script>` element, along with a collaborating function to receive JSONP, the fact that they were defined at design time results in the immediate request, upon the execution of the HTML document. However, this may not always be the desired effect. Utilizing JavaScript, we can resort to script tag injection, thereby obtaining the results at a time of our choosing.

Dynamic Script Tag Injection

When an HTML document is opened within the browser, the parser scans from the top down the markup of the document for any tags that reference external content. For each `<img>`, `<style>`, or `<script>` encountered that may reference an external resource, an HTTP request is initiated. This, however, is not always the desired effect.

Dynamic script tag injection is a technique that relies on JavaScript to configure an HTML `<script>` element at runtime. By creating said tag on the fly, the tag remains absent from the markup, which prevents a resource from being fetched prematurely. Yet, at a point of our choosing, we can insert the configured tag into the body of the document, thereby initiating a request for the indicated JSONP resource. The necessary code to achieve this on demand behavior can be viewed in Listing 9-18.

Listing 9-18. Dynamic Script Tag Injection

```
1 function getScript(url){
2 var script = document.createElement("script");
3     script.src=url;
4     document.getElementsByTagName('head')[0].appendChild(script);
5 }
6 getScript('http://json.sandboxed.guru/chapter9/data/jsonp.php?jsonp=someMethod');
```

Listing 9-18 reveals a function that, when invoked, is responsible for the creation, configuration, and the injection of a script tag within the document of the application being run. The code solely responsible for the dynamic script tag injection has been encapsulated within the getScript function, so that we can generate any number of scripts through a single endpoint (**line 1**). Furthermore, to account for any possible URL to be supplied as the resource of the request, the **getScript** function accepts a URL as a parameter.

Upon an invocation, we utilize the **createElement** method of the document object to create an HTML element of our choosing. As the tag we require is that of a script element, we provide `script` as the parameter and assign the returned element to a variable labeled `script` (**line 2**). Utilizing the script reference, we supply the URL argument as the referenced source via the `src` attribute (**line 3**). From there, we utilize the document object to obtain a reference to the HTML `<head>` element, whereby we will insert our newly crafted HTML `<script>` element. Last, to generate a dynamic tag and trigger our resource to be loaded, we invoke **getScript** and supply to it our JSONP URL. By using JavaScript to inject a script tag into our markup, we have more control over when the resource is loaded. The invocation can be the result of an event, such as a button click.

While **getScript** makes loading JSONP resources on demand a simple task, there are many available libraries, such as jQuery, that extend the code even further, so that it's possible to provide anonymous functions for invocation upon the evaluation of the indicated JSONP request. Such a function that enables this type of behavior can be viewed in Listing 9-19.

Listing 9-19. Dynamic Script Tag Injection with Anonymous Callback Behavior

```
 1 var getJSONP = (function () {
 2  jsonp_callbacks={};
 3  return function(url, fName, callback) {
 4      scriptNode = document.createElement('script');
 5      scriptNode.setAttribute('type', 'text/javascript');
 6      scriptNode.src = url + '?jsonp=' + encodeURIComponent('jsonp_callbacks["' + fName +
        '"]');
 7      jsonp_callbacks[fName] = function (data) {
 8          delete jsonp_callbacks[fName];
 9          callback(data);
10      };
11      document.body.appendChild(scriptNode);
12  };
13 }());
14 getJSONP('http://json.sandboxed.guru/chapter9/data/jsonp.php', 'callback', function
   (data) {
15      console.log(data);
16 });
```

Summary

This chapter pointed out three techniques that can be used to initiate cross-origin requests that fulfill the interchange of JSON. As was indicated, the majority of front-end code remains unchanged. However, it does require a slight amount of modification, with regard to requesting a JSONP resource. In contrast, it will be the onus of the server administrator to configure a resource to be made available to a cross-origin request.

With the conclusion of this chapter, you should find yourself one step closer toward being able to harness the full power of JSON. In the next chapter, we will install and work with Node.js, a platform built on Chrome's JavaScript runtime, so that you can host your own local web server, which can be used to receive, store, retrieve, and transmit JSON, utilizing the configurations required of each of the tactics discussed in this chapter.

The wonderful news is that because Node.js works entirely on the V8 JavaScript engine, you won't be asked to follow along with a language that you might not be used to.

Key Points from This Chapter

- The same-origin policy (SOP) is the security model adhered to by all user-agents.

- The SOP governs a variety of front-end securities.

- The SOP restricts network messages between varying origins.

- SOPs vary according to the degree by which they are enforced between different technologies.

- Use the `in` operator to test whether the `widthCredentials` attribute exists on the `xhr` instance.

- Cross-network errors can be corrected by moving the resource to the same domain as the source origin, or by enabling Cross-Origin Resource Sharing (CORS).

- A domain and its subdomain are not considered authorized by default.

- Origins are considered similar if they possess the same scheme, port, and domain.

- The port address for HTTP is 80, while that for HTTPS is 443

- Certain headers are unable to be altered via `setRequestHeader`.

- SOPs can be circumvented via server-side programming.

- The Access-Control-Allow-Origin header is required to fulfill "simple" requests from varying origins.

- If a request is not simple, it requires "preflight."

- Simple requests use `GET`, `POST`, or `Head` and are limited to four white-listed headers.

- The simple header Content-Type can only be configured as `application/x-www-form-urlencoded`, `multipart/form-data`, or `text/plain`.

- CORS headers can only be used with user-agents that conform to the algorithms of the CORS specification.

- JSONP is JSON wrapped in parentheses and preceded by a function name.

- The client request specifies the function name via the `jsonp` query parameter.

- The SOP does not govern requests of externally referenced content via `<script>`.

- An `ExpressionStatement` cannot start with an opening curly brace.

- A server proxy forwards an authorized request to a remote server.

CHAPTER 10

■ ■ ■

Serving JSON

Up until this point, we have been focusing on JSON primarily from a front-end perspective. However, as a data interchange format, JSON plays an important role on the back end of our applications as well. Therefore, in order to further empower ourselves in the ways of JSON, we will explore how to set up our very own web server, utilizing an open source technology known as Node.js.

Once we have our own server up and running, you will learn how to utilize said server to provide JSON, receive JSON, and even store/persist JSON.

Node.JS

Node.js, commonly referred to as Node, is a runtime environment created by Ryan Dahl that allows us to devise a web server using nothing other than JavaScript. That's right, JavaScript. Now before you begin to presume that this can't be considered a true server, let me assure you that Node is incredibly powerful and extremely efficient. So much so, that it's used by many popular brands, such as Walmart, PayPal, and eBay, to name a few.

Node is built on top of Chrome's V8 JavaScript engine, making JavaScript the ideal language of our server. Furthermore, because Node makes use of the latest V8 code base, our server can utilize the cutting-edge inclusions of the JavaScript API, such as File-System, Web Workers, etc. The benefits don't just stop there either. Because JavaScript is an event-driven language, the functions within Node remain asynchronous and are capable of handling data-intensive applications. Last, Node can run without additional software, such as Apache, being installed, making it simple and convenient to install on either Windows or Mac.

Windows Installation

Upon navigating to nodejs.org/download/, we are immediately presented with the tools that will get us up and running. As there is no reason to take anything but the path of least resistance, we will download and install the Windows Installer (.msi). Whether you chose the 32-bit vs. the 64-bit version is dependent on your current operating system. While most programs designed for the 32-bit versions of Windows are compatible with 64-bit versions, the same cannot be stated for 64-bit software on 32-bit Windows.

To find out if your computer is running a 32-bit or 64-bit version of Windows, in Windows 8 or Windows 8.1, do the following:

1. Open System by right-clicking the Windows button and selecting System from the list.

2. Within the System pane, you can view the system type.

To find out if your computer is running a 32-bit or 64-bit version of Windows, in Windows 7 or Windows Vista, do the following:

1. Open System by clicking the Start button, right-clicking Computer, and then clicking Properties.

2. Under System, you can view the system type.

If your computer is running Windows XP, do the following:

1. Click Start.

2. Right-click My Computer and then click Properties.

    a. If you don't see "x64 Edition" listed, then you're running the 32-bit version of Windows XP.

    b. If "x64 Edition" is listed under System, you're running the 64-bit version of Windows XP.

Once you determine which bit operating system your machine is running, click the corresponding Windows Installer. As I am running a 32-bit version of Windows, as shown in Figure 10-1, I will be installing the 32-bit Node Windows Installer.

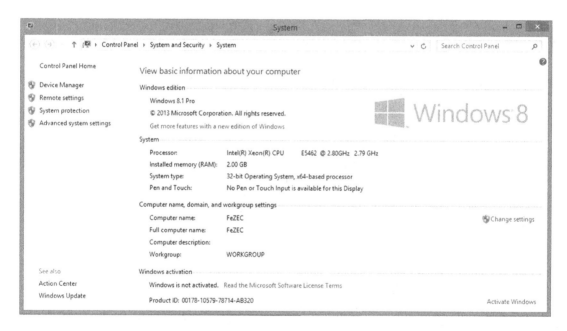

Figure 10-1. *Determining Windows operating system type: 32-bit vs. 64-bit*

By clicking either the 32-bit or 64-bit button, depending on your browser, the `.msi` should begin downloading. Depending on the browser, you may have to acknowledge that you wish the file to be saved. Once the file has been downloaded successfully, navigate to the directory in which it has been downloaded and double-click the installer, to initiate the installation wizard. At this point, the Node setup wizard will walk you through the installation step-by-step. To begin the processes, click Next.

The second screen of the wizard presents us with the license agreement of Node. Before continuing on to the next screen, you must accept the terms in the license agreement. Take this opportunity to read and accept the End-User License Agreement and then click Next to configure the installation.

The following few screens enable you to change the default configurations of the installation. Such configurations determine in which directory to install Node, or how corresponding features should be installed. Unless you feel comfortable enough to modify these settings, you should leave them as they are and continue to the installation screen shown in Figure 10-2.

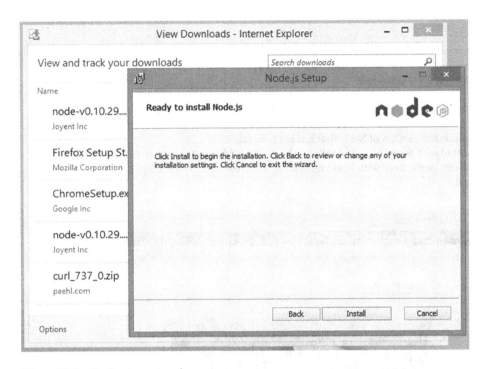

Figure 10-2. *Node setup wizard*

Once you reach this screen, simply click Install, and then sit back and relax for a short moment. You will be presented with confirmation that the Node setup wizard has completed. At this point, feel free to click Finish to exit the wizard. By default, Node and its features are installed globally, and often, system-wide variable changes may not always be recognized until after a reboot. Therefore, before we verify that the installation of Node was successful, it will be wise to reboot.

Once Windows loads, we can verify the installation of Node. We will achieve this with the assistance of the command-line interpreter, also known as the command prompt. To access the command prompt application, right-click your desktop's Start button and choose Run from the list of options. Within the input field, simply type cmd.exe, then click the button labeled "OK."

Figure 10-3 reveals the command terminal in which we can enter commands. The terminal will open to a defaulted folder that exists on the hard drive. Which folder depends on whether you run cmd.exe as an administrator or as a user. If you run it as an administrator, the default folder will be that of a system folder, whereas if you open it as a user, it will reflect your user's folder. Figure 10-3 reveals my directory as C:\Users\UrZA>, which simply reflects the directory that corresponds to the account that I logged in to on the machine. Of course, that account user is named UrZA.

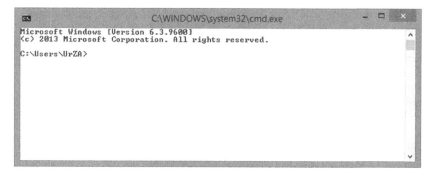

Figure 10-3. *Command prompt interface*

In order to ensure that Node was installed and configured successfully, type node --version within the terminal, then hit Enter. If Node has successfully been configured for your user account, you should be provided with the numerical version of Node that has been installed.

If you are presented with something that reflects the vX.XX.XX format, as shown in Figure 10-4, then congratulations; you can begin work with Node right away. Feel free to fast-forward to the "Building an HTTP Server" section.

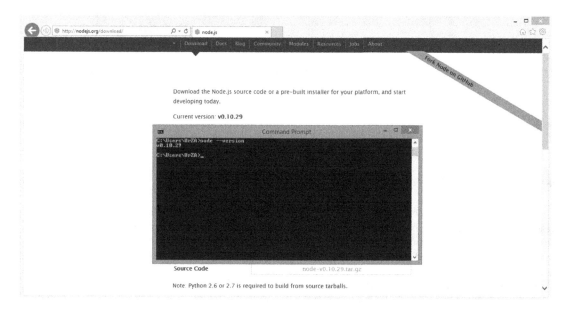

Figure 10-4. *The Node --version command outputs the installed version of Node.js*

If, on the other hand, the terminal outputs the message that Node is not recognized as an internal or external command, operable program, or batch file, it's evident that Node has not been correctly installed. In order to correct this, there are a few steps that can be taken.

The Node installation will install node.exe within the C:\Program Files\nodejs\ directory by default. Take a moment to verify that this executable is indeed present within this folder. If you have altered the destination during the setup process, please navigate to that directory instead. If you do not witness the node.exe executable within the determined directory, the installation may not have successfully completed. Please run the installation wizard once again to rerun the setup process followed by a system reboot.

If you are able to verify the presence of node.exe within the chosen directory, the failure of the command prompt to execute the command node --version may be due to the fact that the directory to which it is installed lies outside the directories utilized by the shell. To be certain as to whether this is the case, type the command PATH within the command prompt. The output shown in Figure 10-5 lists the default directories used by the shell.

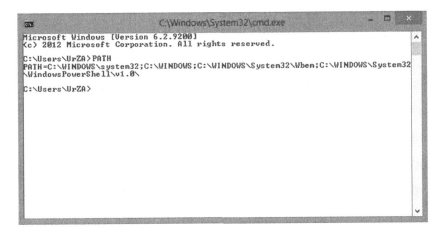

Figure 10-5. *Output of the PATH variable*

As you can see, C:\Program Files\nodejs\ is not among the outputted directories. In this case, we may have to include the installed directory as one of the directories to be used by the shell. This can be achieved by adding the nodejs directory to that of the PATH environment variable. In order to add the necessary directory to our PATH environment, we must navigate to the Control Panel window and type "environment variables" within the input field that reads "Search Control Panel" and hit Enter. This will filter the results in the panel, revealing a result labeled "Edit the system environment variables." Click this result and, on the window that opens thereafter, click the button labeled "Environment Variables...." At this point, you should be presented with a window displaying both User and System variables, as shown in Figure 10-6.

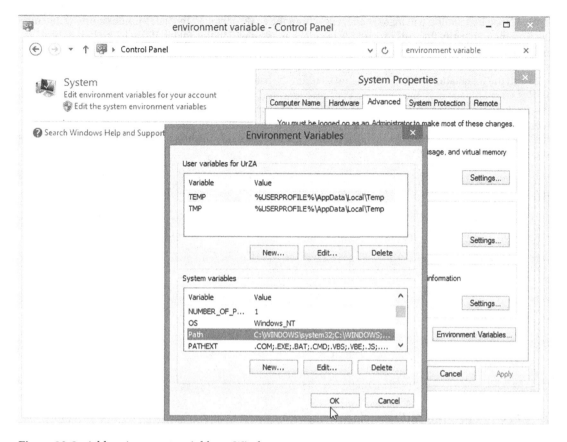

Figure 10-6. *Add environment variables to Windows*

Next, click the New... button immediately below the System variables box. Where it asks for the "Variable name:", supply "PATH." Additionally, for the "Variable value:", supply "C:\Users\UrZA \AppData\ Roaming\npm." (Do not use quotations, and replace UrZA with your user name.) Once those fields are supplied, click OK.

Next, within the System variables section, locate a variable labeled "Path," select it, and click the button labeled "Edit...", located directly below the System variables section. As the Path already exists, we simply have to append our nodejs directory to the list. This is accomplished by typing ;C:\Program Files\nodejs\ to the end of the Variable value field. Note the use of the semicolon (;) before the actual directory. This is used to delimit one path from another.

■ **Note** If you changed the default installation directory, you would have to supply that directory to the PATH environment variable instead.

Once the nodejs directory has been added to our PATH environment variable, accept the changes by hitting OK on all remaining windows. Next, reopen the Command Prompt window and run the following command: node --version.

Mac Installation

Upon navigating to nodejs.org/download/, we are immediately presented with the tools that will get us up and running. As there is no reason to take anything but the path of least resistance, we will download and install the Mac OS X Installer (.pkg). Unlike the installers for Windows/Linux, the Mac Installer provides a universal installer. Go ahead and click the button labeled "Universal," to begin the download of the Mac Installer. Depending on which browser you are currently using, such as Chrome or Firefox, you may receive some form of notification that requires you to confirm that you wish to download the indicated file.

Once the download has completed, locate the Node installer on your system. Ordinarily, files are downloaded to your Downloads folder. Once you locate the installer, double-click the installer, to initiate the installation wizard. At this point, the Node setup wizard will walk us through the installation step-by-step. The initial screen simply informs us of where the package will install node and npm. Feel free to click the button labeled "Continue."

The second screen of the wizard presents us with the Node license agreement. Before continuing to the next screen, you must accept the terms in the agreement. Take this opportunity to read the software license agreement, then click Continue, to agree to the terms of the agreement. Upon agreeing to the terms, we will continue into the configuration portion of the installation.

The next screen enables us to configure the default destination of the installation. Unless you have multiple hard drives, you may only have one option available, as reflected in Figure 10-7. Select the appropriate destination and continue to the installation screen.

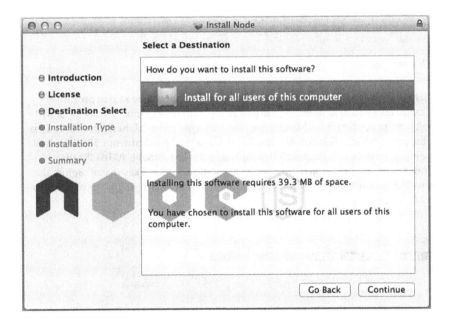

Figure 10-7. *Node Mac setup wizard*

Once you reach this screen, simply click Install, then sit back and relax for a short moment. You will be presented with confirmation that the Node setup wizard has completed successfully. You might note that the Summary screen displays the paths to where both node and the Node Package Manager, or npm, binaries are located. Additionally, it recommends that we ensure that /usr/local/bin is specified as a directory within our $PATH environment variable.

The $PATH environment variable is a colon-delimited list of directories that your shell searches through when you enter a command. The shell searches through each of these directories, one by one, until it finds a directory in which the executable exists. If the path is not configured with the directory that holds our two bin files, they will not be found and, therefore, never executed.

In order to verify that our $PATH variable possesses the /usr/local/bin directory, we must utilize the built-in command line of the Unix OS known as *Terminal*. There are a few ways to access Terminal, but we will rely on Spotlight. Simply clicking the magnifying glass in the top-right corner, or pressing Command and Space at the same time, will provide access to Spotlight. Within the input field to the right of where it states Spotlight, type in "Terminal," without the quotations. This will begin the search and display access to the Terminal application. Select the result shown as the Top Hit, to bring up the Terminal interface.

Within the terminal, type echo $PATH, then hit the Enter key on your keyboard to execute the statement. The list of directories that are configured for your environment should be outputted to the terminal. The directories that are listed within my environment can be viewed in Figure 10-8.

Figure 10-8. Exported $PATH configuration

Among the directories listed, if you are able to verify /usr/local/bin, it should be safe to presume that the node and npm binaries are accessible. If, however, the preceding path is not found within the $PATH environment variable, we will have to configure it. Utilizing the terminal, type nano ~/.bash_profile, then hit Enter. This will bring up the personal initialization file. It is here that we will configure our $PATH variable.

If your .bash_profile is empty, as shown in Figure 10-9, simply add the line export PATH=$PATH:/usr/local/bin, then, on your keyboard, hold down the Control key and press the X key to exit. Before the application terminates, you will be promoted to save the changes, as shown in Figure 10-10. Simply hit Y to save, and proceed to exit .bash_profile.

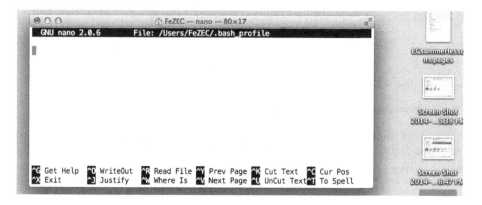

Figure 10-9. Empty .bash_profile content

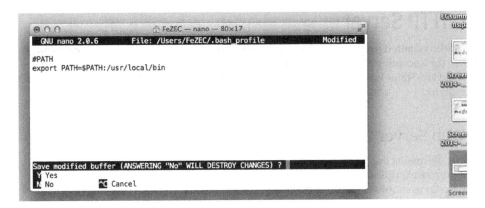

Figure 10-10. Configuring the $PATH environment variable to include /usr/local/bin

■ **Note** The preceding code (shown in Figure 10-10) will not impair your existing environment variables. It will merely append the /usr/local/bin directory to the existing list.

As the code within the .bash_profile is only run prior to a terminal session, close the existing Terminal application and open the application once again. This time, when you type echo $PATH and then hit the Enter key on your keyboard to execute the statement, you should see /usr/local/bin among the list of directories shown.

In order to know whether or not Node was installed and configured successfully, type the command node --version within the console, then hit Enter. If Node has successfully been configured, you should be provided with the version of Node that has been installed.

If you are presented with output that reflects the format vX.XX.XX, such as that shown in Figure 10-11, then congratulations; we can begin working with Node right away. Feel free to click Close, to exit the Node installation wizard and proceed to the section "Building an HTTP Server."

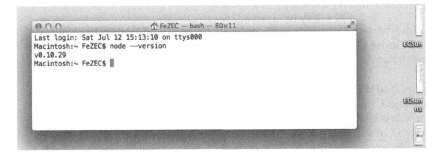

Figure 10-11. node --version resulting in the output of the installed version of Node.js

Building an HTTP Server

With Node installed and configured properly, it is high time to begin building an HTTP server that we can continue to build on in the upcoming chapters. As it was stated at the beginning of this chapter, Node is a platform that utilizes the JavaScript language. Therefore, much of the code that we will be working with will be simply vanilla JavaScript.

Node HTTP Web Server

In this chapter, I will be discussing the components and methods that make up a Node server. While all code will be utilizing pure JavaScript, some of these concepts may seem new to you. With that in mind, I will attempt to keeps things as simple as possible. However, I wish to provide you with an example of what we will be working with. This will, I hope, provide you with a concrete example that you can keep in mind throughout this chapter. Listing 10-1 illustrates an introductory Node server that acts as our foundation for this chapter.

Listing 10-1. Extremely Basic Node Server

```
1 var http = require('http');
2 var server = http.createServer();
3     server.addListener('request', requestHandler);
4     server.listen(1337, '127.0.0.1');
5
6 function requestHandler(request, response) {
7     console.log( request.url );
8     console.log( request.headers );
9     var body="Hello World";
10    response.statusCode = 200;
11    response.setHeader("Content-Type", "text/plain");
12    response.setHeader("Content-Length", Buffer.byteLength( body, 'utf8') );
13    response.end( body );
14 };
15 console.log('Server running at http://127.0.0.1:1337/');
```

Listing 10-1, displays 15 lines of code that make up the content of a simple Node server. The first four lines are all that are required to devise a Node Web Server. The latter nine lines of code demonstrate how to configure a simple response for any and all incoming HTTP requests. Let's walk through the code and discuss each statement.

We begin by loading the built-in HTTP module of the Node platform via the require function. As each module is simply a JavaScript object, we assign the loaded module and then assign it to a well-labeled variable. In this case, that variable is labeled "http" (**line 1**). Utilizing the createServer method exposed by the HTTP object, we establish a new instance of a web server. Next, we assign it to the variable labeled "server," in order to configure the web server (**line 2**). From there, we begin with our first configuration, which is to provide a function to the server as the default handler for all incoming requests to this server instance. When the server receives an incoming request, it dispatches a "request" event notification, to which the associated handler is invoked, thereby handling the request (**line 3**). Last, we configure the server to monitor any incoming transmissions to the specified domain (127.0.0.1), along with the specified port (1337) (**line 4**).

The final portion of code (**lines 6–15**) represents the business logic of the response. The handler that is provided to the server will consistently be provided two arguments for every incoming request. The first argument, the request, represents an object that retains the configurations of the client's request. This object can be used to obtain the method, URL, and the headers of the request, as seen in lines 2–3. The second argument is the response, which, as an object, exposes the necessary properties to configure an HTTP response, as seen in lines 10–13.

Within the body of the request handler, we obtain the reference to the response object and begin to provide it with a status code. We will set this to 200, to reflect the acknowledgment of the request provided (**line 10**). Next, we configure the headers of the response. As we will be providing back the text "Hello World," we use the setHeader method to inform the client of the Content-Type (**line 11**).

Last, we invoke the response object's end method, which not only enables us to provide the response with an entity body, it also signifies the response has been fully crafted, fulfilling the request and providing the response back to the client. The very last line of code serves only to output to the Terminal console that the server has been initiated (**line 13**).

If at this point, if you were to navigate to http://127.0.0.1:1337, you would not be provided with any response from our server. That is because, at this point, we haven't started our Node application. We must inform the Node engine to parse the preceding JavaScript, in order for our server to be operational. To accomplish this, it will be necessary to save the base_server.js within a directory that you will be able to easily navigate to via the command-line utility. You can obtain the location of a file simply by right-clicking the document and selecting "Get Info" for Mac or "Properties" for a PC. To obtain the location of the file in question, you will have to look in the General tab. I have mine saved in the following directory:

```
//PC
C:\Users\UrZA\Desktop\BeginningJSON\chapter10\server

//Mac
/Users/FeZEC/Desktop/BeginningJSON/chapter10/server
```

At this point, if you have closed the Terminal or Command Prompt window, open it once more and type the following:

```
//For PC:
cd C:\Users\UrZA\Desktop\BeginningJSON\chapter10\server

//For Mac:
cd /Users/FeZEC/Desktop/BeginningJSON/chapter10/server
```

However, rather than referencing the location of my file, replace the preceding path with the directory that holds your file. Note that I did not add the name of the file. At this point, within the Terminal application, type node 10-1.js and then hit Return on your keyboard. If you have successfully navigated to the proper directory and provided Node with the proper file name, you should see the statement Server running at http://127.0.0.1:1337/ outputted to the terminal. If, however, you are provided with an error, Error: Cannot find module, you may have accidentally misspelled the file name or navigated into the incorrect directory.

If the problem persists, and the error continues to state that it is unable to find the module provided, simply move base_server.js directly to your desktop. Then, open the console window and type: node ~/Desktop/10-1.js (Mac) or node C:\Users\YourUserNameHere\Desktop\10-1.js (PC), then hit Enter. This time, rather than navigating into the desktop directory before informing Node of the file name to run, execute the Node shell and explicitly specify the full path of the script.

We could have just as easily navigated to the desktop directory first, then typed node 10-1.js. The difference is that when you are within the directory that holds the file, you do not require specifying the path.

Now that we have our server up and running, let's open our preferred browser and navigate to http://127.0.0.1:1337. Upon your arrival, you should see "Hello World" outputted to the screen, as in Figure 10-12.

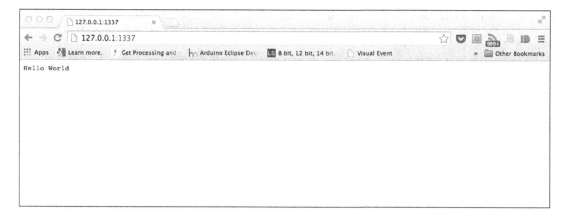

Figure 10-12. *Our first "Hello World" Node Server*

If you were to open your developer console, bring the network pane into view, and refresh the page, you would be able to view the headers of our response, however minimal they may be. What you should see are the following headers:

```
HTTP/1.1 200 OK
Content-Type: text/plain
Content-Length: 11
Date: Mon, 14 Jul 2014 00:19:09 GMT
```

Over the course of this chapter, we will continue to modify the body of code that exists within requestHandler, so that we can serve JSON to our web applications.

Now, exit out of the browser and locate the console window that was used to start up our server and give it focus. While holding the Control key on the keyboard, press the letter *C*, to shut down the application. A running server will not reflect changes to the JavaScript code. It will be necessary to shut down the server instance and start it back up, for any changes to be present.

Node API

The great thing about the Node API is that it's relatively small, given how powerful it is. You can view the entire documentation from the Node web site located at http://nodejs.org/api/. If you find yourself feeling a bit overwhelmed from looking at the table of contents, let me assure you that I am only going to talk about a few aspects of the API. Those aspects are the following modules: HTTP, Path, URL, and File System. Furthermore, for the purpose of this chapter, we will only be regarding a subset of said modules.

Modules

Modules, for all intents and purposes, are nothing more than JavaScript objects. By referencing a specific module, we are able to utilize the interface to which the object exposes. Additionally, as they are broken out into their own context, we can choose to load in only the objects that our server requires, thereby lowering the amount of overhead on the server. While it is possible to create your own modules (following the CommonJS architecture), we will only be considering built-in modules of Node.

Each module in Node (built-in or custom) can be imported into an application via a simple function call. That function is simply `require`. As demonstrated by the signature in Listing 10-2, the `require` function simply expects a singular argument, which represents the module to load in.

Listing 10-2. Signature of the `require` Method

```
require( 'module' );
```

For all built-in modules, we can simply specify the name of the module. The aforementioned modules HTTP, Path, URL, and File System can be imported using their respective names: `http`, `path`, `url`, and `fs`.

For each module specified, a corresponding object is loaded into the application and evaluated. It will be necessary to assign the object returned to an appropriately labeled variable, so that its interface can be utilized at a later point in time. Listing 10-3 demonstrates how we can load and reference the preceding modules.

Listing 10-3. Imported Modules via the `require` Method

```
var http = require('http');
var path = require('path');
var url = require('url');
var fileSystem = require('fs');
```

The first module referenced is that of `http`, and it is essential for any Node server. It is responsible, with the help of several internal objects, for facilitating the mechanisms of an HTTP server.

The HTTP Module

The HTTP module is responsible for devising a server instance and initiating server-side HTTP requests (which will be used for our proxy). It concerns the handling of streams, as well as parsing messages into headers and, possibly, an entity body. In order to remain flexible for any and all possible applications, the HTTP module possesses an extremely low-level API. What this means is that, much like a box of LEGOs, all the individual parts required to build a server have been packaged within Node. However, it will be up to us to connect the individual pieces as we see fit.

The parts that have shipped within the HTTP module box that we will be exploring for the duration of this chapter are `http.IncomingRequest`, `http.ServerResponse`, `http.Server`, `http.ClientRequest`, and `http.Streams`. The two methods outlined in Table 10-1 will be the two methods of the HTTP module that we will use throughout this chapter.

Table 10-1. *Methods of the HTTP Module*

Methods	Description
`createServer([requestListener])`	Returns a new web server object
`request(options, [callback])`	Enables the ability to issue server requests. *Returns an instance `ClientRequest`

http.createServer

The HTTP method createServer is solely responsible for instantiating a server instance that will be used for monitoring connections to our server. I will discuss the server shortly. As you can see from the signature in Table 10-1, an optional callback can be supplied as an argument of the method. This will be the method that will be invoked the moment a request is made of our server. Any provided requestListener must possess the following signature: function (request, response);.

http.IncomingMessage

The first argument provided, request, is an instance of the IncomingMessage Object. IncomingMessage exposes an API that is instrumental in obtaining all parts of the request. Through it, we can obtain the requested URL, the request method, the supplied headers of the request, and the entity body, if one was supplied.

Table 10-2 outlines the interface of the IncomingMessage object that makes it simple for our application to obtain key aspects of the request. However, you may notice there is no attribute for obtaining the entity body. As this is a slightly more complex task, I will discuss how to obtain the entity body in the "The Proxy Server" section.

Table 10-2. *Methods of the IncomingMessage Object*

Methods	Description
url	Returns as a string the URL that is present in the actual HTTP request
Method	Returns the HTTP request method as a string
Headers	Returns an object containing the request headers and values. *Header names are lowercased.

http.ServerResponse

The second argument, the response, is an instance of an object member of the HTTP module known as ServerResponse. It will be through the interface of the response instance that we can provide a response back to the client of the request. The exposed interface of the ServerResponse Object that we will make use of can be viewed in Table 10-3.

Table 10-3. *Methods of the ServerResponse Object*

Methods	Description
response.setHeader(name, value)	Sets a single header value for the response
response.write(chunk, [encoding])	Sends a chunk of the response body. *Can be called multiple times. Possible encodings are binary or utf8.
response.statusCode	Setter method used to generate the status-line of the response. *Expected assignment is a valid HTTP status code.
response.end([data], [encoding])	Signals the end of the response. It can be called with an entity body. *Data must be in string form.

http.Server

The request and response instances supplied to the requestListener method are always supplied by our server instance and for any incoming request. In short, the server instance is an event dispatcher or event emitter, notifying any event listeners to the incoming event via the "request" notification (See Table 10-5). Because the server is an event dispatcher, it's a matter of preference if you wish to designate requestListener at the time of creating the server instance. As an alternative, if you prefer the more object-oriented route, you can choose to listen for the "request" notification, via the server's addListener method (See Table 10-4). The two possible manners, as shown in Listing 10-4, are equivalent.

Table 10-4. *Methods of the Server object*

Members	Description
addListener(event , callback);	Assigns an event handler for a particular event
listen(port, [hostname])	Begins accepting connection on the specified port and hostname

Table 10-5. *Events of the Server object*

Event	Description
request	Emitted each time there is a request. The event handler will receive a request and response instance.

Listing 10-4. Providing a Callback as the Function to Trigger, per Incoming Request

```
var serverA= http.createServer(requestListener);
//or
var serverB=http.createServer();
    serverB.addListener("request", requestListener);
```

In order for our server to monitor the request, we must first establish which connections it is responsible for. In order to do this, we will use the listen method of our server instance. The listen method, as shown in Listing 10-5, can be supplied with two arguments. The first parameter, port, is required, while the second parameter, hostname, remains optional. For the purposes of this book, both will be used.

Listing 10-5. Signature of the listen Method

```
listen( port, [hostname]);
```

Where hostname is required, we will always use the IP address 127.0.0.1, which is simply a way to access one's own computer's network services. The value of the port, on the other hand, is used to afford multiple servers the ability to listen to the same IP. However, by specifying a port, all running servers on 127.0.0.1 will be able to distinguish their incoming requests from the others.

At this point, you should have an understanding of the basic components that are used to craft a rudimentary Node server. Before we continue to learn the remaining parts, let's review, in a simple exercise, what we have learned.

EXERCISE 10-1. YOUR FIRST JSON SERVER

Use the HTTP module and its members to create a server that monitors all incoming traffic on port 1337. Furthermore, utilizing the interface of both the response and request objects, provide the necessary implementation that results in the response headers shown following. The response should satisfy **only** the target resource of the request (shown following).

```
Request Headers
GET /message.json HTTP/1.1
Host: 127.0.0.1:1337
Accept: application/json

Response Headers
HTTP/1.1 200 OK
Content-Type: application/json
Content-Length: 25

{"message":"hello-world"}
```

▪ **Hint**   In order to arrive at the correct Content-Length for the entity body, you must supply the body to the following method: `Buffer.byteLength( data , 'utf8'));`.

Test if you are correct by navigating your browser to your server. Be sure to append a few paths after the URL and port to ensure that only the request is satisfied: `http://127.0.0.1:1337/[paths-here]`.

Listing 10-6 reveals the answer to the previous exercise. We begin by importing our HTTP module (**line 1**). We then invoke its `createServer` method to initialize our server (**line 2**). Additionally, using the optional parameter, we supply the callback method that will be triggered for each incoming request. Utilizing the `listen` method, inform the server to monitor our localhost, with a focus on port 1337 (**line 3**).

Listing 10-6. Answer to Our JSON Exercise

```
1 var http   = require('http');
2 var server = http.createServer(requestHandler);
3    server.listen(1337);
4 function requestHandler( request, response ) {
5    if (request.url === "/message.json") {
6       var body = JSON.stringify({
7                     message : "hello-world"
8                  });
9       response.statusCode = 200;
10      response.setHeader("Content-Type", "application/json");
11      response.setHeader("Content-Length", Buffer.byteLength(body, 'utf8'));
12      response.end(body);
13   }
14 };
15 console.log('Server running at http://127.0.0.1:1337/');
```

174

When an incoming request notification occurs, our `requestHandler` function will be invoked and supplied two objects: `request` and `response` (**line 4**). Per the exercise, our task was to ensure that the response was provided only for the requested /message.json resource. To ensure that we respond only to that resource, we must obtain the requested URL and compare it before we handle it (**line 5**). This is accomplished with strict equality. If, and only if, the requested resource matches /message.json do we configure a response.

Utilizing the `JSON.stringify` method (remember: Node runs on JavaScript), we convert an object into a string (**line 6**). From there, utilizing the `setter` method of the `statusCode` attribute of the `response` object, we assign it a value of 200. This will inform the client that the request was understood (**line 9**). Next, utilizing the `setHeader` method, we supply the Content-Type, which, of course, is `application/json` (**line 10**). In order to calculate the Content-Length, we supply the body variable, which is currently assigned our JSON text, to the `Buffer.byteLength` method. Utilizing the proper encoding, we can arrive at the proper Character-Length (**line 11**).

Remember that Character-Length is not simply the character length but, rather, the length in bytes. While ASCII characters require 1 byte per character, you should remember that JSON is UTF8. Therefore, it is simply safer to rely on the `Buffer.byteLength` method to determine the length of our UTF8-encoded JSON values.

Last, we use the end method of our `response` object to signify that our response has been configured at last. Additionally, we supply our body variable as an argument to the optional parameter.

If we were to run this server and navigate to `http://127.0.0.1:1337/`, we should not be provided with anything. In fact, the request should never be fulfilled. A response is only completed with the invocation of `response.end()`. However, this method will only be triggered if we navigate to `http://127.0.0.1:1337/message.json`. Upon arriving at this URL, we will also be faced with our JSON message outputted to the viewport, as shown in Figure 10-13.

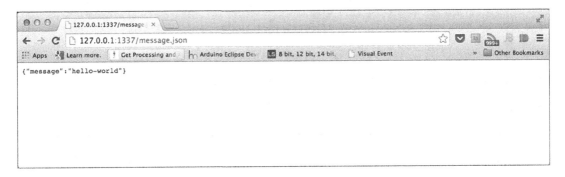

Figure 10-13. *`message.json` outputs the expected JSON*

To keep things simple, the previous exercise only required that you configure a response for a particular request. However, it should be known that all requests be provided a proper response. Failure to use the end method of the `response` object will result in the client waiting until a time-out occurs. You can experience a time-out simply by navigating to `127.0.0.1:1337/`.

A request can be handled in any manner you see fit. The preceding exercise created an object on the fly, but we could just as easily have provided the contents of a JSON document, by tapping into the File System module.

Nevertheless, by monitoring the interface of the `IncomingRequest` instance, whether it's by the exposed URL or any of its configured headers, we can determine how to best satisfy the request. This takeaway will be essential for the remainder of this chapter.

CORS-Enabled Server

If you are following along with the source code provided, take a moment to locate the file labeled "xss-server.js" within Chapter 10. Right-click the file and select "Get-Info," if you're on Mac, or "Properties," for a PC. Within the General tab, locate the absolute path for the file and copy it.

Now, open up a second window of the Command Prompt (PC) or Terminal.app (Mac). Within this second command window, we are going to start our xss-server. At this point, type "node" and then paste the location to the aforementioned xss-server.js. If the address is found, you should see a message informing you that a server is running at http://127.0.0.1:8080.

Ensure that your previous server is still running, by navigating to http://127.0.0.1:1337/message.json. I hope {"message":"hello-world"} is outputted to the screen. If so, the server is ready to receive our request; otherwise, we must start up our exercise server once again.

Now, with both servers running, proceed to http://127.0.0.1:8080. If you are not following along with the source code, navigate your browser to http://json.sandboxed.guru/chapter10/xss-exercise.html. Upon arriving at either of the two destinations, you will be presented with the code for an xhr object configured to make a request to http://127.0.0.1:1337/message.json. Now, open the developer's console, copy and paste the code provided for the request, and execute the code to observe the results. As in our previous chapter, you should be confronted with the infamous network error, as shown in Figure 10-14.

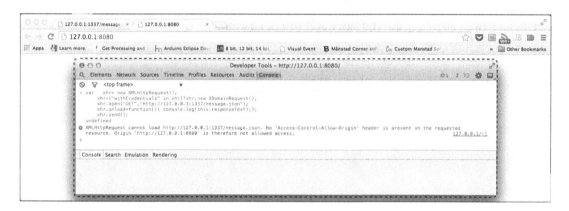

Figure 10-14. Cross-origin network error

However, as we are in control of the server and can configure the headers for message.json, we can resolve this in one of three manners. The first is to incorporate the necessary headers, as outlined by the W3C CORS standard. Second, we can utilize a proxy to make authorized requests on our client's behalf. Third, we can exchange JSON as valid JavaScript via JSONP.

At this point in the chapter, we have everything we require to fulfill a request via the first and third option; however, we have yet to discuss a few particulars that would enable us to devise a proxy. That being said, let's resolve the matter by way of incorporating the CORS header Access-Control-Allow-Origin (see Listing 10-7).

Listing 10-7. message.json with CORS Enabled

```
 1 var http    = require('http');
 2 var server = http.createServer(requestHandler);
 3     server.listen(1337, '127.0.0.1');
 4 function requestHandler( request, response ) {
 5    if (request.url === "/message.json") {
 6        var body = JSON.stringify({
 7                     message : "hello-world"
 8                 });
 9        response.statusCode = 200;
10        response.setHeader("Access-Control-Allow-Origin", '*');
11        response.setHeader("Content-Type", "application/json");
12        response.setHeader("Content-Length", Buffer.byteLength(body, 'utf8'));
13        response.end(body);
14    }
15 };
16 console.log('Server running at http://127.0.0.1:1337/');
```

Listing 10-7 reveals in bold the inclusion of the CORS header and configures its value to that of the wildcard * token. This will provide authorization to all requests from any origin. However, we could have determined whether the source origin via the origin header was exposed via request.headers, to determine if the indicated source origin should be authorized to access the resource. If we determine the source origin to be authorized, we can simply configure the value for the header with the source origin of the incoming message, as seen in Listing 10-8.

Listing 10-8. message.json CORS Enabled for json.andboxed.guru Only

```
 8        //.. code truncated
 9        var sourceOrigin  = request.headers.origin;
10        var originAllowed = (sourceOrigin === "http://json.sandboxed.guru") ?
         sourceOrigin : null;
11        response.setHeader( "Access-Control-Allow-Origin", originAllowed );
12        //.. code truncated
```

The preceding code in Listing 10-8 obtains the origin header from the incoming message via the request object. (In Node, all exposed headers are lowercase.) Utilizing the value returned from this header, we can determine if it is a source origin we are expecting, such as that of json.sandboxed.guru. We can match the value against more values; however, as this is simply for demonstrative purposes, I chose just the one. Utilizing a tertiary operator (a succinct, if else, evaluation), we determine if the source origin should be provided as the value to the Access-Control-Allow-Origin header. If it is a match, we will provide the origin. However, if it is not a match, we will supply the value with null.

With the new line in place, let's restart our server. First, we must shut down the server by pressing Control+C, then we can initialize our server by typing *node*, followed by the name of the exercise.js file. Alternatively, you could hit the up key on your keyboard within the console to use a previous command. Either way, hit Enter, once the proper command is in place, to run the server.

At this point, an attempt to obtain the message.json resource from either http://127.0.0.1:8080 or http://json.sandboxed.guru/chapter10/xss-exercise.html will be successful. Congratulations, you have just configured your first CORS-enabled resource to handle simple requests. At this point, feel free to shut down both servers, as we will shortly modify our code to provide JSONP also.

JSONP Server

A JSONP server, as you recall from Chapter 9, requires us to pad our JSON entity, so that the script engine views it as valid JavaScript. In other words, we cannot return JSON as an entity body whose structural composition is that of a collection (signified by the beginning and ending of the { and } tokens).

While this will not prohibit us from returning JSON, whose structural composition is that of an ordered list, we will still be confronted with the dilemma of obtaining the data upon being evaluated by the script engine. In order to combat this, our JSON must be wrapped or *padded* by the grouping operator and prepended with a function name supplied by the requesting client. The JSONP model establishes that this identifier should be provided as the value to a query string parameter labeled "jsonp."

Let's leverage our existing JSON server to support the JSONP format also, so that if a request for the resource message.json arrives, we can continue to supply it with JSON. However, should the URL possess the jsonp parameter, we can manipulate the JSON to reflect the JSONP model. Because the request.url provides us with a string reflecting the entire URL as it pertains to the request, it will be necessary to use string manipulation to mask the various components that could possibly be reflected in the string. In other words, we will have to isolate any and all query strings from the path of our resource from the provided string. Furthermore, for any query string key provided, it will be necessary to obtain its corresponding value. Only by taking this route can we be certain our conditions for a particular URL will be a match. Additionally, it will allow our server to determine whether to respond with JSON or JSONP. We can validate the conditions accordingly, utilizing some vanilla JavaScript, as demonstrated in Listing 10-9.

Listing 10-9. Skeletal Body of a requestHandler to Extract the Possible jsonp Key-Value from the request.url

```
1 function requestHandler( request , response ){
3    if(request.url === '/message.json') {
4        // return JSON entity
5    } else if(request.url.toLowerCase().indexOf('/message.json?jsonp=') > - 1) {
6        // return JSONP entity;
7    } else {
8        // 404 file not found;
9    }
10 }
11 function getParamKey(key, str) {
12    var regExp = new RegExp(key.toLowerCase() + '=[^&]*');
13    var matchingValue = (str.toLowerCase()).match(regExp);
14    for (var i = 0; i < matchingValue.length; i++) {
15        var replacedValue = matchingValue[i].replace(key + '=', '');
16        matchingValue[i] = replacedValue;
17    }
18    return decodeURIComponent(matchingValue[0]);
19 };
```

Listing 10-9 reflects the skeletal structure to assess whether the requested /message.json resource should be returned as JSON or JSONP. The code begins by assessing whether the request.url matches exactly that of the /messages.json (**line 3**). If this is the case, we will continue to provide the response in JSON form. If, however, the URL requested does not explicitly match that of /messages.json, we further analyze it to determine if the URL in question contains the following substring: /message.json?jsonp= (**line 5**). This is accomplished through the inherited indexOf method possessed by all strings. If the substring is found within the request URI, the character index, as to the beginning of the match, will be supplied as the value of the evaluation. However, if the substring is not found, it returns the integer -1. Therefore, should the value be greater than -1, we can be sure that the request is for message.json and that the client wishes to receive the response as JSONP. If the URL does not reflect any of these conditions, we shall supply the status code of 404 (File Not Found).

Last, in order to extract the value possessed by the jsonp parameter, we will utilize a modified version of our getCookie function, discussed in Chapter 7. This time, however, rather than extracting a particular key from a cookie, we will be extracting the value of a particular parameter. As we will no longer be "getting-cookies" but, rather, obtaining a "parameter-key," we will name this method getParamKey.

The function getParamKey is called with two arguments. The first represents the key to extract, while the second represents the string that is in possession of the key we seek to obtain (**line 11**). Utilizing a regular expression, we analyze the provided string for a possible pattern match (**line 12**). That pattern, of course, is the name of the key, followed by the = token and any subsequent characters, providing that character is not the & token (which would denote the beginning of another key). From there, if the pattern is matched, we store those matches in the matchingValue variable (**line 13**). Next, as our match will reflect the key = value format, we must isolate the value (**line 15**). We can achieve this easily by replacing our key= with and empty string ' ', essentially deleting that portion of our string. Last, we decode the value, in case it is URL-encoded, and then return it to the caller of the function (**line 18**).

■ **Note** When dealing with JSONP, it will be beneficial to ensure that the returned value is not URL encoded, lest we wrap our JSON with a label such as %20someMethod%20.

Let's now revisit our previous code from Listing 10-7 and begin serving up our JSON/JSONP server (see Listing 10-10).

Listing 10-10. Simple JSON and JSONP Server

```
1 var http = require('http');
2 var server = http.createServer();
3 server.addListener("request", requestHandler);
4 server.listen(1337, '127.0.0.1');
5 function requestHandler(request, response) {
6     var body;
7     if (request.url === '/message.json') {
8         // return JSON entity;
9         response.statusCode = 200;
10        response.setHeader("Access-Control-Allow-Origin", "*");

11        response.setHeader("Content-Type", "application/javascript");
12        body = JSON.stringify({ message : "hello-world" });
13    } else if (request.url.toLowerCase().indexOf('/message.json?jsonp=') > -1) {
14        // return JSONP entity;
15        response.statusCode = 200;
16        response.setHeader("Content-Type", "application/javascript");
17        var jsonText = JSON.stringify({ message : "hello-world" });
18        body = getParamKey("jsonp", request.url) + "(" + jsonText + ");";
19    } else {
20        // 404 file not found;
21        response.statusCode = 404;
22        response.setHeader("Content-Type", "text/html");
23        body = "<h1>404<h1> page not found";
24    }
25    (body) ? response.end(body) : response.end();
26 };
```

```
27 function getParamKey(key,str) {
28    var regExp = new RegExp(key.toLowerCase() + '=[^&]*');
29    var matchingValue = (str.toLowerCase()).match(regExp);
30    for (var i = 0; i < matchingValue.length; i++) {
31        var replacedValue = matchingValue[i].replace(key + '=', '');
32        matchingValue[i] = replacedValue;
33    }
34    return decodeURIComponent(matchingValue[0]);
35 };
36 console.log('Server running at http://127.0.0.1:1337/');
```

Listing 10-10 reflects in bold the latest code changes inserted into our earlier json.server, in order to fulfill a request for JSONP. At this point in time, let's run Listing 10-10 and navigate your browser to http://127.0.0.1:1337/message.json. You should find that your browser continues to output the previous message, as shown in Figure 10-13. Now, if you were to append ?jsonp=someMethod to the current URL (http://127.0.0.1:1337/message.json?jsonp=someMethod), you should be presented with the same JSON text, only now it should reflect the JSONP model, as seen in Figure 10-15.

Figure 10-15. Output of JSONP, demonstrating the client-supplied value as the prepended function name

Any value you provide for the jsonp key will continue to be prepended to the padded JSON. As our server is now serving JSONP, let's test its acquisition from another origin. For those following along with the source code, feel free to run the jsonp.html from within the BeginingJSON/chapter10/ directory; otherwise, navigate your browser to http://json.sandboxed.guru/chapter10/jsonp.html. What you should be witnessing is a button labeled "load jsonp," such as that in Figure 10-16.

Figure 10-16. `jsonp.html` *from y, configured to load in JSONP from your local server*

By clicking this button, we will dynamically inject a script tag into our document. As you may have already guessed, the resource that is specified as the external resource to obtain is none other than that of your server. With that being said, and with our server up and running, let's do as the button suggests and load some JSONP.

Much as is illustrated in Figure 10-17, no matter how many times you click the button, the result will always be the same. That result is the reception of JSONP from your server. Congratulations! At this point, you have successfully configured a server to fulfill a JSONP request.

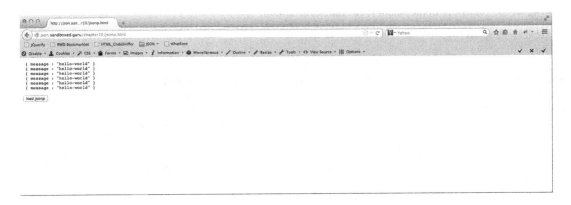

Figure 10-17. `json.sandboxed.guru` *successfully receiving JSONP from your server*

The Proxy Server

Before we delve into the proxy server, we must revisit our previous discussion pertaining to the members of the HTTP module. As you may recall, I had previously mentioned that the HTTP module possesses the ability to make client requests directly from the server. This is achieved via the request method belonging to the HTTP module.

http.request

The request method, the second method of the HTTP module shown in Table 10-2, whose signature is the request(options, [callback]);, provides the server with the ability to configure a client request. This method, as witnessed in the signature, is able to receive two parameters. The first parameter, options, must be provided with an object whose member's make up the request line, in addition to the headers of the request. Such members can be seen in Table 10-6.

Table 10-6. *Possible Keys That Can Belong to the Argument of the* options *Parameter*

Properties	Description
host	A domain name or IP address of the server that issues the request
port	Port of the provided host
method	A string specifying the HTTP request method
path	Requested resource. *Defaults to /
headers	An object containing request headers

The second parameter, callback, represents the function to be triggered as the handler on receiving a response from the remote server. In order to obtain the response, the function indicated as the callback must possess the signature shown in Listing 10-11.

Listing 10-11. Signature of the Request callback Parameter

```
callback( response );
```

As in the case of our earlier review of the requestHandler, the callback function supplied to the method will receive an instance of the IncomingMessage object, from which it will be able to reference the headers and status code of the response. At this point, let's take a moment to put all of this information together into code and walk through it.

Listing 10-12 demonstrates the minimal amount of code to configure a server-side request. We begin by devising an object that will be used to represent the request line of our request. It is supplied with necessary values for the properties host, path, and method (**line 2**). We then provide our configured object as our first argument to the http.request method. Next, we provide an argument as the callback. This function will be used to handle the IncomingMessage object provided by the remote server (**line 3**). Once the request is fulfilled, and a response has been provided, it will be made available to our called function, from which our application can extract the headers and status of the response (**line 5–line 6**).

Listing 10-12. Minimal Code Required to Handle a Server-Side Request Using the http.request Method

```
1 var http = require('http');
2 var options = {  host:"json.sandboxed.guru",
                   path:'/chapter10/data/imagedata.txt',
                   method:"GET"
               };
3 http.request(options, callback);
4 function callback( response ){
5       console.log( response.statusCode );
6       console.log( response.headers );
7 };
```

What should, I hope, be apparent is that our code is missing a means of extracting the entity body of the response. In order to receive the entity body for our `IncomingMessage` object, we must learn how to consume the data directly from the stream.

http.Stream

The `IncomingMessage` object, and all of its instances, is a subclass of a stream. What this simply means is that the interface possessed by a stream is also possessed by any `IncomingMessage` instance.

■ **Note** Obtaining data from `IncomingMessage` applies to any `IncomingMessage` object that possesses an entity body, even for all incoming requests to our server.

A stream, as defined by Node.org, is an abstract interface implemented by various objects in Node. I like to equate a stream to a common garden hose. If you can bring to mind a garden hose, the first thing that you might visualize is a long tube that possesses a relatively small diameter. This small diameter is what ultimately restricts the flow of water, thereby allowing only a finite volume of water to exit per second. Now, envision that garden hose as the cable that connects your computer to a server across the Internet. Similarly, the diameter of this hose represents your bandwidth. The bytes sent from the server are streamed, much like running water through the restricting tube, and arrive at your computer, where they accumulate, only instead of water molecules, our stream consists of data-packets.

There are two events that are dispatched by Node streams, as outlined in Table 10-7, that enable us to consume the streaming data. Those events are `data` and `end`.

Table 10-7. *Events of* `http.Stream`

Properties	Description
data	Enough bytes are available for the stream to consume.
end	All bytes from the stream have been consumed.

The `data` event is fired when enough data becomes available to consume from the stream. Depending on the amount of bytes that make up an entity body, this event may fire multiple times. Each time the `data` event is fired, any callback function will be provided "chunks" of available data. This allows our application to consume the available bytes as they arrive.

The second event, `end`, informs our application that the handler reading from the stream has consumed every bit of data and should not expect anymore.

In order to listen for either of these events, we can attach listeners directly to the provided `IncomingMessage` instance. Listing 10-13 reveals the necessary code required to consume an entity body from our response.

Listing 10-13. Skeletal Body of Code Required to Consume an Entity Body from an `IncomingMessage` object

```
1 var http = require('http');
2 var options = {  host:"json.sandboxed.guru",
                   path:'/chapter10/data/imagedata.txt',
                   method:"GET"
                };
```

```
3   http.request(options, callback);
4   function callback( proxy_response ){
5        console.log( response.statusCode );
6        console.log( response.headers );
7     proxy_response.addListener('data', function(chunkOfData) {
8        //do something with a chunk of data
9     });
10    proxy_response.addListener ('end', function() {
11       //end of stream reached
12    });
13  };
```

Listing 10-13 incorporates (in bold) the necessary listeners for the data and end events to properly work with incoming data, to receive a possible entity body from a response. While Listing 10-13 does not currently provide any particular implementation to handle the provided data, we can honestly do anything with it. We could piece it all back together onto a variable, so that we can read it in its entirety, once the data has been consumed fully. Or, as it will be in the case of our proxy, we can pipe it directly into our response.

At this point in time, if the preceding code from Listing 10-13 were to be executed on the server, the request would never be initiated. Calling the request method does not initiate the actual request. Much like the xhr object in JavaScript, we must trigger the submission of the request. This is accomplished through the ClientRequest instance.

http.ClientRequest

When the request method is invoked, an instance of the ClientRequest object is created and returned to the caller of the method. It will be through the interface possessed of this method that we can provide, along with our request, an entity body.

As shown in Table 10-8, the ClientRequest interface possesses an end method. This method signifies that our request is fully configured, thereby initiating the actual request. Additionally, the end method can accept an optional argument, which allows for the submission of an entity body, along with our request.

Table 10-8. ClientRequest *Methods*

Properties	Description
end([data], [encoding])	Finishes sending the request. *It can be called with an entity body. *Data must be in string, binary, or UTF-8 form.
abort	Aborts a request

Listing 10-14 demonstrates the bare bones of code required when working with a client request. To better understand the code, let's walk through it.

Listing 10-14. Entire Skeletal Structure for Facilitating Proxy Calls

```
1  var http = require('http');
2  var options = {hostname:"json.sandboxed.guru", path:'/chapter10/data/imagedata.txt',
   method:"GET"};
3  var clientRequest=http.request(options, responseHandler);
4     clientRequest.end();
```

```
 5  function responseHandler(proxy_response) {
 6      console.log('STATUS: ' + proxy_response.statusCode);
 7      console.log('HEADERS: ' +proxy_response.headers);
 8      proxy_response.addListener('data', function(chunkOfData) {
 9          //do something with a chunk of data
10      });
11      proxy_response.addListener ('end', function() {
12          //end of stream reached
13      });
14  }
```

The code begins with the inclusion of an http instance (**line 1**). Next, we configure an object with the particulars of the request and assign it to a variable labeled "options" (**line 2**). From there, we initialize our ClientRequest through the http.request method and supply it with the options variable as well as the handler of the provided response (**line 3**). Much as with the response object from our earlier discussions, the ClientRequest has the ability to contain an entity body. For this reason, the request is not invoked immediately. It will be a requirement to use its exposed end method to signify that the request is ready. That being said, and with no body to supply for the request, we invoke the end method on the referenced ClientRequest (**line 4**).

The next block of code pertains to the management of the response from the remote network. Our callback responseHandler is invoked upon the reception of the IncomingMessage. This IncomingMessage is supplied as the argument to our proxy_response parameter (**line 5**), from which we are able to obtain the existing headers (**line 6**) and status code (**line 7**).

From there, we are able to monitor the stream for any incoming data that makes up the entity of the response. Adding an event listener via the addListener method and specifying which event to listen for, we can monitor the incoming bytes of data. The data event will supply the event handler with a chunk of data that can either be used to send back a response with the use of response.write or assembled for internal processing (**line 8**). In the preceding listing, I have opted to assemble the incoming transmission. Each chunk of data provided to the handler is appended onto our existing data variable (**line 9**).

Last, we attach an event listener to monitor for the end event, so that we can be made aware that we have read all the bytes on the provided stream (**line 11**).

EXERCISE 10-2. YOUR FIRST PROXY SERVER

Leveraging the code from Listing 10-14, as well as what you learned earlier in the chapter, building a proxy server should be no sweat. In this exercise, you are asked to devise the necessary implementation that would result in the following (proxy) request headers for the resulting incoming request headers.

```
Request Headers (Proxy)
GET /chapter10/data/imagedata.txt HTTP/1.1
Host: json.sandboxed.guru
Accept: *
```

```
Request Headers (Incoming)
GET /proxy/ HTTP/1.1
Host: 127.0.0.1:1337
Accept: *
```

As this is a proxy, be sure to write all incoming chunkOfData directly to the response. Similarly, don't forget about the headers. Once the stream has been exhausted of all data, be sure to end the response. The answer can be seen in Listing 10-15.

Listing 10-15. Answer to the Proxy Exercise

```
1 var http = require('http');
2 var server = http.createServer( );
3     server.addListener('request',requestHandler);
4     server.listen(1337, '127.0.0.1');
5 function requestHandler(request, response) {
6     if (request.url.toLowerCase().indexOf("/proxy/") >-1 ) {
7             var options = { host:"json.sandboxed.guru",
                               path:'/chapter10/data/imagedata.txt',
                               method:"GET" };
8         var clientRequest=http.request(options, responseHandler);
9             clientRequest.end();
10        function responseHandler(proxy_response) {
11            response.writeHead(proxy_response.statusCode, proxy_response.headers);
12            proxy_response.addListener('data', function(chunkOfData) {
13                response.write(chunkOfData);
14            });
15            proxy_response.addListener ('end', function() {
16                response.end();
17            });
18        }
19    } else {
20        response.statusCode = 200;
21        body = 'proxy calls occur at /proxy/';
22        response.setHeader("Content-Type", "text/plain");
23        response.setHeader("Content-Length", Buffer.byteLength(body, 'utf8'));
24        (body) ? response.end(body) : response.end();
25    }
26 };
27 console.log('Server running at http://127.0.0.1:1337/');
```

Listing 10-15 reveals, in bold, the necessary code required to fulfill the requirements of the preceding exercise. As the code builds on Listing 10-14, I will discuss only the lines that are required to satisfy the exercise.

Per the exercise, a proxy should only occur if it has been determined that an incoming request seeks a resource located within the /proxy/ directory. Utilizing indexOf, we can determine if the /proxy/ substring exists within request.url. If the substring is found, the index returned will be greater than -1, and, therefore, the subsequent block of code will be able to run (**line 6**). Of course, within that subsequent block of code resides our proxy.

Once we initiate our proxy, the supplied callback is provided a reference to an IncomingMessage object. As our proxy is merely making a request on behalf of our client in order to circumvent the same-origin policy, we must simply provide all aspects of the request, unaltered, as the response from our server. Therefore, once we can obtain the headers and status line of the proxy_response, we simply relay them onto the response that we will provide back to our client. This is achieved via the expose writeHead method (**line 11**).

Similarly, we have to route any incoming data chunks to the response of our incoming request. This is accomplished via the write method (**line 13**). Last, once all data has been consumed from the stream, we invoke response.end() to deliver the response back to the requesting client (line 16).

If you were to run this server and navigate to the URL, http://127.0.0.1/proxy/, you should be presented with similar results, as shown in Figure 10-18.

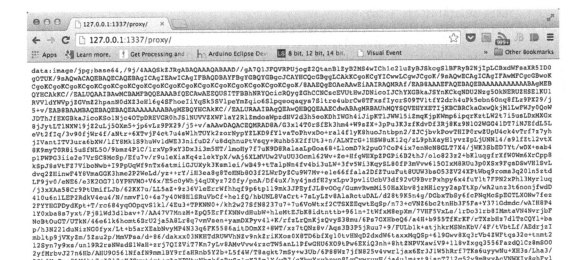

Figure 10-18. *A rather large image whose data has been encoded into Base64*

Currently, our proxy will always and only request, on our behalf, the preceding Base64 data. However, as this is rather limiting, let's modify it to possess the ability to fetch other files as well. On my server, json.sandboxed.guru, within the /chapter10/data/ directory, I have placed the following files: imagesA.json, imagesB.json, and imagesC.json. You may remember these from Chapter 8. Utilizing a singular line of JavaScript, we ensure that these files can be fetched in addition to the existing imagesdata.txt file (see Listing 10-16).

Listing 10-16. Altering Our Proxy to Fetch Additional Files from json.sandboxed.guru

```
1  var http = require('http');
2  var server = http.createServer( );
3      server.addListener('request',requestHandler);
4      server.listen(1337, '127.0.0.1');
5  function requestHandler(request, response) {
6      if (request.url.toLowerCase().indexOf("/proxy/") >-1 ) {
7          var options = { hostname:"json.sandboxed.guru",
                           path:'/chapter10/data/' + request.url.substr(7) ,
                           method:"GET" };
8          var clientRequest=http.request(options, responseHandler);
9              clientRequest.end();
10         function responseHandler(proxy_response) {
11             response.writeHead(proxy_response.statusCode, proxy_response.headers);
12             proxy_response.addListener('data', function(chunkOfData) {
13                 response.write(chunkOfData);
14             });
15             proxy_response.addListener ('end', function() {
16                 response.end();
17             });
18         }
19     } else {
```

187

```
20       response.statusCode = 200;
21       body = 'proxy calls occur at /proxy/';
22       response.setHeader("Content-Type", "text/plain");
23       response.setHeader("Content-Length", Buffer.byteLength(body, 'utf8'));
24       (body) ? response.end(body) : response.end();
25    }
26 };
27 console.log('Server running at http://127.0.0.1:1337/');
```

Listing 10-16 demonstrates how, through simple string manipulation, we can dynamically specify the resource to be requested from the remote server. Through the `request.url`, we can extract any resource that follows the first seven characters, which are precisely how many characters are used to specify /proxy/. From there, the remaining characters within the string can be appended to the value for our `path`. At this point, let's shut down the currently running server, so that we can insert this amendment. Once it's in place, we can start our server back up and navigate to the following:

```
http://127.0.0.1:1337/proxy/imagedata.txt
http://127.0.0.1:1337/proxy/imagesA.json
http://127.0.0.1:1337/proxy/imagesB.json
http://127.0.0.1:1337/proxy/imagesC.json
```

When navigating to any of the preceding destinations, you should be provided with the exact response, as if you directly obtained them from `http://json.sandboxed.guru/chapter10/data/`. The reason why is because we did obtain them directly from the preceding URL, via our proxy.

Congratulations! You have constructed a functioning proxy server.

Summary

This chapter contained a lot of advanced concepts, and you should be truly proud of yourself for making it through. A server is an integral component when it comes to the Internet, and not just for fetching static resources, as you have surely observed. A server, while capable of fetching static files, can in concert with server-side programming, generate the content of the response, evaluate the request, and even initiate requests of its own.

With the ease of the JavaScript language, and Chrome's V8 engine, we were able to conveniently run and manage our own server. With it, we learned how to handle incoming requests, as well as how to configure a response. This chapter also provided a hands-on approach toward circumventing the same-origin policy of the browser. Additionally, you had a glimpse into the concepts of server-side programming, which will serve you well in the future or, at the very least, the next chapter.

In the upcoming chapter, we will continue to leverage the Node platform to create a simple JSON database. This database will allow incoming JSON data to be captured and stored locally on the file system, so that it can be retrieved by later requests.

Key Points from This Chapter

- A Node server can be programmed entirely in JavaScript via the Node's HTTP module.

- end must be invoked on the response instance for a request to be completed.

- Neglecting to invoke end will result in the client's request to time out.

- You must restart your server anytime a change is introduced to the code.

- Node possesses an extremely low-level API.

- Node is non-blocking/event-driven.

- `IncomingMessages` instances represent request/response arguments.

- You can obtain the headers, URLs, and request/status lines from `IncomingMessages`.

- To obtain an entity body from `IncomingMessages`, you must consume data from their stream.

- 127.0.0.1 is a way to access one's own computer's network services.

- Content-Length must specify bytes not character length.

- Ensure that the value supplied with the `jsonp` parameter is not URL-encoded when appending it to the padded JSON.

- With string manipulation, you can respond accordingly to any request.

CHAPTER 11

■ ■ ■

Posting JSON

As should be evident by now, a server has the ability to provide a tailored response to best match the indicated method, resource, and the configured headers of an incoming request. This protocol, when paired with static content, can be utilized by the server software to translate an incoming request into a location for said resource located on its file system. The specified path of the resource is translated via the server software into that of a determined directory, for which a file is thought to exist. The response is either the content of the file or a 404 page.

Similarly, the very same protocol, when paired with a dynamic programming language (such as PHP, .NET, or Java), provides cooperating developers a means of incorporating web services. Such services can be used to persist, update, and retrieve existing data. The difference, per the HTTP/1.1 Specification,[1] lies with the particular method of the request. In this chapter, I will focus on the use of the POST method to provide an entity body to our Node application.

Request Entity Body

There are two sets of HTTP request methods: those that are considered safe, and those that are considered unsafe. Generally speaking, safe methods merely retrieve a resource, whereas unsafe methods seek to provide data with an HTTP request. This resource is referred to as a *payload*. The payload itself may be as complex as a file or as simple as an e-mail address. However, once this information is received, it is often written to a database for later retrieval.

While the preceding sentence may make immediate sense, what might not be so obvious is that without the use of a server-side code to receive and process the incoming payload, the entity provided to a server would serve little to no use. However, once that data is received and handled appropriately, its usefulness is limited to our imaginations and business goals or, as seen in the case of Twitter or Facebook, your fan base.

With the proxy example from the previous chapter, you learned that in order to obtain the payload of an IncomingMessage object, we must consume it via the inherited interface of the stream object. This is accomplished, as demonstrated in Listing 11-1, by attaching an event listener to the incoming request instance, in order to monitor the stream for a data payload. Furthermore, by pairing the listener with a callback capable of receiving incremental chunks of data as an argument, we can consume data from the stream as it is received.

---

[1]R. Fielding et al., *Hypertext Transfer Protocol—HTTP/1.1*, http://tools.ietf.org/html/rfc2616, 1999.

Listing 11-1. Monitoring the Stream for Data

```
1 function requestHandler(request, response) {
2     request.addListener('data', function(chunk) {
3             //do something with data chunk
4             });
   //...truncated
8 }
```

Depending on the format of the payload, whether it's in binary or ASCII, our application may begin to utilize the individual chunks as they enter it. Additionally, by monitoring the stream for the end event, our application can be made aware of when there is no further data to be consumed from the stream, as demonstrated in Listing 11-2.

Listing 11-2. Monitoring the Stream for the end of Data

```
1 function requestHandler(request, response) {
   //...truncated
5     request.addListener(end, function() {
6             //stream no longer has data
7             });
8 }
```

The preceding lines of code, outlined in bold in both Listing 11-1 and 11-2, are essential for obtaining an entity body from an incoming request. However, the actual implementation of code that is utilized within the body is dependent on the needs of the application. Whether the incoming data chunks are immediately parsed or amassed until the stream is drained is a matter of your application's needs and data expectancies. Furthermore, how the data is parsed is absolutely dependent on the Content-Type of the incoming payload. While GET requests can only provide data in the URL-encoded format, POST requests can supply data in a variety of formats. Such formats are the following: multipart/form-data, application/x-www-form-urlencoded, application/xml, text/xml, application/json, and more.

■ **Note** In order to recognize how to parse the incoming information accordingly, it will be helpful to utilize the Content-Type header held by the incoming request via the following snippet: if(request.headers['content-type'].indexOf(substring-to-match-here)>-1){ //condition block }.

HTML Form POST

As a front-end developer, it is likely that you have previously used the standard HTML <form> element to POST data to a server. The <form> element provides a convenient and standard way for a user to supply data via a series of semantic components, such as input fields, check boxes, radio buttons, etc., to a web service that is capable of processing the supplied information on the server.

In order to demonstrate a form POST, we must first devise the HTML markup that can be returned as a resource by our Node application. Listing 11-3 demonstrates the markup that will be provided to any incoming requests for the following resource /index.html.

Listing 11-3. An HTML Form POST

```
1   <!doctype html>
2   <html lang="en">
3   <head>
4       <meta charset="utf-8">
5   </head>s
6   <body>
7       <form action="formPost" method="POST" content="application/x-www-form-urlencoded">
8           First-Name: <input name="fname" type="text" size="25"/>
9           Last-Name: <input name="lname" type="text" size="25"/>
10          <input type="submit"/>
11      </form>
12  </body>
13  </html>
```

The preceding code should not come as a surprise to you, as this is standard HTML markup. The only five lines that we should discuss are those that make up our form. We use the HTML <form> element not only to declare the container, which will hold relevant form elements, but also to configure key aspects of the request (**line 7**). The attribute labeled "action" defines the target resource for which the method is enacted. In this case, I have set the resource to that of formPost. The second attribute, labeled "method," defines the method to be used on the request. This can be a method such as GET or POST, but in this case, we will specify POST. These two attributes will be used in conjunction to make up the request line of our HTTP request.

Last, utilizing the attribute labeled "content," we specify the Content-Type of the data accompanying the request. While there are many possible Content-Types in existence, only three possible values can be applied to an HTML form. These three Content-Types are the following: application/x-www-form-urlencoded, multipart/form-data, and text/plain.

■ **Note** If a form is not configured with the content attribute, the Content-Type that will be used will be that of application/x-www-form-urlencoded.

The next two lines (**line 8** and **line 9**) simply define the input fields that will be used to capture an individual aspect of data. Utilizing the attribute labeled "name," we can establish the key that is used to transport the supplied value. As this form will capture a user's first and last name, I have used fname and lname as the respective keys. Next, we assign the value text to the type attribute. This will identify the input field as requiring user input, so that the browser renders it accordingly.

Last, in order to invoke the submission of the data, we must include a Submit button (**line 10**). This is simply achieved by utilizing yet another input field. However, as you may expect, this input field's type attribute is supplied with that of submit. This will inform the browser to render this input field as a button. Upon the user's click of the button, it will prompt the form to initiate the request.

EXERCISE 11-1. YOUR FIRST NODE FORM POST

ExerciseA.js has begun to incorporate the HTML document from Listing 11-3 into the appropriate conditional block. Continue to supply the remaining ten lines of markup to the following code (Listing 11-4) to complete our index.html resource.

Listing 11-4. ExerciseA.js, a Local Form POST Application

```
1 var http = require('http');
2 var server = http.createServer();
3 server.addListener('request', requestHandler);
4 server.listen(1337, '127.0.0.1');

5 function requestHandler(request, response) {
6   console.log( request.url);
7   request.addListener('data', function(chunk) {
8       console.log(chunk);
9   });
10   request.addListener("end", function() {
11       console.log("end of stream \n");
12   });
13   if(request.url==="/index.html"){
14       response.statusCode = 200;
15       response.setHeader("Content-type", "text/html");
16       response.write('<!doctype html>');
17       response.write('<html lang="en">');
18       response.write('<body>');
       //... add code here;
28   }else{
29       response.statusCode=204;
30   }
31   response.end();
32 };
33 console.log('Server running at http://127.0.0.1:1337/index.html');
```

Once the document has been incorporated into exerciseA.js, use the command-line interface to initiate our server. With the server running, navigate to http://127.0.0.1:1337/index.html, fill in the form with your first and last name, hit Submit, and take note of the data outputted to the command-line window.

If your name coincidently happens to be Ben Smith, then you should have witnessed the following output as shown following:

Server running at http://127.0.0.1:1337/index.html

/index.html
end of stream

```
/favicon.ico
end of stream

/formPost
<Buffer 66 6e 61 6d 65 3d 42 65 6e 26 6c 6e 61 6d 65 3d 53 6d 69 74 68>
end of stream
```

For those whose names are not the equivalent, you should witness something very close to what has been shown in the preceding code. In fact, the data shown in bold is present in your output as well. Let's examine the output in detail, to gain a better understanding of what is occurring.

The moment our server is initialized, our console first outputs a reminder of the URL and PORT, for which our server is running. Additionally, to remind ourselves that we must request the index.html to be presented with our form, I have chosen to include it within the initial output.

By navigating to the URL that is outputted, we arrive at our HTML form. Because the exerciseA application logs each requested resource, the line that immediately follows is /index.html. While that should make sense, what might not be clear are the next three lines.

Following the output of our /index.html request, a message informs us that we have reached the end of our stream. This might be confusing, as you may have expected the end event to fire only after we had submitted our form. However, the reality is that our Node application has been written to monitor for incoming data with each incoming request. As the request for our index.html page was not accompanied by any data what so ever, as the stream is empty, the end event naturally fires. This check happens needlessly for every single incoming request and is made evident with each subsequent request.

The next line is one I wanted to discuss because it often confuses a lot of Node newcomers. Often, when debugging code, newcomers are curious as to why their code appears to fire multiple times after receiving an HTML document. The reason is that user-agents initiate a request that is not apparent to the end user. That request is for the icon that appears in the browser's window tab for the displayed HTML Document. This is known as the favicon and is a 16×16 image that can be used as the icon that will identify your page should someone choose to bookmark it. An example of a favicon can be seen in Figure 11-1. As this is yet another incoming request on our server, the messaging end of stream follows. Lastly, as initiated by the submission of our form, an incoming request for /formPost is outputted to our console.

Figure 11-1. Microsoft favicon

■ **Note** So as not to cause added throughput on our server, an application should only attempt to consume data from the stream of a client the requested method has determined to be an unsafe method, such as POST.

Following the output of said resource appears to be a sequence of alphanumeric characters. To keep things as simple as possible, I can assure you this is not gibberish but, rather, hexadecimal format. I won't go into too much detail, but, ultimately, each grouping of characters represents an alphanumeric character. In the preceding output, **66** represents **f, 6e** represents **n, 61** represents **a,** etc. If I were to continue to explain the next three values, you would be able to recognize the gibberish is actually spelling out "**fname=**."

While reading hexadecimal is far better than reading binary, it is absolutely no substitute for plain text. Therefore, let's shut down our current server and modify the buffer to output plain text. This is accomplished by defining the encoding via the setEncoding method exposed on our request instance. The code, request. setEncoding('utf8');, defaults all incoming data as UTF-8. At this point in time, let's shut down our server and incorporate this line of code just before our data event listener. Once this code is in place, restart our exerciseA application and perform a form POST once again. This time, you should observe the following output:

```
//..truncated output
fname=Ben&lname=Smith
end of stream
```

Congratulations! You have received your first HTML form POST. As you can clearly read from the output, the entity body is provided in the form of a key/value pair, similar to that of a GET. The notable difference is that the data is not preceded by the ? token. As we have been working rather extensively with key/value pairs, it should be a cinch to extract our data values from their keys, utilizing our getParamKey function from the previous chapter. Once again, let's shut down our server and incorporate the getParamKey function, shown in Listing 11-5, into our existing server.

Listing 11-5. The getParamKey Function

```
function getParamKey(key, str) {
    var regExp = new RegExp(key.toLowerCase() + '=[^&]*');
    var matchingValue = (str.toLowerCase()).match(regExp);
    for (var i = 0; i < matchingValue.length; i++) {
        var replacedValue = matchingValue[i].replace(key + '=', '');
        matchingValue[i] = replacedValue;
    }
    return decodeURIComponent(matchingValue[0]);
};
```

The incorporation of getParamKey will enable us to extract the values for the supplied keys that make up the entity body. For the form POST we have been working with, those keys are fname and lname. By providing these identifiers along with the received data chunk to getParamKey, we can easily obtain their values. At this point in time, let's shut down our currently running server and insert the necessary code required to log out the value for our two variables, by tapping into the getParamkey function. Once you have implemented the code that would result in Listing 11-6, restart the server, use the form to submit your name once again, and observe the results.

Listing 11-6. Parsing x-www-form-urlencoded Data

```
var http = require('http');
var server = http.createServer();
server.addListener('request', requestHandler);
server.listen(1337, '127.0.0.1');

function requestHandler(request, response) {
  console.log(request.url);
  request.setEncoding('utf8');
  request.addListener('data', function(chunk) {
      console.log(getParamKey("fname", chunk));
      console.log(getParamKey("lname", chunk));
  });
```

```
    request.addListener("end", function() {
        console.log("end of stream \n\r");
    });

    if(request.url === "/index.html") {
      response.statusCode = 200;
      response.setHeader("Content-Type", "text/html");
      response.write('<!doctype html>');
      response.write('<html lang="en">');
      response.write('<body>');
      response.write('<form action="formPost" method="POST" content="application/x-www-form-
urlencode">');
      response.write('First-Name:');
      response.write('<input name="fname" type="text" size="25"/>');
      response.write('Last-Name:');
      response.write('<input name="lname" type="text" size="25"/>');
      response.write('<input type="submit"/>');
      response.write(' </form>');
      response.write(' </body>');
      response.write('</html>');
    } else {
        response.statusCode = 204;
    }
     response.end();
};

function getParamKey(key, str) {
    var regExp = new RegExp(key.toLowerCase() + '=[^&]*');
    var matchingValue = (str.toLowerCase()).match(regExp);
    for (var i = 0; i < matchingValue.length; i++) {
        var replacedValue = matchingValue[i].replace(key + '=', '');
        matchingValue[i] = replacedValue;
    }
    return decodeURIComponent(matchingValue[0]);
};
console.log('Server running at http://127.0.0.1:1337/index.html');
```

Running the preceding code, should no errors be present, will have undoubtedly outputted the values that had been supplied to both input fields. Now that we have this extracted information, we could potentially alter the data of the response or even store the supplied information within a database. You will learn more about persisting data via back-end programming in the next chapter.

While forms are a convenient way for a visitor to supply a few fields of basic information, such as first name and last name, the possible Content-Types that can be used with a form lack the ability to maintain the structure of data such as that of JSON. However, in order to transmit the JSON data type, we will have to leverage an XMLHttpRequest object.

Processing a JSON POST

As has been stated throughout this book, JSON is a highly interoperable data format with many advantages. It can easily be read by humans; it is succinct, thereby keeping file size to a minimum; it can group as well as retain the structure of data; and, as a text-based format, JSON can be stored/retrieved and parsed without degrading its integrity. Of course, to utilize this functionality, our server-side application must possess the ability not only to obtain any and all incoming JSON but to parse it as well. In order to keep things backward compatible, we will build upon our code base from exerciseA. This way, if a visitor has JavaScript enabled, the data contents will be provided to our server via Ajax as JSON. However, if the user does not have JavaScript enabled, our form will continue to work as intended in the URL-encoded data format, via a full-page load.

As was stated earlier, an HTML form element can only send one of three Content-Types, and JSON is not one of them. Therefore, in order to send JSON, we must leverage our acquired knowledge of Ajax. Listing 11-7 reveals the ajax function that was discussed in Chapter 8. For the most part, the ajax function remains unchanged, with the exception that the request line has been updated to reflect the new formPost resource.

Listing 11-7. Progressively Enhancing Our HTML Form with Ajax

```
<script>
 function ajax() {
     var xhr = new XMLHttpRequest();
     xhr.open("POST", "formPost");
     xhr.setRequestHeader("Content-Type", "application/json");
     var input = document.getElementsByTagName("input");
     var obj = {
         fname : input[0].value,
         lname : input[1].value
     };
     xhr.send(JSON.stringify(obj));
   return false;
 }
</script>
```

If you recall from Chapter 8, we used the preceding function to POST two HTML form fields, First Name and Last Name, to a server, using the application/json Content-Type. Obtaining the values directly from the input fields, and then adding them as the members of an object, which was immediately serialized, accomplished this. The form, with the use of its onsubmit attribute, invoked the ajax function when its Submit button was clicked.

If you are following along with the source code provided for Chapter 11, locate the json-form.js file. This file incorporates the ajax function, shown in Listing 11-7, along with a few additional code amendments. One such amendment is the assignment of our function as the value of the form's onsubmit attribute: **<form action="formPost" method="POST" onsubmit="return ajax();">**.

Furthermore, as this application will be used to demonstrate the reception of JSON, rather than our previous key/value pairs, I have incorporated a means to isolate the values for fname and lname in a manner befitting of JSON. Because our Node application is written entirely in JavaScript, I have merely incorporated the use of JSON.parse, as shown in Listing 11-8. In order to distinguish the x-www-form-urlencoded format from that of incoming JSON, we will incorporate conditions that determine whether a particular Content-Type exists as a substring of request.headers['content-type'].

■ **Note** The implementation of the ajax function progressively enhances the capability of our form to transmit the captured data of a user via Ajax, without impairing the experience for those visitors who may have JavaScript turned off.

Listing 11-8. Determining the Content-Type of Incoming Data

```
request.addListener('data', function(chunk) {
  if(request.headers['content-type'] ].indexOf('application/json')>-1){
    var json=JSON.parse(chunk);
    console.log(json.fname);
    console.log(json.lname);
  }else if(request.headers['content-type'].indexOf('application/x-www-form-urlencoded)>-1){
  }
});
```

Be sure to shut down any Node applications that you may have running, and start up json-form. When you navigate to http://127.0.0.1:1337/index.html, you should not witness any visual differences, as we have not altered our form, only the format for which it is supplied. This time, when you submit the form, the output displayed in the command-line interface should resemble that of Figure 11-2.

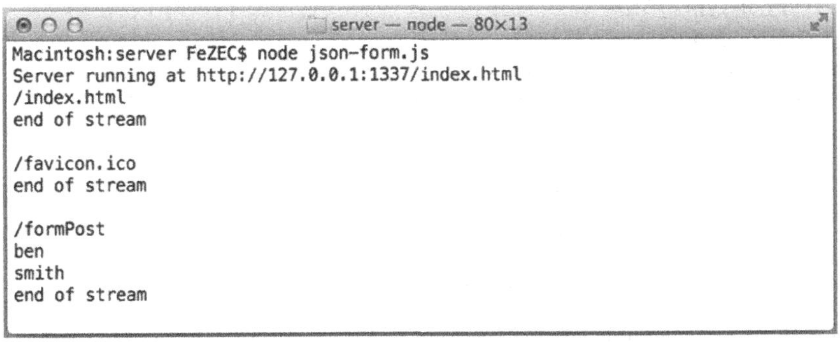

```
Macintosh:server FeZEC$ node json-form.js
Server running at http://127.0.0.1:1337/index.html
/index.html
end of stream

/favicon.ico
end of stream

/formPost
ben
smith
end of stream
```

Figure 11-2. *Logging out* end of stream *when all data has been consumed*

As clearly illustrated in Figure 11-2, the fields of our data have been successfully parsed and individually outputted. Congratulations, you have parsed your first, albeit simple, JSON POST! Before you begin your celebration dance, I do wish to point out one thing. In our json-form application, in addition to our exercise application, we were attempting to parse the incoming data before we had reached the end of the stream, as illustrated in Figure 11-2. While this is not a problem for these two simple examples, we could easily run into issues when the incommoding data is extremely large. As you witnessed in the previous chapter, the data event is capable of firing multiple times, each time supplying more data to our application. In that particular example, the file that was being transferred was 1.5MB in size.

As the data being transmitted to our application within this chapter is minimal, there is no need to ˙ expect the data event to fire multiple times. However, this might not always be the case. Therefore, in order to ensure that we have received every last chunk of incoming data before attempting to parse it, we should accumulate all incoming data onto a variable (see Listing 11-9). Only once the end event has fired should our application attempt to parse our data.

Listing 11-9. Retaining All Incoming Data onto a Variable

```
1 function requestHandler(request, response) {
2     console.log(request.url);
3     console.log(request.headers);
```

```
4     var incomingEntity = '';
5     request.setEncoding('utf8');
6     request.addListener('data', function(chunk) {
7         incomingEntity += chunk;
8       });

9      request.addListener("end", function() {
10         console.log("end of stream \n");
11         console.log(incomingEntity);
12         if (request.headers['content-type'].indexOf("application/json") > -1){
13             //handle JSON payload
14         }else if(request.headers['content-type'].indexOf("application/x-www-form-
urlencoded")> -1){
15             //handle x-www-form-urlencoded payload
16         }
17       });
18     if (request.url === "/index.html") {
19         response.statusCode = 200;
20         response.setHeader("Content-type", "text/html");
21         //...truncated code
22     } else {
72         response.statusCode = 204;
73         response.end();
74     }
75   }
76 console.log("response-end");
```

Listing 11-9 demonstrates the use of a variable labeled "incomingEntity," which will be used to retain all incoming chunks of data. Because UTF-8 is a text-based format, we can use string manipulation to join incoming chunks of data together. However, we will not attempt to read said data until we are certain we have received it all. Once the end event is dispatched, we can safely log, parse, or inspect the accumulated data retained by an incoming entity.

EXERCISE 11-2. INCOMING ENTITY BODY

In order to minimize the amount of code used within the preceding sections, our server has neglected to respond to any request for /formPost. Instead, we have been informing the browser, via the 204-status code, that the resource being requested is without content. However, now that we have the ability to parse the information as it enters, let's output, as the response, the full name received.

Because our existing form has been enhanced utilizing JavaScript, it is certain that visitors who do not have JavaScript enabled will require a proper response to be provided in the HTML format. This, of course, will result in a full-page load. However, for those individuals who do have JavaScript enabled, we should continue to provide them with JSON.

Be sure to check the responses from the application via the Network tab of the developer console, with JavaScript both turned on as well as off. Compare your results with Listing 11-10.

Regardless of whether JavaScript is enabled or disabled, our exercise application, whose code should reflect that of Listing 11-10, is capable of properly parsing the payload provided. Furthermore, the application responds with a corresponding Content-Type, which enables the results to be viewed by our visitor, regardless of whether JavaScript is on or off.

Listing 11-10. Answer to Exercise/Incoming Entity Body

```
1 var http = require('http');
2 var server = http.createServer();
3 server.addListener('request', requestHandler);
4 server.listen(1337, '127.0.0.1');

5 function requestHandler(request, response) {
6   console.log(request.url);

7   if (request.method === "POST") {
8       var incomingEntity = '';
9       var data;

10      request.addListener('data', function(chunk) {
11          incomingEntity += chunk;
12      });

13      request.addListener("end", function() {
14          console.log("end of stream \n");
15          console.log("Raw entity: " + incomingEntity);

16          if (request.headers['content-type'].indexOf("application/json") > -1){
17              data = JSON.parse(incomingEntity);
18              if (request.url === "/formPost") {
19                  response.statusCode = 200;
20                  response.setHeader("Content-Type", "application/json");
21                  response.end(incomingEntity);
22              }
23          }else if(request.headers['content-type'].indexOf("application/x-www-form-
            urlencoded")>-1){
24              if (request.url === "/formPost") {
25                  response.statusCode = 200;
26                  response.setHeader("Content-Type", "text/html");
27                  var fname = getParamKey("fname", incomingEntity);
28                  var lname = getParamKey("lname", incomingEntity);
29                  response.write('<!doctype html>');
30                  response.write('<html lang="en">');
31                  response.write('<body>');
32                  response.write('</span>' + fname+ ' ' +lname +'</span>');
33                  response.write('</body>');
34                  response.end();
35                  return;
36              }
37          }
38      });
```

```
39      } else if (request.method === "GET") {
40          if (request.url === "/index.html") {
41              response.statusCode = 200;
42              response.setHeader("Content-Type", "text/html");
43              response.write('<!doctype html>');
44              response.write('<html lang="en">');
45              response.write('<body>');
46              response.write('<form action="formPost" method="POST" onsubmit="return ajax();"
                                content="application/x-www-form-urlencoded">');
47              response.write('First-Name:');
48              response.write('<input name="fname" type="text" size="25"/>');
49              response.write('Last-Name:');
50              response.write('<input name="lname" type="text" size="25"/>');
51              response.write('<input type="submit"/>');
52              response.write('</form>');
53              response.write('<script>');
54              response.write('function ajax(){');
55              response.write('var xhr = new XMLHttpRequest();');
56              response.write('xhr.open("POST", "formPost");');
57              response.write('xhr.setRequestHeader("Content-Type", "application/json");');
58              response.write('xhr.setRequestHeader("Accept", "application/json");');
59              response.write('var input = document.getElementsByTagName("input");');
60              response.write('var obj = {');
61              response.write('fname : input[0].value,');
62              response.write('lname : input[1].value');
63              response.write('};');
64              response.write('xhr.send(JSON.stringify(obj));');
65              response.write('return false;');
66              response.write('}');
67              response.write('</script>');
68              response.write(' </body>');
69              response.write('</html>');
70              response.end();
71          } else {
72              response.statusCode = 204;
73              response.end();
74          }
75      console.log("response-end");
76  };
77  function getParamKey(key, str) {
78      var regExp = new RegExp(key.toLowerCase() + '=[^&]*');
79      var matchingValue = (str.toLowerCase()).match(regExp);
80      for (var i = 0; i < matchingValue.length; i++) {
81          var replacedValue = matchingValue[i].replace(key + '=', '');
82          matchingValue[i] = replacedValue;
83      }
84      return decodeURIComponent(matchingValue[0]);
85  };
86  console.log('Server running at http://127.0.0.1:1337/index.html');
```

As it stands now, our application possesses the ability to handle two varieties of incoming payloads. This, of course, can always be enhanced to further handle even more. The code, as it stands now, can only satisfy incoming payloads from the same origin, and not simply because our code neglects to configure the Access-Control-Allow-Origin header. Rather, our code neglects to satisfy a user-agent's preflight request.

Preflight Request

As you may recall from Chapter 9, while our application is able to receive communications from other servers, the user-agents of modern browsers will interfere with most client requests when they are made from varying source origins. Previously, we discussed how user-agents prohibit our applications from receiving a response provided by a server located at originA from being obtained by a client request from originB, due to the same-origin policy (SOP).

In Chapters 9 and 10, you learned how to circumvent the SOP so that we could obtain the response. We learned of three ways in which we could successfully do so, with the simplest of all techniques being the inclusion of the Access-Control-Allow-Origin header. While the aforementioned header has the ability to authorize the source origin, thereby allowing the client to obtain a proper response, the Access-Control-Allow-Origin header alone is not responsible for authorizing an HTTP POST from varying origins.

As explained earlier, GET requests are considered safe methods because they generally fetch a resource. I state *generally* because, as you have seen earlier, an application can be programmed to do as it sees fit. However, per the specification, GET requests do not incur side effects such as that of a POST method. Therefore, the only matter at hand is whether or not the source origin is authorized to receive the resource provided, which, of course, is determined with the Access-Control-Allow-Origin header.

On the other hand, a method such as POST is considered an unsafe method. This means that it can cause side effects on the server and even the response. Therefore, the user-agent can't shoot first and then ask for authentication later. In other words, the user-agent can't simply allow the request to occur and then determine if the source origin has proper authorization before returning the response. Instead, it must first proceed with what is referred to as a preflight request.

Preflight is a term that is defined by Webster as "preparing for or preliminary to flight."[2] As you may have guessed, *preflighting* is a term that originated in the aviation industry and represents a series of checks and tests that are conducted by the pilot preflight, to ensure that it will be a safe and successful one. Generally speaking, the use of preflight is to determine the risks, if any exist. While the term certainly better suits aircrafts than Ajax, the process of preflighting reduces the likelihood of irreparable damage that could otherwise take place by blindly allowing an unsafe request to occur.

In order to preflight our request, the user-agent acts sort of like a bouncer at a club—checking everybody's identification and comparing them against the club's rules and regulations. Such rules may be the maximum number of total occupants, in addition to minimum age restrictions. Should all club criteria be met, the bouncer allows a patron to enter the premises. Otherwise, the bouncer turns them away, forcibly, if need be.

As discussed previously, HTTP headers are used to facilitate the request/response between the client and the server. However, in the case of preflight, our bouncer, the user-agent, utilizes headers to determine if the server has any rules that may prevent an unsafe request from entering, by preceding our actual request with that of another, as depicted in Figure 11-3.

---

[2]Merriam Webster Online Dictionary, "preflight," http://www.merriam-webster.com/dictionary/preflight, 2015.

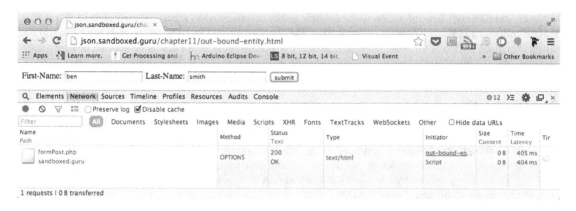

Figure 11-3. *An unauthorized preflight request*

Figure 11-3 demonstrates the necessary preflight request and its use of the OPTIONS request method.

OPTIONS Request Method

The request method OPTIONS, as outlined in the original 1999 HTTP/1.1 specifications, can be used to determine the options and/or requirements associated with a given resource. Additionally, it can be used to reveal the capabilities of a server. Furthermore, the request receives such information without implying any action to be performed on the specified resource. Therefore, it will not initiate the retrieval of said resource. For this reason, OPTIONS is considered a safe method.

Generally speaking, a request for a resource utilizing the OPTIONS method reveals, by way of the configured headers, which request headers and possible request methods are capable of being used with incoming requests for the indicated resource.

As this point in time, if you are following along with the source code that accompanies this chapter, locate and run, within your browser, out-bound-entity.html. If you are not following along with this chapter's source code, you can navigate the browser of your choice to the following URL: http://json.sandboxed.guru/chapter11/out-bound-entity.html. Upon your arrival to either the local or online version of the out-bound-entity.html resource, you will view the form shown in Figure 11-4.

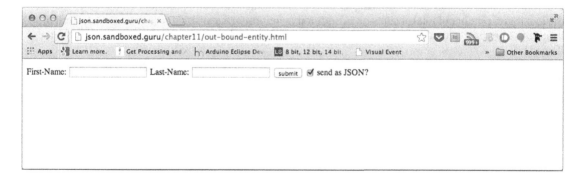

Figure 11-4. *Form that makes cross-origin requests to* http://127.0.0.1:1337/formPost

You may note that it's not unlike the one used by our `incomingEntityBody` application. The most notable difference between this form and the previous form is the inclusion of a check box located to the right of the Submit button. In the previous exercise, I had you disable JavaScript, which caused the form post to be submitted in a different format from when JavaScript was turned on. The result is that when JavaScript was turned off, the browser parsed the response rather than the `xhr` object. This resulted in a new page being presented on the screen. As the source origin of the request and the response occurred from the same origin, the response appeared natural. However, this would not be the case if the form from `exampleA.com` resulted in a full-page reload from `exampleB.com`, as this would be rather apparent to the end user. Therefore, I have included this check box, which uses JavaScript to toggle between the `application/x-www-form-urlencoded` format and the `application/json` format. We will keep it checked to send as JSON for the meantime.

If you no longer have the `incomingEntityBody` application running, start the server once again, so that we can attempt to submit our form from a varying origin. Additionally, open the Network tab on your developer toolbar, to observe the HTTP request. Upon the submission of your form, the results, as shown in your developer toolbar, should reflect those shown in Figure 11-3. Rather than a `POST` occurring, an `OPTIONS` request takes place. In fact, our `POST` does not even appear in the list at all. The reason why is because the user-agent has not yet received the proper preflight authorization from the server regarding the `formPost` resource that would result in our request taking place. Let's inspect the headers of the `OPTIONS` request that occurred.

By navigating to the "Headers" aspect within the Network tab, you should be able to review the configured headers of the preflight request. Those headers should reflect the ones that I have listed below, with the exception of the headers outlined in bold.

```
Access-Control-Request-Headers:  accept, content-type
Access-Control-Request-Method: POST
Cache-Control: no-cache
```
Origin: http://json.sandboxed.guru
```
Pragma: no-cache
```
Referer: http://json.sandboxed.guru/chapter11/out-bound-entity.html
User-Agent: Mozilla/5.0 (Macintosh; Intel Mac OS X 10_9_4) AppleWebKit/537.36 (KHTML, like Gecko) Chrome/36.0.1985.143 Safari/537.36

Of the headers listed, there are three that you might recognize from Chapter 9, which defined the headers of the CORS specifications. Those headers are Access-Control-Request-Headers, Access-Control-Request-Method, and Origin.

As you may recall, the Origin header is added by the user-agent to inform the server as to the source origin of the request, of which the server can determine whether or not to authorize the source origin, via the Access-Control-Allow-Origin header. What you may not know is that the other two headers are intended for similar use. However, rather than communicate the need for authorization among origins, they require authorization for the configured headers of our request, as well as the specified method to be enacted on the target resource.

To ensure the safety of the request, the user-agent, as per the CORS specification, extracts all headers from the actual Ajax request and configures them as a comma-delimited value for the preflight CORS-supported header Access-Control-Allow-Headers. Likewise, the request method specified in the request line of our actual request is extracted and configured as the value to yet another preflight CORS header labeled "Access-Control-Request-Method."

Once the server receives these three headers, it is able to authorize or deny the request simply by configuring the request with the corresponding preflight CORS response headers. Those headers, as shown in Table 11-1, are the following: Access-Control-Allow-Headers and Access-Control-Allow-Methods.

Table 11-1. *CORS Preflight Headers*

Header	Role	Configures
Access-Control-Request-Headers	Indicates which headers will be used in the actual request	User-Agent
Access-Control-Request-Method	Indicates which method will be used in the actual request	User-Agent
Access-Control-Allow-Methods	Indicates, which methods can be used during the request for a targeted resource	Server
Access-Control-Allow-Headers	Indicates which header field names can be used during the request of the targeted resource	Server

If, and only if, all values configured by the user-agent, are reflected in the configured values of the response will the actual request take place. Unlike the Access-Control-Allow-Origin header, which can be configured with the wildcard * token, the Access-Control-Allow-Methods and Access-Control-Allows-Headers headers must explicitly declare, in a comma-delimited fashion, all accepted header fields and methods for the identified resource.

As it stands now, we are unable to review the response within the network tab, and for good reason. Up until this moment, our incomingEntityBody application has only required the ability to respond to incoming requests that utilize GET and POST. Until we implement a response for the OPTIONS request method, the request will continue to wait for one.

Currently, the requestHandler within our incomingEntityBody application distinguishes between GET and POST methods. Depending on which request method is being used, the appropriate code block is run, resulting in the fulfillment of the request. Monitoring for the OPTIONS request is as simple as adding yet another condition, as seen in Listing 11-11.

Listing 11-11. Including the Ability to Respond to Preflight Requests

```
1 //... code is truncated
6 function requestHandler(request, response) {
7   console.log(request.url);
8     if (request.method === "POST") {
9       //... code is truncated
51    } else if (request.method === "GET") {
52      //... code is truncated
88    } else if( request.method==="OPTIONS"){
89    }
90    console.log("response-end");
91 };
```

To keep things simple, Listing 11-11 reveals the code as it stands within incomingEntityBody, only I have condensed the areas that are not relevant to the current discussion. As you can see on lines 88 and 89, a new code block has been added to respond to any incoming OPTIONS request. Within this block, we can properly configure a response to reflect which headers and methods are allowed on either a global level or for an individual resource. For the purpose of this demonstration, we will be configuring the headers on a per-resource basis.

Listing 11-12 begins by configuring the appropriate status code that acknowledges the request was properly received (**line 89**). From there, we determine if the resource being requested by the client is for that of /formPost (**line 90**). If this is, in fact, the resource being requested, the response will be configured utilizing the appropriate CORS headers.

Listing 11-12. Demonstrating the Configuration of the Preflight CORS Headers

```
88 } else if( request.method==="OPTIONS"){
89    response.statusCode = 200;
90    if (request.url === "/formPost") {
91        response.setHeader('Access-Control-Allow-Origin', '*');
92        response.setHeader('Access-Control-Allow-Headers', 'Content-Type, Accept,
                             Accept-Language, Accept-Encoding, User-Agent, Host,
                             Content-Length, Connection, Cache-Control');
93        response.setHeader("Access-Control-Allow-Methods", 'GET, POST, OPTIONS');
94    }
95    response.end();
96 }
```

The first configured header is used to authorize the source origin. The second configured header is used to inform the user-agent of any and all headers that are authorized for the following resource. As you can see, each header field that our resource requires must be added to the Access-Control-Allow-Headers header. These configured values may regard valid HTTP/1.1 headers in addition to custom headers. In this case, I have configured the values with typical fields (**line 92**). These configured fields for the Access-Allow-Request-Headers header can certainly possess more that what I have listed. The third configured header regards the authorized methods that can enact upon the targeted resource. As this book only considers three HTTP/1.1 methods, GET, OPTIONS, and POST, I have provided all three (**line 93**).

Last, regardless of which resource is requested, we submit the response, as it is currently configured, and conclude the incoming request (**line 95**). Upon the reception of the response, the user-agent will compare and contrast its configured headers with those returned by the server.

```
CORS Preflight Request Headers
Access-Control-Request-Headers:  accept, content-type
Access-Control-Request-Method: POST
Origin: http://json.sandboxed.guru

CORS Preflight Response Headers
Access-Control-Allow-Headers: Content-Type, Accept, Accept-Language,Accept-
      Encoding, User-Agent, Host, Content-Length, Connection, Cache-Control
Access-Control-Allow-Methods: GET, POST, OPTIONS
Access-Control-Allow-Origin: *
```

If the configured values of the CORS preflight request headers can be matched (case-insensitive) against the corresponding CORS preflight response headers, only then will the actual request be initiated. Otherwise, the actual request will be canceled.

With our new configured headers in place, let's run the application that possesses the code, as shown in Listing 11-12, and perform another form submission once again. Upon the submission of the form, you should see that the preflight request has been performed and succeeds and, therefore, is followed by our actual request, as shown in Figure 11-5.

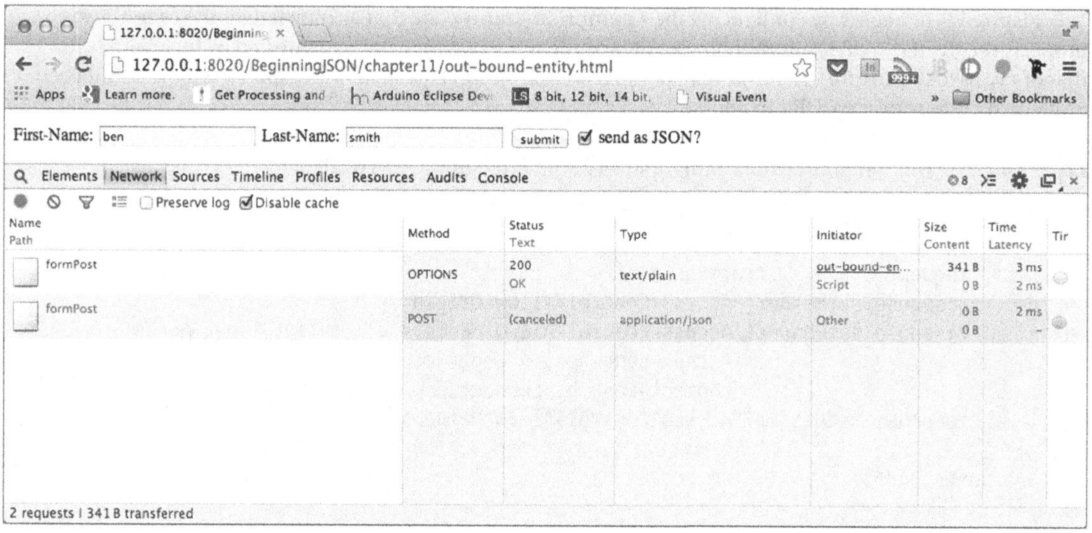

Figure 11-5. *Authorized preflight request followed by an unauthorized source origin request for* formPost

As depicted by Figure 11-5, the preflight request has been approved and follows up with our actual request. However, due to a network error, our request for the /formPost resource is canceled. The reason for the network error is outputted within the console tab. While the network error will vary depending on the browser being used to make the request, it should be immediately apparent as to why the request was canceled.

```
XMLHttpRequest cannot load http://127.0.0.1:1337/formPost. No 'Access-Control-Allow-Origin'
header is present on the requested resource. Origin 'http://127.0.0.1:8020' is therefore not
allowed access.
```

As explained via the preceding messaging provided by Chrome, the request resulted in a network error. This is due to the fact that the source origin has not been provided sufficient authorization to receive the response. However, this is simple enough to resolve by including the Access-Control-Allow-Origin header as a configured header of the response. At this point in time, let's make this proper amendment, shown in bold in Listing 11-13, and then initiate the request once more.

Listing 11-13. Authorizing formPost for All Source Origins

```
 1  ...//truncated code
13      request.addListener("end", function() {
14          console.log("end of stream \n");
15          console.log("Raw entity: " + incomingEntity);

16          if (request.headers['content-type'].indexOf("application/json")>-1) {
17              data = JSON.parse(incomingEntity);
18              if (request.url === "/formPost") {
19                  response.setHeader("Access-Control-Allow-Origin","*");
20                  response.statusCode = 200;
21                  response.setHeader("Content-Type", "application/json");
22                  response.end(incomingEntity);
23              }
```

```
24          }else if(request.headers['content-type'].indexOf("application/x-www-form-
            urlencoded")>-1) {
25              if (request.url === "/formPost") {
26                  response.statusCode = 200;
27                  response.setHeader("Access-Control-Allow-Origin","*");
28                  response.setHeader("Content-Type", "text/html");
29                    var fname = getParamKey("fname", incomingEntity);
30                    var lname = getParamKey("lname", incomingEntity);
31                  response.write('<!doctype html>');
32                  response.write('<html lang="en">');
33                  response.write('<body>');
34                  response.write('</span>' + fname+ ' ' +lname +'</span>');
35                  response.write('</body>');
36                  response.end();
37                  return;
38              }
39          }
40      });
41  ...//truncated code
```

If we were to run the application with the inclusion of the bold code from Listing 11-13 and resubmit our form, the results this time would be authorized, resulting in the output above our form, as shown in Figure 11-6.

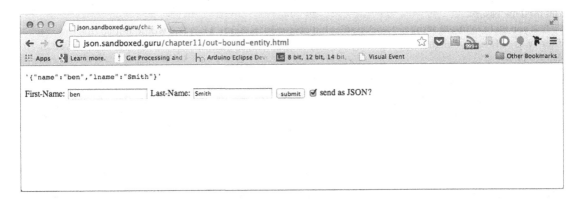

Figure 11-6. *Successful Ajax POST from a remote origin*

Additionally, if you were to uncheck the check box beside the Submit button, we could alter the Content-Type of the payload from `application/json` to `application/x-www-form-urlencoded`. Because our server is implemented to respond with an appropriate Content-Type that reflects the format of an incoming payload, the transmission of the two Content-Types can be clearly identified via the response, as shown in Figure 11-7.

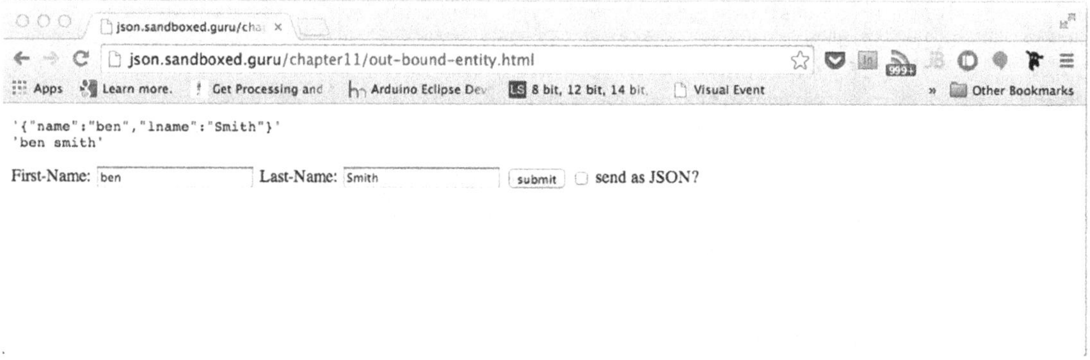

Figure 11-7. *Successful form POST*

Congratulations! You have just created a server that can accept incoming JSON payloads from both local and remote origins.

What Determines Preflight

It should be made known that the real reason I had incorporated the check box into the preceding form was not truly to demonstrate the ability for our form to alternate between two Content-Types. Rather, I incorporated it to emphasize the conditions under which the user-agent determines if a preflight request is deemed necessary.

If you were to monitor the network traffic that occurred in Figure 11-7, you would notice that the there was only one preflight request, as signified by the OPTIONS request method. This can be observed in Figure 11-8.

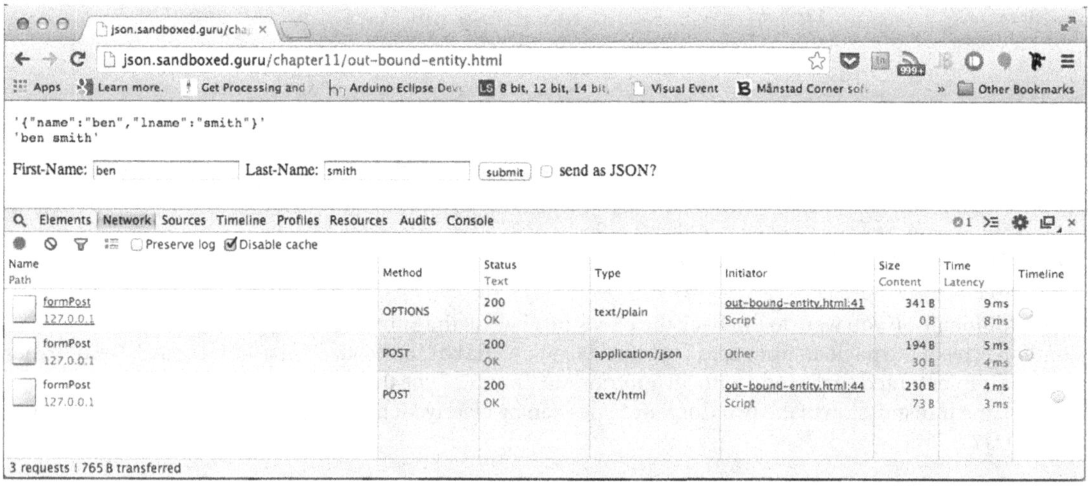

Figure 11-8. *One reflight request, two POST requests*

As clearly shown in Figure 11-8, the form received two responses of varying Content-Types. One response was supplied as `application/json,` while the other was supplied as `text/html`. Both responses are output as they are received in the upper-left corner of the document. However, as seen in the Network tab, three requests were made, of which only one is a preflight request.

As was stated in Chapter 9, for legacy purposes, HTTP requests that are only configured with simple request headers and simple request methods do not require the use of preflight. However, if the requests are made from varying origins, they will require proper authorization to obtain the response. This is achieved by configuring the Access-Control-Allow-Origin header. While simple request methods refer to requests that utilize either GET, POST, or HEAD as their request methods, what constitutes simple request headers is slightly more elaborate, as quoted by the CORS specification.[3]

> *A header is said to be simple, if the header field name is an ASCII case-insensitive match for Accept, Accept-Language, or Content-Language or if it is an ASCII case-insensitive match for Content-Type and the header field value media type (excluding parameters) is an ASCII case-insensitive match for application/x-www-form-urlencoded, multipart/ form-data, or text/plain.*

What this means for varying origins is that if your server is expecting an incoming payload whose Content-Type is not among the three that can be configured with an HTML form element, such as JSON, it will be mandatory for your application to anticipate a browser's need for preflight. Conversely, your Ajax request may be denied if the server does not utilize these headers.

Summary

Typically, when we use APIs belonging to Twitter or Facebook, we tend to overlook what might be required of a server to make these interactions possible. Generally, we take a lot of what is taking place behind the scenes for granted. This chapter has attempted to shed some light on this matter.

We regarded what it takes to receive and process incoming data. As it turns out, POSTing JSON data can be slightly more intricate than you may have previously believed, especially when dealing with cross-origin requests.

When considering a request from a varying origin, any attempt to use an unsafe method immediately results in what is regarded as a preflight request. Only requests that use simple methods and simple headers are able to make a request without the use of preflight. Furthermore, as you have learned, any attempt to transmit the Content-Type `application/json` results in a preflight request. Preflight, of course, is only required when the request occurs from a source origin that varies from the origin of the server being posted to. In either case, this chapter has now prepared you to account for both.

Now that you have learned to process data, you will be able to apply this knowledge in the next chapter.

Key Points from This Chapter

- GET requests only have one MIME type, whereas POST requests have many.

- Incoming payloads can be both simple and complex.

- One must consume incoming data by monitoring the stream for the `data` event.

- When all data has been consumed from the stream, the `end` event is fired.

---

[3]World Wide Web Consortium (W3C), Anne van Kesteren, ed. "Cross-Origin Resource Sharing," `www.w3.org/TR/cors/`, January 16, 2014.

- The HTML <form> element can only transmit three Content-Types.

- Determining the Content-Type for incoming data is beneficial with regard to processing the received data.

- Buffers are used to read bytes from the stream.

- Preflight reduces the likelihood of malicious behavior.

- Preflight makes use of the OPTIONS request method.

- There are two preflight headers that must be properly configured by the server in order to authorize a source origin.

■ ■ ■

CHAPTER 12

Persisting JSON: II

The last time I discussed the persistence of JSON, it was strictly from a front-end perspective. However, as promised, this chapter will consider the persistence of JSON from a back-end perspective.

You may be familiar with the terms *SQL* and *MySQL*, as they are both rather popular databases. These databases store data in rows, within a table. With the assistance of the SQL, Structured Query Language, data can be extracted from the table and returned to the requesting client. However, what you may not be so familiar with is the term *NoSQL databases*, which, as you may surmise, refers to a category of databases that do not rely on the SQL query language (or at least not heavily).

NoSQL databases, such as CouchDB and MongoDB, store their data as JSON within individual documents, rather than as rows within a table. Storing data in this fashion has been shown to provide a great amount of scalability, as well as flexibility, compared to traditional SQL databases.

CouchDB

As prominently stated on the CouchDB web site, located at `http://couchdb.apache.org`, Apache CouchDB™ is a database that uses JSON for documents, JavaScript for MapReduce indexes, and regular HTTP for its API. Because CouchDB leverages the open source technologies of the Web, it itself is an entirely open source project.

Installing CouchDB, as with Node, requires very little effort and is as easy as downloading the appropriate installation package. CouchDB is available for Mac, Windows, and Ubuntu Linux, but this book will only cover the installation on Mac and Windows.

Windows Installation

Open your browser to `http://couchdb.apache.org/` and scroll down until you find the red Windows (x86) download button. At the time of this writing, the version of CouchDB that will be downloaded is 1.6.1. This will direct you to the Apache Download Mirrors site, which makes a few suggestions pertaining to where you should download the CouchDB setup executable. Unless you have a preference for which mirror you make use of, click the mirror link directly below the words "We suggest the following mirror site for your download." This will initiate the download. Depending on the browser being used, you may be prompted to run, save, or cancel the download.

When the download has completed, and you are ready to begin the installation, locate the directory for which the download was saved and run the executable. Once the application runs, you'll be presented with the initial screen of the setup wizard. At this point, feel free to click Continue and accept the Apache license agreement.

The third screen of the installation presents you with the default location for the installation. Unless you have a reason for this to change, continue with the defaulted location by clicking Next. Unless you would like to place the program's shortcut within a folder other than Apache CouchDB, click Next.

The final screen presents you with two check boxes that have already been checked off. Keep these both active and continue once again by clicking Next, to proceed to the installation screen. The installation screen reflects the chosen configurations for one final review before the installation begins. If you are satisfied with the present settings, click Install.

When the installation has concluded, and you receive the "Completing the Apache CouchDB Setup Wizard" message, you can click Finish. At this point, and only if you left both check boxes selected, CouchDB will already be running. To ensure that the installation has been successful, navigate your browser to the following address: `http://127.0.0.1:5984/`. You should be presented with similar JSON output shown in Figure 12-1.

Figure 12-1. *Successfully running CouchDB*

If you are seeing this message, congratulations; CouchDB has been successfully installed.

Mac Installation

Open your browser to `http://couchdb.apache.org/` and scroll down until you find the red Mac OS X (10.6+) download button. At the time of this writing, the version of CouchDB that will be downloaded is 1.6.1. This will direct you to the Apache Download Mirrors site, which makes a few suggestions pertaining to where you should download the CouchDB setup executable. Unless you have a preference for which mirror you make use of, click the mirror link directly below the words "We suggest the following mirror site for your download." This will initiate the download. Depending on the browser being used, you may be prompted to run, save, or cancel the download. Feel free to hit Save.

Once the download has completed, and you are ready to begin the installation, locate the directory for which the download was saved. Locate the `Apache-CouchDB` file and double-click it to unzip the contents of the archive, to reveal the Apache CouchDB application. The beauty of the Mac installation is that the application is self-contained and ready to run simply by double-clicking the app. As the file is an app, feel free to move the file into the Applications directory before running.

At this point, if you are ready to launch the CouchDB application, go ahead and double-click the Apache `CouchDB.app`. Now you should have CouchDB running in the background. To ensure that you have successfully launched CouchDB, simply navigate your browser to the following URL: `http://127.0.0.1:5984/`.

You should be presented with similar JSON output to that shown in Figure 12-2.

Figure 12-2. *Successfully running CouchDB*

If you are seeing this message, congratulations; CouchDB has been successfully installed.

Working with CouchDB

What makes CouchDB unique as a database, other than storing data within individual documents, is the fact that its API is nothing more simple than HTTP requests. Whether we're taking about databases or the documents within them, our ability to receive, update, add, and delete are all made possible via the eight standard HTTP request methods to http://127.0.0.1:5984. As with our Node applications, CouchDB is running a server that monitors all incoming requests on the port 5984. For each incoming request, an appropriate response is provided.

Because the API is nothing more than standard requests, incorporating CouchDB with Node is a piece of cake. Before we begin to incorporate CouchDB with our Node application, let's first take a look at the interface that accompanies CouchDB.

Futon

As was stated earlier, the API of CouchDB is made up entirely of HTTP requests. Rather than requiring new adopters of CouchBD to create an interface of their own to monitor and work with databases instantly, the developers at CouchDB have provided us with a local interface that wraps all HTTP requests for us within a series of visual elements. This interface has been dubbed "Futon."

Futon is a simple HTML interface that leverages HTTP requests to provide us with an easy way to work with our data. At this point, navigate your browser to http://127.0.0.1:5984/_utils/. Upon your arrival you will be presented with the view shown in Figure 12-3.

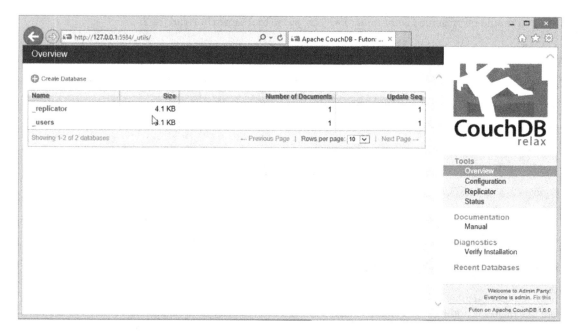

Figure 12-3. *Futon utilities interface*

Each Futon interface is divided into two halves. The left-hand portion of the view is the prominent view and is used to easily work with and create data. The second component, toward the right-hand side of the screen, provides us with an easy way to access a variety of utilities provided by the CouchDB application. From within this column of the Futon interface, you can access documentation, update the configurations for the application, and even run diagnostics.

The view reflected in Figure 12-3 represents the overview interface. Within this view, we are presented with a table of currently existing databases. By default, CouchDB comes preinstalled with two. These are the following: _replicator and _users. While it's nice that Couch provides us with these, it will be more interesting to work with our own. New databases can be easily created directly from this interface via the Create Database button located just above the table of existing databases.

Constructing Your First Database

Creating our first database via Futon is as easy as can be. Simply click the Create Database button to begin the process. Upon clicking, Futon provides us with a prompt asking for us to label our database. As this chapter will work toward the creation of a guestbook for our Node applications, we will provide the label "guestbook." Clicking Create will create the database and results in the updated interface shown in Figure 12-4.

■ **Note** A guestbook is a way for visitors who arrive at a site to leave their names and possible comments.

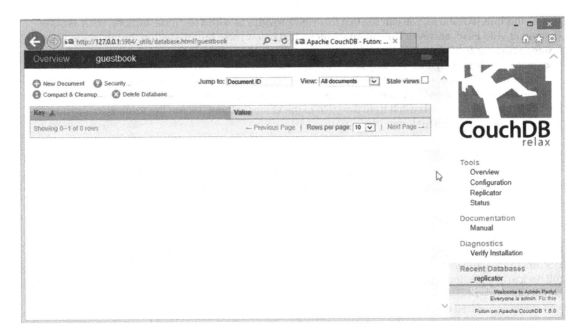

Figure 12-4. *No documents within guestbook*

As identified by the breadcrumbs in the upper-left-hand corner, this interface no longer regards the overview but, rather, our recently created database. This Futon interface provides us with the necessary tools to work with a particular database. In this case, that particular database is our guestbook database.

Here, we would be able to see all JSON documents that have been stored within; however, as we have just created this database, it remains empty for the time being. Let's add our first piece of content by clicking the button labeled "New Document." By clicking this button, we find ourselves viewing yet another interface that resembles that shown in Figure 12-5.

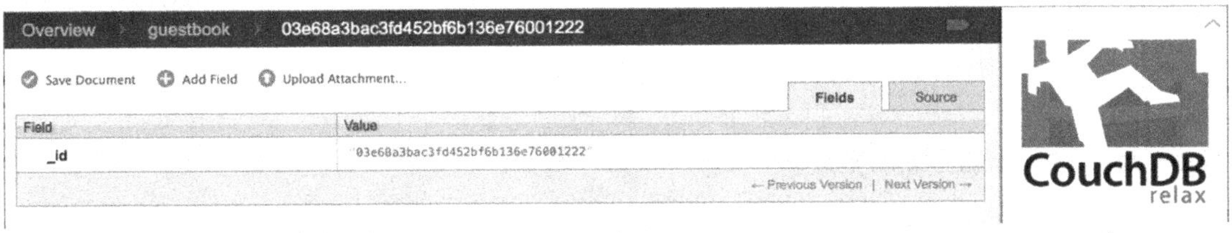

Figure 12-5. *Overview of a guestbook document*

This interface, as illustrated by the breadcrumb, concerns an individual document. Remember that all data is saved individually as a JSON document. By default, each document created is provided with a GUID (Globally Unique Identifier). Because GUIDs are globally unique, the value shown in my figure will undoubtedly be different from the GUID your document has been provided with. Although this view provides you with an input field allowing you to adjust this value, you are generally discouraged from doing so. The reason is that this GUID is the identifier that will be used to locate this file. Depending on how many documents you are expecting to store, you may find yourself running out of proper names to provide each document.

Because the document _id represents the resource itself, if you were to have visited http://127.0.0.1:5984/guestbook/*03e68a3bac3fd452bf6b136e76001222*, replacing my GUID with yours, you would have made a GET request for the contents of the file we are currently modifying.

217

As this interface shows, you can see that this view provides us with a few more buttons, such as Save Document, Add Field, and even Upload Attachment. Just below these buttons within the tab labeled "Fields," resides a singular field and value. From this view, we will be able to provide key/value pairs to our JSON document simply by assigning as many keys and values as we desire.

Utilizing the button labeled "Add Field," we will add two more fields to this document. Upon clicking Add Field, a new "unnamed" row will appear. Let's change the name from "unnamed" to "handle." Next, by hitting Tab, the focus will switch from the Field to the Values column. Within the Value field, provide the string value @CouchDB and hit Enter.

■ **Note**   It's important to note that fields should not be provided with double quotes, as they will be applied behind the scenes. Furthermore, all strings provided for Values should always have double quotes.

Once again, click Add Field and replace the "unnamed" field with that of "message." Then once again hit Tab, to provide the value of "greetings and salutations" and hit Enter. Last, click the button labeled "Save Document," to write these changes into the document. CouchDB provides versioning to ensure the ability to roll back to any previous changes. For this reason, you may note that CouchDB has inserted a field on your behalf labeled "_rev." This simply refers to the current document revision.

While we utilized the Add Field button to include key/value pairs to our document, you could have switched the manner in which we inputted our members by toggling from the Fields view to the Source view. Once within Source view, by double-clicking the presented source, you would note that the presented JSON becomes editable, as shown in Figure 12-6. If you are utilizing the Source route, always make sure that you are providing valid JSON.

Figure 12-6. *JSON Source input field*

Congratulations, you have created your very first data entry in the guestbook database. In order to view the JSON text of this entry, click the icon shown in Figure 12-7.

Figure 12-7. *Performing a quick request for the current view*

Clicking the button shown in Figure 12-7 is simply an easier way to navigate our browser to the current document similarly, as shown previously. Whether you use the button or physically type in the full URI, you will be presented with the raw JSON, as revealed in Figure 12-8. Figure 12-8 shows our recently created document with accompanying handle and message.

Figure 12-8. *JSON revealed for @CouchDB signature*

At this point, let's revisit the overview interface by navigating to http://127.0.0.1:5984/_utils/. This time, arriving at the overview interface lists our guestbook among the default two. From here, we can easily access our guestbook database by clicking the name "guestbook" within the list.

By selecting the guestbook database, the Futon interface drills down from the overview to our guestbook database specifically. The last time we were within this interface, the table possessed zero documents. However, this time, a single document is presented within the table, as shown in Figure 12-9.

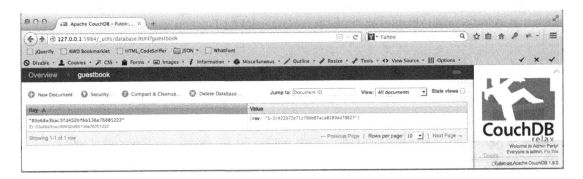

Figure 12-9. *All existing documents listed for guestbook*

Figure 12-9 shows a two-columned table consisting of the labels "Key" and "Value" and, within it, our recently created document. This can be identified by the GUID we were working with earlier. Furthermore, by clicking the GUID listed in the column labeled "Key," we can review the individual content retained by that document.

As I stated earlier, Futon, similar to a user-agent, initiates a series of HTTP requests on our behalf behind the scenes. If you were to open up your developer's toolbar and navigate to the Network tab, you would be able to find a GET request for the following request: http://127.0.0.1:5984/guestbook/_all_docs.

At any point in time, we can query our database for any and all entries it holds, by navigating to the aforementioned URL. As the later portion of the URL, _all_docs, suggests, we should expect to view every saved document pertaining to our guestbook database. Upon your arrival to the preceding URL, you should be presented with something that resembles the following JSON:

```
{"total_rows":1,"offset":0,"rows":[ {"id":"03e68a3bac3fd452bf6b136e76001222","key":"03e68a3b
ac3fd452bf6b136e76001222","value":{"rev":"1-2c422372e71c79db87aca8289dd78827"}} ]}
```

The preceding output displays a complex JSON structure providing an overview of all documents possessed by our guestbook database. Held within the member labeled "rows," it reveals an array whereby each reflected document can be easily traversed, and its "id" can be obtained. As you recall, this is the identifier by which the server refers to a document.

The resource used before, _all_docs, reflects a unique JSON document. What makes this document unique is that all of its retained data reflects the results for a particular query. That query being the following:

Capture the id and current revision for documents affiliated with our guestbook database. Additionally insert the id as the value of the "key" field.

In the CouchDB nomenclature, all documents that are used to reveal the results of a query are referred to as a *view*.

Creating Views

Creating a custom JSON representation of the data held by our database is what the CouchDB nomenclature refers to as a *view*. A view, in its most atomic form, is a JavaScript map function whose signature and implementation reflect the following code:

```
function( doc ){
  emit( key , value);
}
```

■ **Note** A map function is applied against all elements within a list, to produce a particular result set.

The initial parameter doc represents the parsed JSON content of a document, which exists within the database. With a process similar to a JavaScript for loop, each and every document that exists within our database is supplied to this very function. From within the body of the function, and utilizing pure JavaScript, we can analyze the provided JavaScript object to extract particular keys and values to construct a new object that reflects the needs of a particular view. Once we have determined what we wish to provide as a row within this result, we will supply it as the value argument of the emit method. The emit method is a global method provided by CouchDB to capture a key and data value as a row within a particular view.

The great thing about the emit method is that it can be called as many or as few times as you like per document. Additionally, the key provided mustn't be unique. Unlike a traditional key/value pair, the parameter labeled "key" is used strictly to sort or filter results that are captured within this view. By providing taxonomy, we can obtain all rows that exhibit this particular key.

■ **Note** Each call to emit creates a corresponding row in the produced document.

While this may sound inefficient, depending on the amount of saved documents within the database, the reality is that it's only inefficient the very first time this view is queried. Any subsequent request for a view that has previously been run will only be executed against any documents that may have been updated, deleted, or added.

Creating Our First Custom View

Let's begin to devise our first view. If you are not currently within the guestbook view, navigate your browser to http://127.0.0.1:5984/_utils/ and click the guestbook database. On the right-hand side of the screen, you will see a drop-down menu labeled "View:", as seen in Figure 12-10. Be sure to select "Temporary view...."

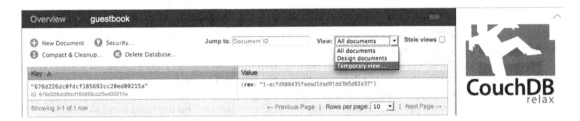

Figure 12-10. *Creating a temporary view*

Upon your selection, you will be presented with a screen similar to that shown in Figure 12-11.

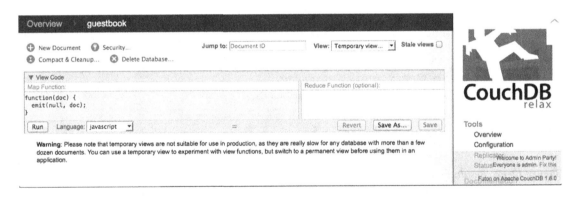

Figure 12-11. *An anonymous map function*

The interface illustrated in Figure 12-11 is what we will use to design a custom query, a.k.a. a view. On the left-hand side of the screen, just below the label "Map Function," you can see the anonymous function I was discussing earlier. Utilizing the interface, we can begin reading particular members from the supplied document and begin the retrieval for the rows of our view.

While we have a view that provides the IDs and revisions to all documents, let's create a view that will output all captured handles and their corresponding message, by updating the map function to reflect the following code (Listing 12-1):

Listing 12-1. A Specific map Function Implementation

```
function(doc) {
  if(doc.handle){
    emit(doc.handle, { "handle":doc.handle, "message": doc.message, "_id":doc._id} );
  }
}
```

Listing 12-1 demonstrates an implementation that constructs a view, which will reveal the handles, messages, and the ID of each document within the guestbook database. Furthermore, using a simple condition to determine if a handle does not exist, we can choose whether or not a particular document should be present. With this code in place, click the button labeled "Run" to observe the results of our view.

Clicking Run should reveal a singular row reflecting its findings, as seen in Figure 12-12. As we only have one document in our database, only one document has been supplied to our function. Let's add a second entry to our guestbook database, but first, let's save this temporary view as a permanent one. Any temporary view can be converted into a permanent one simply by clicking "Save As..." on the right-hand side of the screen.

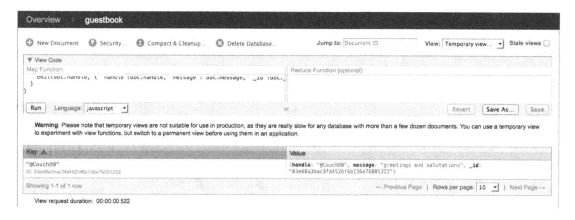

Figure 12-12. *Results for our custom query*

Clicking this button will bring up a prompt asking for the name of a design document, as well as the unique name for our recently created query (a.k.a. view). At this point, provide the name of a document as _design/guests and provide the view name "signatures," as shown in Figure 12-13. Once you have entered the appropriate names, click Save. Because everything is saved as a JSON document, you, too, can access the raw JSON for the view we just devised.

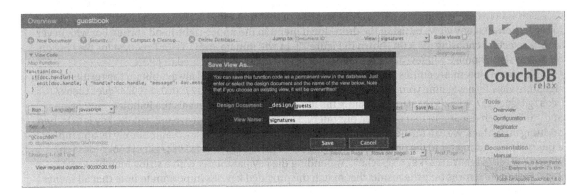

Figure 12-13. *Creating a permanent view*

The design document labeled "guests" is an example of a string id versus a GUID. Because design documents are more likely to be requested specifically rather than iterated over, it makes more sense to use a name that is easy to remember. Because the name of the resource, "guests," is the actual name of the file, we can always obtain its raw JSON by simply visiting the following URL: http://127.0.0.1:5984/guestbook/_design/guests.

It is worth noting that all documents pertaining to a view are prefixed with _design/. This denotes a view from an ordinary document.

Once more, let's get back to our database by navigating your browser once more to http://127.0.0.1:5984/_utils/ and clicking the guestbook database. To create another entry into our database, click New Document. Let's add a second document, to reflect the handle @apache, and provide it with the following message: "Hello World." When this is completed, click Save.

At this point, you should now have two entries within the guestbook database. You can easily navigate back to our guestbook database by selecting it from the breadcrumb in the header. Upon your arrival, you should witness the two documents of our database, as revealed in Figure 12-14. You may immediately recognize that the rows of our view no longer resemble the outputted table as previously shown in Figure 12-9.

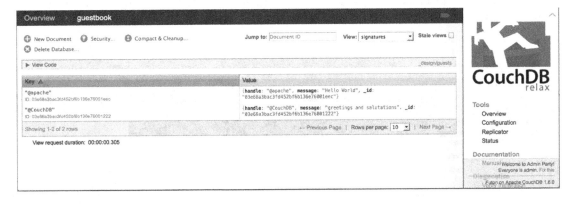

Figure 12-14. *Two rows of signatures within the guestbook*

This is because the database currently makes use of the "signature" view we recently created. Feel free to toggle between any views by using the drop-down menu in the upper-right-hand corner. For whichever view is selected, choosing the icon shown in Figure 12-14 will initiate an HTTP GET request for the chosen resource. The response will reveal for the chosen query all matches presented in JSON.

No matter how many entries your guestbook DB is provided, you can always obtain the results of your signature view by navigating your browser to the following URL: `http://127.0.0.1:5984/guestbook/_design/guests/_view/signatures`. Visiting the aforementioned URL reveals the handles, message, and `_id` for each document that matched our query. Furthermore, because we utilized the key label when emitting our values, we can further filter our search to that of a particular key/value simply by appending a query string parameter to the preceding URL, like so: `http://127.0.0.1:5984/guestbook/_design/guests/_view/signatures?key="apache"`. Appending the key parameter with a string matching our @apache handle returns only the results that match the provided key. It's important to note that all *strings provided to the* key *parameter must be wrapped in double quotes.*

We can even sort our list by providing yet another query parameter. At our disposal for sorting, we can use either ascending or descending. Regardless of which parameter you choose to use, the value which it requires is that of a `true` or `false`. Visiting the following URL will present our rows, in alphabetical order: `http://127.0.0.1:5984/guestbook/_design/guests/_view/signatures?ascending=true`.

Connecting Node and CouchDB

As was stated earlier, CouchDB possesses its own REST API for working with databases, documents, and views. In fact, it's 100% possible to add/remove documents, views, and databases with nothing other than standard HTTP requests. I hope from what you have previously observed that this will not come as a shock to you.

Because CouchDB's API is available through the URL, we can both persist and query data from either a browser or server. If we were to work with CouchDB via the client side, we could rely on Ajax, whereas on the server side, we can incorporate the use of an instance of the `http.ClientRequest`.

It must be made known that because CouchDB runs on its own port, any and all client-side requests beyond those made by Futon will require the incorporation of all appropriate CORS headers. By default, CouchDB does not have these enabled, but it does offer the ability to activate them via the configuration view, shown in Figure 12-15, located at `http://127.0.0.1:5984/_utils/config.html`. We will discuss how to properly configure CouchDB to enable CORS in Chapter 14.

Figure 12-15. CouchDB configuration interface

Simply because the HTTP methods required to work with CouchDB are beyond the scope of this book, for simplicity, we will incorporate CouchDB with Node and use yet another module to streamline such HTTP calls into a simple API. The module that we will be working with is known as Cradle.

Cradle for Node

While Node itself includes a variety of modules, one that it does not ship with is Cradle. Cradle is a third-party, high-level CouchDB client module that has been created to easily and asynchronously work with CouchDB and Node applications. Due to its extremely high-level API, we will remain shielded from the HTTP methods that have not been covered in this book. If you wish to learn more about Cradle, feel free to navigate to its GitHub page: https://github.com/flatiron/cradle.

Installing Cradle is very easy. Simply use the command-line interface to navigate to the top directory, which contains the chapter12 source code. For me, that would be the following locations:

```
//PC
C:\Users\UrZA\Documents\Aptana Studio 3 Workspace\BeginningJSON\chapter12\
//Mac
/Users/FeZEC/Documents/Aptana Studio 3 Workspace/BeginningJSON/chapter12/
```

Simply type cd, followed by the location of your chapter12 directory, and hit Enter. Next, type in the following command and hit Return on your keyboard:

```
npm install cradle
```

This will initiate a download of all required packages for the particular module into a folder labeled node_modules, within the chapter12 directory. If your console outputs a series of lines that all display errors, as shown in Figure 12-16, you will be required to run the same command as the administrator.

```
Macintosh:chapter12 FeZEC$ npm install cradle
npm WARN package.json cradle@0.6.7 No repository field.
npm ERR! Error: Attempt to unlock cradle, which hasn't been locked
npm ERR!     at unlock (/usr/local/lib/node_modules/npm/lib/utils/locker.js:44:11)
npm ERR!     at cb (/usr/local/lib/node_modules/npm/lib/cache/add-local.js:30:5)
npm ERR!     at /usr/local/lib/node_modules/npm/lib/cache/add-local.js:47:20
npm ERR!     at /usr/local/lib/node_modules/npm/lib/utils/locker.js:30:7
npm ERR!     at /usr/local/lib/node_modules/npm/node_modules/lockfile/lockfile.js:167:38
npm ERR!     at OpenReq.Req.done (/usr/local/lib/node_modules/npm/node_modules/graceful-fs/graceful-fs.js:144:5)
npm ERR!     at OpenReq.done (/usr/local/lib/node_modules/npm/node_modules/graceful-fs/graceful-fs.js:64:22)
npm ERR!     at Object.oncomplete (fs.js:107:15)
npm ERR! If you need help, you may report this *entire* log,
npm ERR! including the npm and node versions, at:
npm ERR!     <http://github.com/npm/npm/issues>

npm ERR! System Darwin 13.3.0
npm ERR! command "node" "/usr/local/bin/npm" "install" "cradle"
npm ERR! cwd /Users/FeZEC/Documents/Aptana Studio 3 Workspace/BeginningJSON/chapter12
npm ERR! node -v v0.10.29
npm ERR! npm -v 1.4.14
npm ERR!
npm ERR! Additional logging details can be found in:
npm ERR!     /Users/FeZEC/Documents/Aptana Studio 3 Workspace/BeginningJSON/chapter12/npm-debug.log
npm ERR! not ok code 0
```

Figure 12-16. *Cradle installation error*

On a Mac, this can be achieved by preceding the aforementioned command with sudo, making the entire command sudo npm install cradle. Once you press Enter, you will be asked for your login password.

On a PC, you will have to close the command prompt and open it from the Start menu. Depending on the version of Windows, you may find within your startup menu two listings for the command prompt; only one is followed by "Admin." Choose this particular command prompt and retry the preceding command.

If, on the other hand, you do not see the Admin command prompt within your startup menu, right-click on the singularly listed command prompt, to reveal the menu option "run as admin." Go ahead and run as admin and retry the command.

A successful installation reveals a node_module folder within the specified path, at which point our module is ready to be used.

■ **Note** Due to a bug in the latest Node.js Windows installable, Windows users may be receiving the following message: "Error: ENOENT, stat 'C:\Users\[USER_NAME]\AppData\Roaming\npm." If this is the case, to correct the problem, you will have to type the command mkdir C:\Users\[USER_NAME]\AppData\Roaming\npm, where [USER_NAME] is replaced with the login name of your user.

Incorporating the Cradle Module

Once the Cradle module has been successfully installed into our top-level directory, we can begin working with it by incorporating it into a Node application via require(). Furthermore, as long as the CouchDB server is running, we can use the following snippet of code shown in Listing 12-2 to configure our http.ClientRequest to connect to it.

Listing 12-2. Including and Configuring Cradle with CouchDB

```
1 var cradle = require('../node_modules/cradle');
2 var DBConnection = cradle.Connection;
3 var couchDB = new DBConnection('127.0.0.1', 5984, {
4   cache : true,
5   raw : false,
6   forceSave : true
7 });
```

The code shown in Listing 12-12 simply demonstrates the inclusion of the Cradle module within the Node application, in addition to opening a connection to our CouchDB server. The path provided to the require method reflects the path our node_module folder created, relative to the directory holding our Node application. Once the Cradle object is obtained via the require method, it is assigned to a variable labeled "cradle" and then used to open a connection to the CouchDB server.

Working with Databases

As you will soon come to learn, Cradle possesses an extremely high-level API that allows us to simply and conveniently work with databases and CouchDB. Furthermore, the API that we will be working with is object-oriented. This means that the API is exposed solely as an inherited interface of an initialized object. In this particular case, that object is a database instance. Listing 12-3 demonstrates how to create such a reference.

Listing 12-3. Creating a DB Reference

```
var gbDataBase = couchDB.database('guestbook');
```

The code shown in Listing 12-3 leverages the method labeled "database," exposed by our couchDB instance, to initialize a Cradle database object. With this object, we will be able to work with documents and views that pertain to this particular database. What is important to understand is that the preceding code is not actually connected to CouchDB at the moment. Remember that HTTP is a stateless protocol. The moment a response is provided, the connection between the client and server are closed. Instead, our gb reference is nothing more than a wrapper that will be used to concentrate requests for a particular database. In this particular case, that database is labeled "guestbook." Once a reference to a particular database is created, we can reference its exposed API, to begin receiving and sending data between Node and CouchDB.

Cradle Database API

Because CouchDB's interface is exposed via mere HTTP requests, what will actually occur under the hood of the Cradle API will be a series of HTTP requests to the CouchDB server. However, as Cradle itself is a wrapper, it will perform these low-level tasks on our behalf. This allows us to focus on the five key methods of the API, shown in Table 12-1.

Table 12-1. Methods of a Cradle Wrapper

Methods	Description
create();	Used to create a database
exists(callback);	Used to determine if a database currently exists
get(id[,id] , [object], callback);	Used to fetch a particular document
view(id, [object] ,callback);	Used to query an existing view
save([id], object , callback);	Used to save a document to the current database. This can be used to save either a view or an entry.

The methods shown in Table 12-1 are the sole methods we will be working with in this chapter. Now, if that is not simple enough, then consider the following: four out of the five methods outlined above provide functionality of the sort we have already become familiar with from the previous sections.

create

The first method that we will review is the create method. Use of the create method provides our Node application with the ability to initialize a database within CouchDB. Use of the method is as simple as invoking the method upon a database reference, as seen in Listing 12-4.

Listing 12-4. Invoking the Creation of Our Database Reference

```
1 //..truncated code
8 var gbDataBase = couchDB.database('guestbook');
9    gbDataBase.create();
```

Listing 12-4 invokes the create method upon our existing gbDataBase instance. The code is equivalent to us having pressed the "Create Database..." button within the Futon interface.

Apache CouchDB prevents us from creating a database that possesses the same name as a database that currently exists. Because our CouchDB application is currently in possession of a database labeled "guestbook," the code from Listing 12-4 silently fails. This can be considered both a good thing and a bad thing. On one hand, it's great to know that you don't have to be concerned with possibly overwriting an existing database by mistake. However, on the other hand, you may rather be made aware if a database of the same name exists, so that you can provide a new name to the DB. For that, our DB instance exposes the exists method.

exists

The exists method is an asynchronous method used to determine if a database currently exists. The advantage of such a method is to determine whether a database already exists, lest we insert values to a table we did not intend to.

As an asynchronous method, the invocation of the exists call must be provided with a callback function. It is this function, whose signature reflects that of Listing 12-5, that will be triggered once Cradle has determined whether the database exists or not.

Listing 12-5. Callback Signature of the exists Method

```
function(err, exists);
```

As Listing 12-5 reveals, the callback supplied must be capable of receiving two arguments. The first parameter, err, accounts for any error that may have occurred, such as a network error. If no error has occurred, the argument provided will be that of null. The second parameter, exists, indicates whether the given database exists or not. The argument it will be provided if an error is not thrown will be that of a Boolean value.

Using these two parameters, we can determine the appropriate conditions that determine which code blocks to execute, as shown in Listing 12-6.

Listing 12-6. Determining If a Database Exists

```
 1 //...truncated code
 9 gbDataBase.exists(function(err, exists) {
10   if(err) {
11     console.log('error', err);
12   }else if (exists) {
13     console.log('the guestbook db exists');
14   }else {
15     console.log('database does not exists.');
16     gbDataBase.create();
17   }
18 });
```

Utilizing our gbDataBase reference, Listing 12-6 invokes the exists method exposed by the gbDataBase instance and supplies an anonymous function as the callback (**line 9**). Upon the callbacks invocation, it will be supplied with either an error instance or that of a Boolean. Utilizing both of these parameters, we can determine whether or not they possess a value to determine what blocks of code should be run.

If there is an error, our application will be provided with the ability to handle it (**line 10**). If the file exists, we can perform the invocation of another database (**line 13**). Last, if the database does not exist, we can successfully create it, utilizing the previously discussed `create` method (**line 16**).

If you were to execute Listing 12-6 in its totality, you would notice that the following is output in the command line: `the guestbook db exists`. Of course, this is expected, as we already had created the guestbook database. One good thing about this is that we also have a few documents stored within our guestbook database. This will become helpful when we review the next method in the Cradle interface.

get

The get method, as you may suspect, initiates HTTP requests utilizing the `GET` request method. The get method is used to obtain documents that are associated with the targeted database in an asynchronous fashion. The method's signature, as outlined in Table 12-1, reveals that the get method expects to be invoked with a possible three arguments. These arguments represent the document by its ID, an object, and a callback function.

The first parameter, `id`, can be provided either as a singular identifier or as an array of multiple document IDs supplied as an array. If you recall, a document ID is generally a GUID, such as `03e68a3bac3fd452bf6b136e76001222`, unless the document you seek is the result of a design document, in which case, it's you who must supply the full path to the query you are seeking to utilize, such as `_design/guests/_view/signatures`.

■ **Note** Every document possessed by a database can be obtained by supplying `_all_docs` as the string.

The second parameter of our get method is that of an object. The object itself represents the provision of optional query string parameters that we wish to accompany the request. Such parameters can be `ascending`, `descending`, `limit`, `key`, `startkey`, and, last, `endkey`, used to manipulate the resulting rows returned by our views.

The first two keys, `ascending` and `descending`, are self-explanatory. These parameters are used to sort the set of results in either an ascending or descending manner. The factor that determines whether an item comes before or after depends on the value that established the "key" used with the query. In the case of our guest/signature, the key was each user handle. The value that can be supplied to either of these keys is 1 or 0, whereby 1 equals `true` and 0 is `false`.

The parameter `limit` is used to express the maximum amount of desired results to be returned. This value should be expressed in the form of an integer.

The key parameter, as you may recall, must be provided a value of a string wrapped with double quotes. Providing this parameter can reduce the entire result set to that of a subset of rows whose keys match the value supplied. Providing `key="@CouchDB"` would result in our signature's query only displaying one result.

The final two parameters, `startkey` and `endkey` are used to return a subset of the original set of results whose keys are determined to exist within the indicated boundaries.

The provision of any query string you choose to apply to the `GET` request is required to appear as a key/value member of the object. Listing 12-7 demonstrates the use of the optional parameter to establish the use of the `limit` and `key` parameters. If you do not plan on using any parameters, just provide `null` as the value.

Listing 12-7. Query String Parameters Supplied As Members of an object

```
var queryString = { limit:1, key:"@CouchDB" };
```

The final parameter that must be provided to get is that of a callback. The callback whose signature can be seen in Listing 12-8 is required to possess two parameters.

Listing 12-8. Callback Signature for get

```
function(err, res);
```

Because get is an asynchronous method, it is necessary to provide a callback, so as to be informed when the operation has concluded. Furthermore, as outlined in Listing 12-8, our callback will be provided with an argument for either of the two outlined parameters, err and res. The first parameter, err, will be provided with an instance in the event that an error has occurred. Such an error may be related to network traffic or a server error. On the other hand, if everything is successful, our callback function will be provided with the appropriate JSON response.

Utilizing these two parameters, we can ensure the appropriate body of code is executed, lest we cause our own errors. Listing 12-9 demonstrates a GET request for our all_docs query.

Listing 12-9. Obtaining All Documents for the Target DB

```
 1 var cradle = require('../node_modules/cradle');
 2 var DBConnection = cradle.Connection;
 3 var couchDB = new DBConnection('127.0.0.1', 5984, {
 4  cache : true,
 5  raw : false,
 6  forceSave : true
 7 });

 8 var gbDataBase = couchDB.database('guestbook');

 9 gbDataBase.exists(function(err, exists) {
10  if (err) {
11   console.log('error', err);
12  } else if (exists) {
13   console.log('the guestbook db exists');
14  } else {
15   console.log('database does not exists.');
16   gbDataBase.create();
17  }
18 });
    /*obtain all documents*/
19 gbDataBase.get('_all_docs', { limit:1 }, function(err, res) {
20  if (err) {
21    console.log('error', err);
22  } else if (res) {
23    console.log(res);
24  } else {
25    //.. do something else
26  }
27 });
```

Listing 12-9 demonstrates the use of the get method to obtain a particular document from the guestbook database. In this particular case, that document is a query for all documents. Furthermore, we have chosen to limit the returned results to a maximum of one document. Running the preceding Node application results in the following output:

```
[ { id: '03e68a3bac3fd452bf6b136e76001222',
    key: '03e68a3bac3fd452bf6b136e76001222',
    value: { rev: '2-d91c1f744fe10e74dc5a2e8f23c13315' } } ]
```

As you can see, we have received a single result from the original set of results. Because we could potentially be working with a vast amount of results, CouchDB conveniently inserts each JSON result within an array structure, so that it can be easily traversed. As I hope you may be able to witness, the preceding output is no longer JSON but, rather, a JavaScript object. You can note this is the case, owing to the missing double quotes that would otherwise surround the keys if it were JSON. What this means is that we don't have to attempt to parse the returned JSON text, as Cradle has already performed this for us. Therefore, the response provided can immediately be traversed, and its members accessed. Let's remove the limit parameter and output only the ID of each row. Listing 12-10 outlines in bold the changes to our get method.

Listing 12-10. Logging the ID of Each Returned JSON Document

```
 1 //..truncated code
   /*obtain all documents*/
19 gbDataBase.get('_all_docs', { limit:1 }, function(err, res) {
20  if (err) {
21   console.log('error', err);
22  } else if (res) {
23     var len = res.length;
24     for (var i = 0; i < len; i++) {
25         console.log(res[i].id);
26     }
27  } else {
28   .. do something else
29  }
30 });
```

Listing 12-10 traverses each of the indexes within the provided JavaScript array until all have been reached. With each value obtained, we log out the corresponding ID, resulting in the following output below:

```
03e68a3bac3fd452bf6b136e76001222
03e68a3bac3fd452bf6b136e76001eec
_design/guests
```

As you can see from the output, our guestbook database is currently in possession of three documents, two of which possess GUIDs as their identifiers, and one of which utilizes a string. Knowing what is currently retained within our database and what was outputted, we could easily deduce that these two GUIDs represent our two guestbook entries, while the latter represents our query. However, now that we have obtained the resulting identifiers, we could easily obtain the values retained by each ID with subsequent use of the get method.

view

While the results of a view can be obtained via get, a simpler method is to use the view method. Because view actually wraps get, it invites us to provide a more succinct path to our query. As I mentioned within the section on get, a design document can be obtained by specifying a full path, such as the following: '_design/guests/_view/signatures'. However, this path can appear rather long and be cumbersome to work with.

With view, you have the ability to query a view simply by omitting _design and _view from the preceding path, resulting in the more succinct path guest/signatures. Each design document and its view can easily be fetched by simply joining the two names together with a forward slash. You may recall "Design Document" and "View Name" as the titles of fields shown in Figure 12-13.

The view method possesses a few more behaviors that can improve efficiency, but they are beyond the scope of this book. However, aside from those unmentionables, the view method continues to function in precisely the same manner as get. It continues to require the object parameter for added query parameters, and last, because it is an asynchronous function, it requires a callback function whose signature is the same as that provided to get. At this point, let's query our guestbook database for any and all signatures left behind (see Listing 12-11).

Listing 12-11. Querying Our DB for All Signatures

```
var cradle = require('../node_modules/cradle');
var DBConnection = cradle.Connection;
var couchDB = new DBConnection('127.0.0.1', 5984, {
 cache : true,
 raw : false,
 forceSave : true
});

var gbDataBase = couchDB.database('guestbook');

gbDataBase.exists(function(err, exists) {
 if (err) {
  console.log('error', err);
 } else if (exists) {
  console.log('the guestbook db exists');
 } else {
  console.log('database does not exists.');
  gbDataBase.create();
 }
});

/*obtain an existing view*/
gbDataBase.view('guests/signatures', null, function(err, res) {
 console.log(res);
});
```

Listing 12-11 reveals in bold the latest change to our running base code. Rather than using the get method exposed by our gbDataBase instance, we opt for the more succinct method of defining our path with view. Running the preceding Node application results in the following output:

```
[ { id: '03e68a3bac3fd452bf6b136e76001eec',
    key: '@apache',
    value:
     { handle: '@apache',
       message: 'Hello World',
       _id: '03e68a3bac3fd452bf6b136e76001eec' } },
  { id: '03e68a3bac3fd452bf6b136e76001222',
    key: '@CouchDB',
    value:
     { handle: '@CouchDB',
       message: 'greetings and salutations',
       _id: '03e68a3bac3fd452bf6b136e76001222' } } ]
```

The preceding code outputs the two presently saved signatures and messages provided by both @apache and @CouchDB. Because view leverages the get method, we can opt to provide our request with the addition of query string parameters. Listing 12-12 demonstrates a query that filters the preceding results with the use of the key parameter.

Listing 12-12. Filtering All Signatures for a Particular Key

```
//.. truncated code

/*obtain an existing view*/
gbDataBase.view('guests/signatures', {key:"@CouchDB"} , function(err, res) {
    console.log(res);
});
```

Listing 12-12 replaces the null primitive with that of an object whose sole member is that of the key parameter. The preceding code will result in the HTTP GET request for the following URL: 127.0.0.1:5984/ guestbook/_design/guests/_view/signatures?key="@CouchDB". By providing a key, the result set will be filtered there by returning a subset of results whose keys match those of "@CouchDB". Running the preceding listing outputs the following:

```
[ { id: '03e68a3bac3fd452bf6b136e76001222',
    key: '@CouchDB',
    value:
     { handle: '@CouchDB',
       message: 'greetings and salutations',
       _id: '03e68a3bac3fd452bf6b136e76001222' } } ]
```

As you can see, the output displayed only reveals a signature left by the handle @CouchDB. If it just so happened that @CouchDB signed our guestbook more times, all of those results would be returned.

With that being said, the next method will provide us with the ability to create more documents.

save

The save method, as the name suggests, allows us to save documents for the targeted database. As its signature reveals in Table 12-1, the save method anticipates three parameters: id, object, and callback.

The first parameter, id, is used to provide an identity to the document being created. As you have undoubtedly witnessed, any and all documents have a corresponding ID. These are usually generated as GUIDs by CouchDB; however, they can also represent the name of a design document. To keep things flexible, save enables us to opt in to supplying an ID as the first parameter. If an ID is not provided, CouchDB will generate it automatically. If, however, an ID is provided, it will replace the ID that will have been generated by CouchDB.

If the document being created represents a view, you will be required to supply an appropriate ID. Remember: All views must be prefixed with _design/ in order for CouchDB to differentiate between ordinary documents and design documents.

The second parameter that will be supplied to save is that of the document's content. If we were to re-create our initial document with save, it would be provided with the following object:

```
{
    "handle": "@CouchDB",
    "message": "greetings and salutations"
}
```

Providing ordinary document content is fairly straightforward. On the other hand, if we were to re-create our "signatures" view, the object that would be required reflects the one following:

```
views: {
 signatures: {
  map:"function(doc) {emit( doc.handle, {handle:doc.handle, message:doc.message, _id:doc.
id}); }";
 }
};
```

Because a design document will be saved as its own JSON document, it is necessary to use the members that define its content appropriately. While at a glance this might be confusing, the reality is that this will always be the format for constructing a map function.

Note the complex structure of the preceding object. All design documents begin with a key labeled views, where views represents the top-level object and is used to reference yet another complex structure.

The complex structure of views consists of any number of object members, in which each member represents an individual query. In the preceding outline, the member signatures represents a possible query associated with our view.

Each query references an object whose only allowable members are the following two: map and reduce. While both map and reduce can be used simultaneously, this chapter does not make use of the reduce member and, therefore, it has been omitted. We will be working exclusively with map.

The member map holds a string value whereby that string can be evaluated by CouchDB to produce our actual query.

The final parameter of the save method is that of a callback. As an asynchronous method, save requires a callback to invoke when the operation has concluded. As outlined in Listing 12-13, the callback provided should possess the following parameters: err and res.

Listing 12-13. Callback Signature for save

```
function(err, res);
```

Depending on whether an error has occurred, the `err` parameter will either be supplied with an object or a `null` primitive. Furthermore, if an error has not occurred and the response is successful, we will be able to reference that response via the `res` parameter. Using these two parameters, we can ensure that the appropriate body of code is executed, lest we cause our own errors.

Creating Documents via Cradle

Having learned how to work with the save method, let's attempt to create some new documents, beginning with yet another guestbook signing, as seen in Listing 12-14.

Listing 12-14. Creating a Document via Cradle

```
1 //..truncated code

/*signing of our guestbook*/
19  gbDataBase.save({
20    handle : "@CouchDB",
21    message : "welcome and thank you",
22  time : new Date()
23    }, function(err, res) {
24    if (err) {
25      console.log('error', err);
26    } else if (res) {
27      console.log(res);
28      }
29 });
```

Listing 12-14 demonstrates the implementation required by Cradle to create a new document for our guestbook database. As you can see, we opted out of providing this document with a specific ID. As I have previously stated, it's often best to allow this value to be generated by CouchDB.

The body of our document has been devised to possess a user's name and message, in fields labeled "handle" and "message." In addition to the previous fields, this document also possesses a field that reflects the time of its creation. While our previous documents lack this "time" field, it is one of the benefits of using NoSQL databases over SQL databases. I will discuss this in more detail shortly.

■ **Note** Cradle methods require the provision of an object that will be stringified prior to its transmission to CouchDB, where it will be encapsulated within a document as JSON.

Last, we have provided a callback to be notified as to whether the document has been successfully created or not. Running Listing 12-14, should no network issues be present, will result in the following output:

```
{ ok: true,
  id: '03e68a3bac3fd452bf6b136e760064b4',
  rev: '1-66821f76618071e197e2c3aa79ecf722' }
```

As you can see, upon the creation of a document, CouchDB responds with the details of that newly created document. As signified by the ok field and its value of true, we can rest assured that CouchDB has successfully stored our document, in which case, we would be able to see it through the Futon interface.

Upon navigating your browser to http://127.0.0.1:5984/_utils/database.html?guestbook/_design/guests/_view/signatures, CouchDB will present you with three signatures. Sure enough, as seen in Figure 12-17, our most recent document appears within the signature results. Furthermore, the inclusion of the new field, time, did not have any negative impact on our signature query. Because our query did not anticipate a field labeled as "time," that value, whether it exists or not, has no bearing on that particular function.

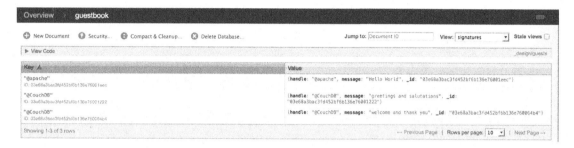

Figure 12-17. *Cradle document successfully created in CouchDB*

The last time we visited the preceding URL, only two documents were presented. Upon this query, as discussed early on in this chapter, any new changes are resubmitted to the anonymous function and accounted for as a row within the provided results.

Now that we have more than one result whose key is that of @CouchDB, let's revisit our ability to filter results for an identified key simply by appending ?key="@CouchDB" to the preceding URL. Upon receiving a response to http://127.0.0.1:5984/guestbook/_design/guests/_view/signatures?key="@CouchDB", you will find yourself presented with two rows.

SQL databases that make use of tables to store data require all fields that will be used for a project to be made known up front, so that a column can be used to retain that value. This behavior requires that all data utilize each predetermined field. If a value for those fields is not specified, a default value must be provided, lest there be an error while running a query.

On the other hand, NoSQL databases do not rely on tables to store data. Instead, they store data in individual documents, like those we have been working with. Because each document represents its own body of data, it can possess any variety of fields it chooses.

Creating Design Documents via Cradle

As we have just recently stored a document that makes use of the time in which it was created, we should devise a query that can map all documents for our guestbook database into their own view. One thing we will have to keep in mind is that if an object does not possess the time field, we must make certain not to populate our view with the current document. Such a query is reflected in Listing 12-15.

Listing 12-15. Creating a Design Document to Possess Multiple Views

```
 1 //..truncated code

19 /*saving of a view*/
20 gbDataBase.save('_design/guests', {
21 views : {
22  sigTime : {
23   map : "function( doc ){ "+
24              "if(doc.time){" +
25               "emit(doc.handle,{ handle:doc.handle, time:doc.time,
                  message:doc.message });" +
26              "}" +
27           "}"
28  },
29  signatures : {
30   map : "function(doc) {" +
31              "emit(doc.handle,{ handle:doc.handle,message:doc.message });" +
32           "}"
33  }
34 }
35 }, function(err, res) {
36  if (err) {
37   console.log('error', err);
38  } else if (res) {
39   console.log(res);
40  }
41 });
```

Listing 12-15 outlines in bold the key elements of our new design document. The first item I will discuss is that saving a design document with the name of a document that exists will overwrite the original content of that document. In the preceding listing, I am opting to save the current design document with the name of an existing one, in order to show you that you can have multiple views within a design document.

Using the save method and the required complex structure for a design document, this view will be used to provide two queries regarding our guestbook. These two queries are signatures and sigTime. The view signatures is, in fact, the same query used previously; however, as this update will be overwriting the existing _design/guests document, we must provide this view in addition to our sigTime, lest it be deleted. However the view sigTime reflects an entirely new query, which will be used to create a view to reveal only documents that possess the time field.

As you can see within the lines of 24 and 26, our map function determines if the document supplied does indeed possess a field labeled time. Only if the field is present will our function emit a new row for this view. Running, Listing 12-15, should no network issues be present, will result in the following output:

```
{ ok: true,
  id: '_design/guests',
  rev: '2-b0723b44888089eeecf790a1c3e37824' }
```

You may be able to note that the result returned is no different than that we received when saving an ordinary document. However, what is different, aside from the IDs, is that as this file has been updated, its revision now reflects version 2.

Now that we have two views, let's visit our Futon interface once again and take a moment see the results it provides. Figure 12-18 reveals our two views within the drop-down menu at the top-right-hand side of the interface.

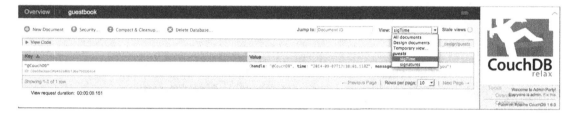

Figure 12-18. *sigTime and signatures successfully created as queries of guests*

As you can see from Figure 12-18, both queries reside under the same document ID, yet either can be used to provide its own set of results. Feel free to toggle between the two views and note how the results vary.

EXERCISE 12-1. PERSISTING INCOMING DATA

In Chapter 11, you learned how to receive, authorize, and process incoming JSON. Using a form along with Ajax, we have been posting users' first and last names to our Node application. Up until now, we have not been retaining those names. In fact, all we have been doing is returning the extracted values as the entity body of the request. Using Cradle, create a new database labeled "visitors" and retain all incoming names.

Last, provide the incoming request with the response supplied by CouchDB with each use of the save method. You can compare your code with that of Listing 12-16.

Hint: Remember that Cradle provides all response as JavaScript objects. However, a response can only be supplied as a string.

Listing 12-16 leverages the code in Listing 11-3 from Chapter 11 and incorporates the changes discussed in this chapter. The additions from this chapter appear in bold.

Listing 12-16. Incorportaing Cradle with an Existing HTTP Node Application

```
/*require*/
var cradle = require('../node_modules/cradle');
var http = require('http');

/*HTTP*/
var server = http.createServer();
server.addListener('request', requestHandler);
server.listen(1337, '127.0.0.1');
```

```
/*Cradle*/
var DBConnection = cradle.Connection;
var couchDB = new DBConnection('127.0.0.1', 5984, {
 cache : true,
 raw : false,
 forceSave : true
});
/*create visitors database*/
var gbDataBase = couchDB.database('visitors');
    gbDataBase.create();

/* handle incoming requests */
function requestHandler(request, response) {

 if (request.method === "POST") {
  var incomingEntity = '';
  var data;

  request.addListener('data', function(chunk) {
   incomingEntity += chunk;
  });

  request.addListener("end", function() {
   if (request.headers['content-type'].indexOf("application/json") > -1) {
    data = JSON.parse(incomingEntity);
   } else if (request.headers['content-type'].indexOf("application/x-www-form-urlencoded") > -1) {
    data = parseQueryStringToObject(incomingEntity);
    return;
   }
   saveToDB(data, response);
  });

 } else if (request.method === "GET") {
  if (request.url === "/index.html") {
   response.statusCode = 200;
   response.setHeader("Content-type", "text/html");
   response.write('<!doctype html>');
   response.write('<html lang="en">');
   response.write('<body>');
   response.write('<form action="formPost" method="POST" onsubmit="return ajax();"
   content="application/x-www-form-urlencoded">');
   response.write('First-Name:');
   response.write('<input name="fname" type="text" size="25"/>');
   response.write('Last-Name:');
   response.write('<input name="lname" type="text" size="25"/>');
   response.write('<input type="submit"/>');
   response.write('</form>');
   response.write('<script>');
   response.write('function ajax(){');
   response.write('var xhr = new XMLHttpRequest();');
   response.write('xhr.open("POST", "formPost");');
```

```
    response.write('xhr.onload=function(){ alert(this.responseText);};');
    response.write('xhr.setRequestHeader("Content-Type", "application/json");');
    response.write('xhr.setRequestHeader("Accept", "application/json");');
    response.write('var input = document.getElementsByTagName("input");');
    response.write('var obj = {');
    response.write('fname : input[0].value,');
    response.write('lname : input[1].value');
    response.write('};');
    response.write('xhr.send(JSON.stringify(obj));');
    response.write('return false;');
    response.write('}');
    response.write('</script>');
    response.write(' </body>');
    response.write('</html>');
    response.end();

  } else {
    response.statusCode = 204;
    response.end();
  }
} else if (request.method === "OPTIONS") {
  response.statusCode = 200;
  if (request.url === "/formPost") {
    response.setHeader("Access-Control-Allow-Origin", '*');
    response.setHeader("Access-Control-Allow-Headers", 'Content-Type, Accept,
        Accept-Language,Accept-Encoding, User-Agent, Host, Content-Length, Connection,
        Cache-Control');
    response.setHeader("Access-Control-Allow-Methods", 'GET, POST, OPTIONS');
  }
  response.end();
}
console.log("response=-end");
};
console.log('Server running at http://127.0.0.1:1337/index.html');

var saveToDB = function(obj, response) {
 gbDataBase.save(obj, function(err, res) {
  response.setHeader("Access-Control-Allow-Origin", "*");
  if (err) {
   response.statusCode = 500;
   console.log('error', err);
  } else if (res) {
   response.statusCode = 200;
   var stringResponse = JSON.stringify(res);
   response.setHeader("Content-Type", "application/json");
   response.setHeader("Content-Length", Buffer.byteLength(stringResponse, 'utf8'));
   response.write(stringResponse);
  }
  response.end();
 });
};
```

240

```
var parseQueryStringToObject = function(queryString) {
 var params = {}, queries, temp, i, l;
 // Split into key/value pairs
 queries = queryString.split("&");
 // Convert the array of strings into an object
 for ( i = 0, l = queries.length; i < l; i++) {
  temp = queries[i].split('=');
  params[temp[0]] = temp[1];
 }
 return params;
};
```

Summary

This chapter demonstrated the persistence of JSON from the perspective of the server. In contrast to persisting data via the client, as we achieved in Chapter 7, persisting data on the server can offer a whole lot more advantages.

For starters, visitors cannot delete their data simply by clearing cache or deleting their cookies. As the database resides behind HTTP requests, our application can safeguard the data from specific requests, thereby offloading the control of what is saved/deleted to our application. Additionally, because all data is being retained in a centralized location rather than on visitors' browsers, we can perform unique queries to organize our data and make connections between those using our applications.

CouchDB is a convenient way in which we can construct a document-oriented database. Furthermore, because the content within each document is JSON, our applications are more flexible than those of traditional SQL databases.

Key Points from This Chapter

- CouchDB is a NoSQL database.

- NoSQL databases store their data as JSON within individual documents.

- CouchDB leverages the power of JSON and JavaScript to create a powerful and open source database.

- CouchDB's API is simply HTTP requests.

- Futon is a wrapper that allows us to get up and running with CouchDB immediately.

- A query in CouchDB is referred to as a *view*.

- A document that contains a view is referred to as a *design document*.

- The emit function populates a new row.

- emit can be called as many or as few times per document as you like.

- Cradle is a Node module that can be installed to wrap all HTTP requests.

■ ■ ■

CHAPTER 13

Working with Templates

Generally speaking, a template is a tool that is used to structure as well as provide consistency among interchangeable parts. The benefit, with regard to interchangeable parts, is that they can be used both interchangeably and indistinguishably within an existing structure, provided they adhere to a template. The ability to allow for interchangeability is beneficial in all walks of life. The flexibility that templates offer has reinforced their utility as dependable tools in the development of modern web sites. The pairing of templates and web development has been proven to alleviate the tightly coupled architecture concerning layout and the data that it utilizes.

Owing to their nature, templates have become the backbone of many platforms, resulting in the prevalence of content management systems (CMS) such as WordPress, Drupal, and more. For the most part, these platforms use dynamic server-side programming to embed content from a database layout. However, with the prevalence of Ajax, and the fact that change is constant, it was only a matter of time before templates were being applied to the front end. Today, there is a variety of templating engines available to choose from. A few examples are Dust, JSRender, Moustache, and Handlebars, all of which rely on JSON.

Templating Engine

A templating engine, with regard to front-end development, is simply a library that binds data with markup on the fly or otherwise dynamically. This could occur at runtime or even performed at design time.

Up until now, while we have not been using a templating engine, we have been performing a similar functionality nonetheless. You may recall that in Chapter 8, we used JavaScript not only to trigger an XMLHttpRequest but to additionally append the returned JSON result set of book covers to our HTML document. This was achieved by the code shown in Listing 13-1.

Listing 13-1. An Ajax Request with the Incorporation of Markup

```
<!DOCTYPE html>
<html lang="en">
<head></head>
 <body>
  <ul id="image-container"></ul>
  <script>
    function loadImages() {
        var ul= document.getElementById("image-container");
        var xhr= new XMLHttpRequest();
            xhr.open("GET", "data/imagesA.json");
            xhr.onload = function() {
                var data= JSON.parse( this.responseText );
                var list = data.images;
```

```
                    for (var i = 0; i < list.length; i++) {
                        var image = list[i];
                        var listItem = document.createElement("li");
                        var img = document.createElement("img");
                            img.src = image.url;
                            img.alt = image.title;
                        listItem.appendChild(img);
                        ul.appendChild(listItem);
                    };
                };
                xhr.send();
        };
        loadImages();
    </script>
  </body>
</html>
```

The preceding listing relies on string manipulation and DOM scripting to augment the returned JSON data set at runtime into a presentable list of images utilizing HTML elements, as shown in Figure 13-1.

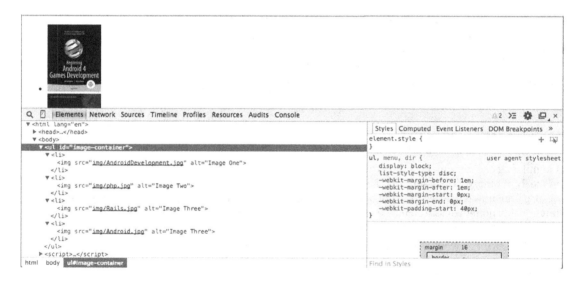

***Figure 13-1.** Revealing the markup of our dynamic inclusion of loaded data*

In the preceding example, the HTML elements required to produce the layout have been entangled with our HTTP request, which makes our application convoluted. Not only is our markup not located where it ought to be, in an HTML document, but in their object-oriented form, the elements are not instantly recognizable as HTML elements.

```
var listItem = document.createElement("li");
var img = document.createElement("img");
    img.src = image.url;
    img.alt = image.title;
    listItem.appendChild(img);
```

The preceding isolated code is the presentational style that will be adopted by each item that exists within our data set, making the JavaScript code our template. While this works, the code itself is not very optimal or legible, for that matter. Furthermore, as we are integrating HTML within JavaScript, we are thereby making readability and maintainability all the more challenging. Last, as JavaScript, we lose the innate ability of most IDE's to validate our template as proper markup at design time.

Use of a templating engine has the ability to change all of that; however, it requires that we think a bit more abstractly, as you will soon see.

Handlebars

Handlebars itself is not a programming language but, rather, a JavaScript templating engine. However, it does, for all intents and purposes, possess its own lingua franca and syntax, to enable the desired templating behavior.

As stated on the Handlebars web site, located at handlebarsjs.com, "Handlebars provides the power necessary to let you build **semantic templates** effectively with no frustration." What this means is that rather than using JavaScript to define our templates, as in the preceding example, Handlebars utilizes a more elegant templating system that employs the semantic tags of HTML. This will manage to keep our code clean and extensible.

Installation

In order to make use of the Handlebars library, we must first obtain the latest source code to incorporate into our HTML documents. We can obtain the latest source code by navigating to http://handlebarsjs.com/ and clicking the bright orange button labeled "Download: 2.0.0." (See Figure 13-2.) This will download the latest version of the Handlebars source code (currently version 2.0.0).

Figure 13-2. Handlebars main page

As shown in Figure 13-2, you can witness a link just below the orange button. This hyperlink reads "Download: runtime-2.0.0." These two items are not one in the same and are used for different purposes, so be sure to click directly on the button. Clicking this button will begin the download process. Feel free to save the file to a location of your choosing.

■ **Note**   The runtime 2.0.0 library is only to be utilized by templates that have been pre-compiled.

Once the download has completed, navigate to the directory in which it was saved. Once you have located the handlebars-v2.0.0.js file, move it to a more suitable location for use in our exercises. If you are following along with the source code for this chapter, you will note that I have already provided this chapter with the handlebars-v2.0.0 JavaScript file located within the directory structure at BeginningJSON/chapter13/js/libs/. If you have been working with your own folder structure, feel free to move handlebars-v2.0.0 to a location relative to your HTML documents.

Once the Handlebars library has been downloaded, all one must do is incorporate it within each HTML document intended to use the templating engine. This is easily achieved by incorporating an external script via the HTML <script> element, as seen in Listing 13-2.

Listing 13-2. Including the Handlebars Library

```
<!DOCTYPE html>
<html lang="en">
 <head>
   <script src="js/libs/handlebars-v2.0.0.js"></script>
 </head>
 <body>
   <script>
      alert(Handlebars);
   </script>
 </body>
</html>
```

Listing 13-2 incorporates the Handlebars version 2.0.0 templating engine into the head of the page utilizing the HTML <script> tag. Furthermore, to ensure that the library is properly incorporated, I have chosen to output the global Handlebars reference. If an alert of [Object, Object] is displayed within the alert box, then congratulations, you have successfully loaded the Handlebars object. This is a global object that exposes a few methods that will be used to work with our Handlebars templates. We are now ready to begin defining templates with Handlebars.

Working with Handlebars

The libraries name, *Handlebars*, is a nod to the tokens it makes use of to demarcate placeholders within a template. These tokens are the opening and closing curly braces, ({, }), which, when turned in the appropriate 90-degree direction, resemble a handlebar moustache, hence the name *Handlebars*. These handlebars are then used to demarcate an expression within a template.

A Basic Expression

A basic expression, or placeholder, as it is commonly referred to, is the building block of the Handlebars templating engine. Simply enough, the placeholder syntax is none other than the reference to a key, wrapped within two curly braces, such as the following {{key}}. This placeholder is referred to as an *expression*, because, at runtime, it will be replaced by the value of a key/value pair possessed by a collection with a member that matches the specified key. Furthermore, it is the most basic expression within Handlebars and is used to replace static elements, such as strings and/or numbers. You will learn about more complex expressions in a later section. First, however, let's ease into the immersion of Handlebars by analyzing the use of a Handlebars basic expression (see Listing 13-3).

Listing 13-3. Simplest Use of a Handlebars Template

```
<!DOCTYPE html>
<html lang="en">
 <head>
  <meta charset="utf-8">
  <script src="js/libs/handlebars-v2.0.0.js"></script>
 </head>
 <body>
  <script type="application/x-handlebars" id="Handlebar-Name-Template">
   <span> {{name}} </span>
  </script>
  <script type="application/javascript">
   var initialTemplateWrapper = document.getElementById("Handlebar-Name-Template");
   var initialTemplateContent = initialTemplateWrapper.innerHTML;
   var dynamicTempate = Handlebars.compile(initialTemplateContent);
   var markupOutput = dynamicTempate({ "name" : "ben" });
      document.getElementsByTagName("body")[0].innerHTML = markupOutput;
  </script>
 </body>
</html>
```

Listing 13-3 reveals in its entirety a succinct Handlebars template and the few lines of JavaScript code required to make our template functional. Running the preceding listing results in the document revealing the name ben, surrounded by opening and closing span tags. In order to best understand what is taking place in Listing 13-3, the upcoming sections will break down the preceding code into four topics.

Defining a Handlebars Template

Defining a Handlebars template is a simple process of designing a semantic layout using ordinary HTML elements and denoting, inline, any basic expression to be replaced with actual data at a later point in time. Before we get into the syntax of the language, let's begin by analyzing the design of a simple template. The most basic implementation of a template that can be designed in Handlebars is one that uses a single placeholder, as shown in Listing 13-4.

Listing 13-4. A Single Expression Template

```
1  <!DOCTYPE html>
2  <html lang="en">
3   <head>
4    <meta charset="utf-8">
5    <script src="js/libs/handlebars-v2.0.0.js"></script>
```

```
 6   </head>
 7   <body>
 8     <script type="text/x-handlebars-template" id="Handlebar-Name-Template">
 9       <span class="name">{{name}}<span>
10     </script>
11   </body>
12   </html>
```

Listing 13-4 demonstrates a simple template that makes use of a single placeholder to be filled in dynamically once data is provided. The lines in bold define our Handlebars template. Let's walk through these lines of code, to better understand what is taking place.

Listing 13-4 begins as any ordinary HTML document. However, what makes this page extraordinary is the incorporation of the Handlebars library. We utilize the script tag to load into the document the external Handlebars library, so that we can begin making use of its templating engine (**line 5**). Of course, along with a template engine, we require a template. The code highlighted in bold makes up a Handlebars template. However, the surrounding `<script>` tag plays a rather important part in the template as well.

It may come as a shock, but our template is not considered JavaScript, as noted in the `type` attribute of the script tag. Rather, the script type is assigned the value of `text`. To be more specific, it's a particular subset of `text` that defines a Handlebars template. I will explain why this is important shortly. The content within our script tag, as denoted by the type, is that of our Handlebar template.

Within the template, which we have defined, is nothing more than a single placeholder contained within a `<span>` element. The two braces that surround our placeholder easily identify a basic expression within a Handlebars template. An expression, as we have learned in JavaScript, is simply the evaluation and return of data. In other words, the basic expression, `{{name}}`, will later be interpolated with the value retained by a member that matches the expression, within the given context of the data provided. Furthermore, as the term *template* implies, every time we reference this particular template, we can expect to generate an HTML span tag with an arbitrary name within.

If we were to run the preceding listing, I'm afraid we'd be presented with an empty document, as shown in Figure 13-3. The reason why is simple. Currently, our document lacks any HTML markup to render. If you were expecting our template to render, the reason why it doesn't is owing to the use of the `<script>` tag that surrounds it.

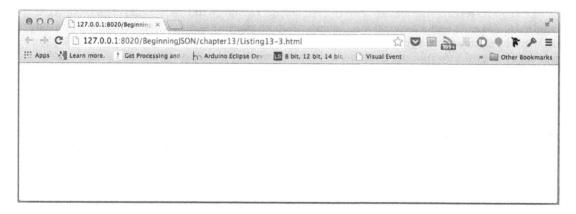

Figure 13-3. *An empty document*

■ **Note** By default, the `<script>` tag exhibits a CSS display property of none.

The Role of <script>

Wrapping our template within the script element provides several advantages. The first is that it cleverly removes our template from being rendered by the document, lest we reveal our placeholders to our visitors. Per the W3C spec, any script tag will forgo rendering, as it will be supplied to the appropriate script engine to be evaluated. However, as our Handlebars template does not define JavaScript, the last thing we want to do is supply our Handlebars template to the script engine, where it would be parsed as such. For this reason, we provision the type attribute with a scripting language that our browser will not be able to recognize. In our example, we have provided the scripting language of `text/x-handlebars-template`.

Signifying that our script contains a Handlebars template not only thwarts the user-agent from supplying it to a script engine but helps to immediately identify it as a Handlebars template to any and all developers.

Provided we use the script tag as outlined previously, our template provides zero impact to the document. This is one of the greatest advantages that accompanies our Handlebar templates. This enables us to define a template inline. While this may not seem to be much at first, there is a lot to be said from a maintainability standpoint, by associating our template within the markup that will utilize it.

Last, a final benefit of our script element is that, as with all elements, we can refer to it by a particular ID. In our existing example, our template can be referenced via the identity `Handlebar-Name-Template`. Having the ability to reference our template by ID will become necessary, as you will soon see in the upcoming section.

Compiling a Template

At this point, all we have managed to do is define a template that our template engine will use. However, as you have just recently discovered, a template alone has no effect on our document. In order for a template to work, it must be provided to the Handlebars library, so that it can be compiled into a JavaScript function. For this, we are required to provide the content for the script ID, `Handlebar-Name-Template`, to the compile method exposed by the global Handlebars object. Adding five lines of code to our existing markup achieves this, as shown in Listing 13-5.

Listing 13-5. Compiling Our `Handlebar-Name-Template`

```
1  <!DOCTYPE html>
2  <html lang="en">
3    <head>
4     <meta charset="utf-8">
5     <script src="js/libs/handlebars-v2.0.0.js"></script>
6    </head>
7    <body>
8      <script type="text/x-handlebars-template" id="Handlebar-Name-Template">
9        <span class="name"> {{name}} <span>
10     </script>
11     <script type="application/javascript">
```

```
12        var templateWrapper = document.getElementById("Handlebar-Name-Template");
13        var templateContent = templateWrapper.innerHTML;
14        var tempateFunction = Handlebars.compile(templateContent);
16     </script>
17    </body>
18    </html>
```

Listing 13-5 reveals, in bold, the five lines that are used to transform our template into a function that can be called repeatedly and be provided a JSON argument. As indicated by line 11, the ability to compile a template requires just a bit of good old-fashioned JavaScript.

The first line of JavaScript code (line 12) is used to target the specific template that we wish to compile. Leveraging the document method getElementById and supplying the value of Handlebar-Name-Template easily obtains a reference to the HTML script element containing our template. To keep our code clean and readable, I assign the returned element to that of a variable labeled templateWrapper.

The next step is to extract the text that occurs between the script element's opening and closing tag. For this we use the innerHTML property, and once again, we assign the returned value to another variable. In this case, that variable is labeled templateContent. Once we have a reference to our template, all that is left is to provide it as the argument to the compile method exposed by our global Handlebars object.

Giving Context to Our Template

Supplying a template to the compile method results in the return of a JavaScript function, which can be assigned to a variable so that it can be called over and over again. As revealed by the signature displayed in Listing 13-6, this function, when invoked, accepts a JSON argument.

Listing 13-6. Signature of Our Template Function

```
function( object );
```

The object provided to the function is referred to in Handlebars nomenclature as the *context*. The context is named such because it represents the model and/or data set from which all Handlebars expressions (placeholders) derive their value. (See Listing 13-7.)

Listing 13-7. A Compiled Template Is Used to Render JSON Data into Markup

```
10    //..truncated code
11    <script type="application/javascript">
12      var templateWrapper = document.getElementById("Handlebar-Name-Template");
13      var templateContent = templateWrapper.innerHTML;
14      var templateFunction = Handlebars.compile(templateContent);
15      var outputMarkup = templateFunction({ "name":"ben" });
17      alert( outputMarkup );
16    </script>
17    </body>
18    </html>
```

Listing 13-7 adds to our existing code base the two lines shown in bold. The first new line (line 15) invokes templateFunction and provisions it with a JSON collection consisting of one key/value pair. You may note that the key which our JSON possesses is equivalent to the label with the placeholder used by our template. This is not simply a matter of coincidence. I mentioned earlier that interchangeable parts could be used both interchangeably and indistinguishably within an existing structure, providing they adhere to the structure of a template. In other words, the label used to represent our placeholder is replaced, or interpolated, with the corresponding value of a key of the same name, if it exists as a member on the context provided. When a template is compiled via `Handlebars.compile`, it is transformed into a JavaScript function. When said function is invoked with JSON as an argument, the implementation of the function relies on string manipulation to assign values from our JSON to our placeholders and returns, upon its conclusion, a string. This is not unlike our Ajax request in Listing 13-1. The only difference is that the JavaScript function is not created at design time, but, rather, it is created on the fly at runtime. This takes place the moment the reference to `Handlebars.compile` is parsed by the script engine. Once the function has been executed, the result is provided back to the caller of the function.

The second line of code added to our page simply alerts us to the result, as shown in Figure 13-4.

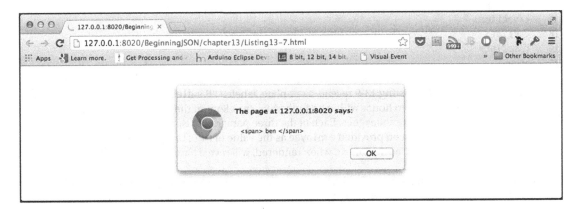

Figure 13-4. *The rendered output of data*

As revealed by Figure 13-4, the output that results from `templateFunction` is none other than the string representation `<span> ben </span>`. At this point, we can append the resulting string to our HTML document with some very simple DOM scripting. Furthermore, each invocation of our template function can be provided with varying contexts, thus allowing the resulting output to vary with each invocation, as shown in Listing 13-8.

Listing 13-8. Repeated Use of `templateFunction` with Varying Contexts

```
var outputMarkup;
    outputMarkup = templateFunction({ "name":"ben" });
      console.log( outputMarkup );  // <span> ben </span>
    outputMarkup = templateFunction({ "name":"ivan" });
      console.log( outputMarkup );  // <span> ivan </span>
    outputMarkup = templateFunction({ "name":"michael" });
      console.log( outputMarkup );  // <span> michael </span>
```

Multiple Placeholders

A template needn't consist of a single placeholder. Because a placeholder is simply a reference to a key within a provided context, it's entirely possible to construct templates that reference multiple placeholders. However, it generally helps to begin with just the one. Listing 13-9 demonstrates how multiple placeholders can be used to produce a more complex template.

Listing 13-9. Use of Multiple Placeholders Within a Template

```
   //..truncated code
 8 <body>
 9   <section id="directory">
10    <script type="application/x-handlebars" id="Handlebar-Employee-Template">
11     <div class="employee">
12       <p> firstName: {{fName}} </p>
13       <p> lastName:  {{lName}} </p>
14       <p> contact:   {{phone}} </p>
15     </div>
16    </script>
17   </section>
18   <script>
19   </script>
20 </body>
```

The markup used within Listing 13-9 reveals a template, labeled "Handlebar-Employee-Template." This particular template is intended to house within an individual `<p>` element the first and last name, as well as the contact number, of one of my colleagues. Each of the three paragraphs is, furthermore, contained within a parenting `<div>` tag that has been provided employee as the value of the class attribute. By providing a class identifier to the template, each context, when rendered, will reveal a uniformly styled element upon its inclusion into the document.

With our template having been defined, all that remains is to provide the implementation that compiles Handlebar-Employee-Template, as well as supply it a context or two to be rendered. (See Listing 13-10.)

Listing 13-10. The JavaScript Code Required to Insert Data into a Document, with the Proper Presentation

```
17  //Truncated code...
18 <script type="application/javascript">
19    var initialTemplateWrapper = document.getElementById("Handlebar-Employee-Template");
20    var initialTemplateContent = initialTemplateWrapper.innerHTML;
21    var templateFunction = Handlebars.compile(initialTemplateContent);

22    var dataA = templateFunction( {"fName" : "Ben",     "lName" : "Smith", "phone" :
      "555-1234"} );
23    var dataB = templateFunction( {"fName" : "Ivan",    "lName" : "Bravo" , "phone" :
      "555-5678"} );
24    var dataC = templateFunction( {"fName" : "Michael", "lName" : "Chang" , "phone" :
      "555-9090"} );

24    var directory = document.getElementById("directory");
          directory.innerHTML  = dataA;
          directory.innerHTML += dataB;
          directory.innerHTML += dataC;

25 </script>
```

As the code from Listing 13-10 reveals, the implementation and utilization of a template are equivalent, regardless of the number of placeholders. This is due to the magic of the Handlebars scripting engine. Executing the preceding code results in the rendering of each context to be included within the directory, as shown in Figure 13-5.

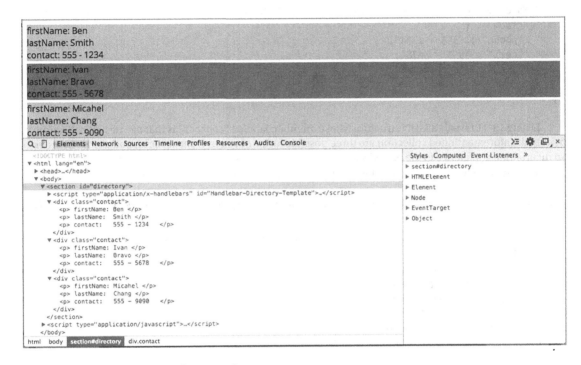

Figure 13-5. *Directory listing of my coworkers*

■ **Note**   I have not revealed any styling in the listings, to keep code to a minimum. However, I have applied a minimal amount of styling to the `employee` class.

One of the features that makes JSON a superior data format is that it is capable of retaining the hierarchical structure of data. As we have seen in previous chapters, JSON allows us to nest structural composites, resulting in more complex JSON structures.

Complex JSON Structures

A great templating engine can easily work with complex data, and Handlebars is definitely up to the task. Because all Handlebars placeholders reference the topmost structure of the provided context, any and all nested members within a data collection can be referenced with the simple use of dot notation.

Our previous example demonstrated how we could use Handlebars to output an employee directory, revealing the contact number per colleague. However, in the case of an urgent matter, it's always best to have alternate methods of contacting an individual. Let's revisit our previous `Handlebar-Employee-Template`, and reconstruct it to make use of the nested structure shown in Listing 13-11.

Listing 13-11. A Complex JSON Structure

```
var complexJSON =
{
    "fName" : "Ben",
    "lName" : "Smith",
    "contact" : {
        "phone" : "555 - 1234",
        "cell" : "555 - 5678",
        "email" : "ben@example.com"
    }
};
```

Listing 13-11 reveals a JSON structure whose member, labeled "`contact`", is that of a nested collection. Within the aforementioned collection are three possible forms of contact: `phone`, `cell`, and `email`. In order to incorporate a reference to the nested values into our template, we simply employ the use of dot notation within our placeholders, as seen in Listing 13-12.

Listing 13-12. Handlebar Template Relying on Dot Notation to Reference a Nested Collection

```
<section class="directory">
 <script type="application/x-handlebars" id="Handlebar-Employee-Template">
  <div class="employee">
    <p> firstName: {{fName}} </p>
    <p> lastName:  {{lName}} </p>
    <p> work:      {{contact.phone}} </p>
    <p> email:     {{contact.cell}} </p>
    <p> cell:      {{contact.email}} </p>
  </div>
 </script>
</section>
```

If we were to compile the template from Listing 13-12 and supply as the context `complexJSON` from Listing 13-11, our document would render the results shown in Figure 13-6.

Figure 13-6. *Rendered template utilizing dot notation*

While dot notation can be sufficient for working with nested structures, it can become rather cumbersome and repetitive. Furthermore, when working with many properties or deeply nested structures, our template can become bloated and unwieldy. For this reason, the Handlebars engine supplies us with more versatile expressions.

Block Expressions

As stated on the Handlebars web site, "Block expressions allow you to define helpers that will invoke a section of your template with a different context than the current." Although I have yet to discuss *helpers*, the key takeaway from the previous sentence is that block expressions are special expressions that can be used to change the working context within our templates. In the upcoming section "Block Helpers," you will see how they can be paired with helpers.

As the term *block* implies, a lock expression is used to define a subset or group of expressions within a template. In other words, block expressions are used as containers for other expressions, wherein the expressions residing within a block expression are subject to the context defined by the block itself. This is similar to the CSS cascading effect, which child HTML elements can inherit from their parents. Furthermore, because a block expression is a special form of expression, a block expression has the capability to be the parent for another block expression. Listing 13-13 reveals the syntax of a block expression.

Listing 13-13. Syntax of a Block Expression

```
{{#Expression}}
        //anything that happens here is within the context of Expression
{{/Expression}}
```

As shown in Listing 13-13, the syntax of a block expression is much more complex than that of its counterpart the basic expression. Further examination of the syntax reveals similarities between the two. It would appear that a block expression is made up of two special basic expressions. The first expression is prefixed by a hash token (#), while the latter basic expression is simply prefixed by the solidus token (/). The two tokens that I have mentioned are used to denote the beginning and end of a block.

Any and all expressions contained within said block will inherit the context established by the block expression. What do I mean by "established by the block expression"? Like any basic expression, the block references a placeholder that will be replaced with the value for the defined key shown in Listing 13-13 as "Expression", thus altering the context for any nested expressions.

Incorporating block expressions within a template is as simple as determining where our template would benefit from a change in context. Let's revisit Handlebar-Employee-Template from Listing 13-12 and establish a new context that will allow us to remove all uses of dot notation. (See Listing 13-14.)

Listing 13-14. Use of a Block Expression to Alter the Current Context

```
<section class="directory">
 <script type="application/x-handlebars" id="Handlebar-Employee-Template">
  <div class="employee">
    <p> firstName: {{fName}} </p>
    <p> lastName:  {{lName}} </p>
      {{#contact}}
    <p> work:  {{phone}} </p>
    <p> email: {{cell}} </p>
    <p> cell:  {{email}} </p>
      {{/contact}}
  </div>
 </script>
</section>
```

Listing 13-14 employs a block expression in order to reflect, as the new context, contact, exposed by the current context. Mind you, the item held at contact is a collection of three keys, phone, cell, and email. From there, all placeholders contained within our block will be replaced with the values possessed by the matching keys held by the new context, thus eliminating the need for dot notation, in order to obtain references to phone, cell, and email.

■ **Tip**   A block expression can be used to work your way down a complex JSON structure.

If we were to compile the template from Listing 13-14 and supply as the context complexJSON from Listing 13-11, our document would render the same result shown previously in Figure 13-6.

Block Expressions and Arrays

One extremely powerful inclusion of the block expression, aside from being used to establish a new context, is how it will loop over the indexes of an array, if that is what the expression evaluates to. In other words, if the key defined by our block expression evaluates to that of an array, each item held by all indexes of said array are individually set as the new context for any and all expressions within the block. This is especially important, because the Handlebars engine will assemble, in one shot, several data sets contained within an ordered list.

With that being said, Listing 13-15 incorporates within our initial Handlebar-Employee-Template from Listing 13-9 a block expression, shown in bold.

Listing 13-15. Incorporating a Block Expression

```
<body>
  <section id="directory">
    <script type="application/x-handlebars" id="Handlebar-Employees-Template">
    {{#employees}}
    <div class="employee">
        <p> firstName: {{fName}} </p>
        <p> lastName:  {{lName}} </p>
        <p> contact:   {{phone}} </p>
    </div>
    {{/employees}}
    </script>
  </section>
</body>
```

This very minor inclusion adds an extremely large amount of automation to our template. Up until this point, the code required to augment multiple individuals into our directory consisted of obtaining computed data, augmenting it, and inserting this into our DOM three times over. However, the inclusion of the new block expression can supply an arbitrary number of employees to our template with a single data provision.

Because both our template and data must possess a relationship in order for our template to work, it requires the provision of JSON that complements our block expression. The JSON provided must possess at least one key/value pair whose label is that of employees. Furthermore, the value which employees must retain is that of an array, whose indexes are composed of individual collections pertaining to a particular employee, as shown in Listing 13-16.

Listing 13-16. An Ordered List of Individual Employees

```
{
    "employees" : [
        {"fName" : "Ben",     "lName" : "Smith", "phone" : "555 - 1234" },
        {"fName" : "Ivan",    "lName" : "Bravo", "phone" : "555 - 5678" },
        {"fName" : "Michael", "lName" : "Chang", "phone" : "555 - 9090"}
    ]
};
```

Listing 13-16 reveals a JSON structure that complements the block expression shown in Listing 13-15. If we were to compile the template from Listing 13-15 and provide the preceding JSON to the resulting function, the resulting string returned would reflect the following markup:

```
<div class="employee">
 <p> firstName: Ben </p>
 <p> lastName:  Smith </p>
 <p> contact:   555 - 1234   </p>
</div>
<div class="employee">
 <p> firstName: Ivan </p>
 <p> lastName:  Bravo </p>
 <p> contact:   555 - 5678   </p>
</div>
<div class="employee">
 <p> firstName: Michael </p>
 <p> lastName:  Chang </p>
 <p> contact:   555 - 9090   </p>
</div>
```

All that would be left for our code to do would be to append the preceding string into our document so that it can be rendered. The full source code can be viewed in Listing 13-17.

Listing 13-17. Utilizing a Block Expression to Render Three Employees from One JSON Argument

```
<body>
  <section id="directory">
    <script type="application/x-handlebars" id="Handlebar-Employee-Template">
    {{#employees}}
    <div class="employee">
    <p> firstName: {{fName}} </p>
    <p> lastName:  {{lName}} </p>
    <p> contact:   {{phone}} </p>
    </div>
    {{/employees}}
    </script>
  </section>
  <script type="application/javascript">
    var initialTemplateWrapper = document.getElementById("Handlebar-Employee-Template");
    var initialTemplateContent = initialTemplateWrapper.innerHTML;
    var templateFunction = Handlebars.compile(initialTemplateContent);

    var dataA = templateFunction({
          "employees" : [
```

```
                        {"fName" : "Ben", "lName" : "Smith", "phone" : "555 - 1234" },
                        { "fName" : "Ivan", "lName" : "Bravo", "phone" : "555 - 5678" },
                        {"fName" : "Michael", "lName" : "Chang", "phone" : "555 - 9090"}
                    ]
    });

    var directory = document.getElementById("directory");
    directory.innerHTML += dataA;
  </script>
</body>
```

Executing Listing 13-17 renders the results shown in Figure 13-5. While the results are the same, the difference in labor speaks for itself.

EXERCISE 13-1. ENHANCING THE DIRECTORY

While our employee directory is making use of the latest Handlebars techniques, thereby reducing the amount of JavaScript required to add new employees to our directory, we have managed to revert back to displaying only one form of contact per employee. Using the information learned thus far about Handlebars expressions, rewrite the directory template to account for the following JSON as its context:

```
{
    "employees" : [
    {
        "fName" : "Ben",
        "lName" : "Smith",
        "contacts" : {
            "phone" : "555 - 1234",
            "cell" : "555 - 5678",
            "email" : "ben@example.com"
        }
    }, {
        "fName" : "Ivan",
        "lName" : "Bravo",
        "contacts" : {
            "phone" : "555 - 9012",
            "cell" : "555 - 9034",
            "email" : "ivan@example.com"
        }
    }, {
        "fName" : "Michael",
        "lName" : "Chang",
        "contacts" : {
            "phone" : "555 - 9035",
        }
    }]
}
```

You may note that Michael does not possess a cell or e-mail for this exercise. Take note of this when your template is rendered. You can compare your template to Listing 13-18.

If your template resembles that of Listing 13-18, then, congratulations; you are on your way to mastering the Handlebars engine.

Listing 13-18. Answer to the Preceding Exercise

```
<section id="directory">
 <script type="application/x-handlebars" id="Handlebar-Employee-Template">
  {{#employees}}
    <div class="employee">
    <p> firstName: {{fName}} </p>
    <p> lastName:  {{lName}} </p>
    {{#contacts}}
        <p>phone: {{phone}}</p>
        <p>cell:  {{cell}}</p>
        <p>email: {{email}}</p>
    {{/contacts}}
    </div>
  {{/employees}}
 </script>
</section>
```

Rendering the template from Listing 13-18 reveals that a Handlebars template outputs fields, whether or not an existing member within the provided context can replace the basic expression. As in the case of Michael, who lacked a cell as well as an e-mail address, Handlebars did not omit these fields, as shown in Figure 13-7.

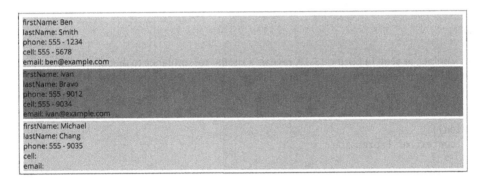

Figure 13-7. *Rendering of empty fields*

Applying Logic to Logic-less Templates

As was stated earlier, Handlebars templates are logic-less, which simply means that they do not incorporate the use of JavaScript operators. This is extremely beneficial, because it increases the readability, reusability, and maintainability of our templates, by ensuring the separation of presentation from functionality. Similarly, it separates our HTML from our JavaScript. However, at times, we will find it quite necessary to apply logic into our presentation. For this reason Handlebars incorporates helpers.

Helpers

In order to decouple logic from presentation, Handlebars does not permit the coupling of logic within a template—and rightfully so. HTML, CSS, and JavaScript should remain as separate from one another as possible. However, this is not to say that Handlebars templates cannot reflect the use of logic at all. In fact, the Handlebars library provides us with the necessary framework in which we can pair logic with templates in a way that is sure to decouple the logic from our layout.

In order to decouple the two, the Handlebars library relies on what are referred to as helpers. A helper is merely an expression, which, at runtime, resolves to a function of the same name. Only in the runtime environment are our template and logic intertwined. This is contrary to design time (our source code), during which our template will only exhibit what appears to be yet another expression, thus ensuring an optimal amount of separation from our presentation.

There are two types of helpers: custom and built-in. Because custom helpers are an advanced topic, this chapter will not discuss them. Rather, I will discuss the variety of remarkably useful helpers that Handlebars includes, so that we can incorporate them into our templates immediately.

Built-in Helpers

Unlike custom helpers, which, as you may suspect, offer more fine-tuned logic, hence increased complexity, built-in helpers are included to supply basic logic to Handlebars templates. The helpers that I will be discussing are each, if, unless, and else.

As you may surmise from their names, the aforementioned built-in helpers facilitate the most basic of JavaScript faculties. As you will find, the built-in helpers that I will be discussing will all coincide with a block expression. Helpers that are used with block expressions are referred to in the Handlebars nomenclature as *block helpers*.

Block Helpers

The syntax for a block helper, as seen in Listing 13-19, reveals a similar resemblance to that of a block expression. The sole difference between the two is that it is the name of the helper that defines the block.

Listing 13-19. Syntax of a Block Helper

```
{{#helper Expression}}
    // Within the context of Expression
{{/helper}}
```

As you can see from Listing 13-19, a block helper is a block used to apply specific logic to some context, Expression. In the case of the block helper, it is the name of the helper that succeeds the beginning and ending tokens of the block. Although the syntax varies from our earlier discussion of a block expression, a block helper is still a block, and, therefore, for all expressions within, is business as usual. In other words, all expressions within are subject to the new context brought about by the block helper.

The each Helper

The each helper is a remarkable helper that traverses all keys for a given context. The difference between each and the default behavior of the block expression, however, is that each will iterate over both collections as well as an ordered list. As with a block expression, each item held by the traversed key will be set to the current context for any and all expressions within the block. Listing 13-20 reveals the syntax for the each block helper.

Listing 13-20. Syntax of the each Helper

```
{{#each Expression}}
    //evaluate against the current context
{{/each}}
```

As shown in Listing 13-20, the each block helper defines a block that will traverse all keys belonging to the evaluated context, Expression. The each key provides a tremendous amount of automation that can be added to our template. It can be used like a block expression to iterate an array, or it can also be used to iterate over a collection of key/value pairs. Listing 13-21 makes use of both, to reveal the each helper's versatility.

Listing 13-21. Revisiting Our Directory with the Assistance of the each Helper

```
<script type="application/x-handlebars" id="Handlebar-Employee-Template">
{{#each employees}}  //traverse an array
  <div class="employee">
    <p> firstName: {{fName}} </p>
    <p> lastName:  {{lName}} </p>
    {{#each contacts }} //traverse a collection
        <p>{{@key}}: {{this}}</p>
    {{/each}}
  </div>
{{/each}}
</script>
```

Listing 13-21 updates our previous Handlebar-Employee-Template. This time, it reflects the necessary code that takes advantage of the each helper. As you can see, our template will traverse our array, employees, and our object, contacts. You may notice that our template no longer explicitly includes the placeholders phone, cell, and email. In their place is a single line of code: <p>{{@key}}: {{this}}</p>. Because the use of each sets the value of each traversed key as the current context for all subsequent expressions within the block, our aforementioned placeholders will not be evaluated. This is because each value of each key held by our contacts collection is a string. For this particular reason, the Handlebars engine provides special placeholders that can be used to refer to specific parts of a context.

These special placeholders are {{@key}} and {{this}}. The placeholder {{@key}} refers to the key for which the current context is held, while, conversely, the placeholder {{this}} refers to the value of said key. These come in especially handy when iteration is involved.

Utilizing these two special placeholders, we can achieve the original output of our various methods of contact. Providing the data model shown in Listing 13-22 results in the rendering of Figure 13-8.

Listing 13-22. Complex JSON

```
{
    "employees" : [
     {
         "fName" : "Ben",
         "lName" : "Smith",
         "contacts" : { "phone" : "555 - 1234", "cell" : "555 - 5678", "email" :
         ben@example.com }
     }, {
         "fName" : "Ivan",
         "lName" : "Bravo",
         "contacts" : {  "phone" : "555 - 9012",  "cell" : "555 - 9034", "email" :
         ivan@example.com }
     }, {
         "fName" : "Michael",
         "lName" : "Chang",
         "contacts" : { "phone" : "555 - 9035", }
     }]
}
```

Figure 13-8. *Rendering of fields that exist*

As you can see, the effect is nearly the same as the output from the earlier exercise within this chapter. What you may recognize, however, is that only phone has been outputted for Michael. This is because the each helper traverses only the keys that exist.

The if Helper

The if helper is a handy helper that can be used to add conditional logic to a block expression and takes on the implementation shown in Listing 13-23.

Listing 13-23. Syntax of the if Helper

```
{{#if Expression}}
    //evaluate against the current context Expression
{{/if}}
```

Listing 13-23 reveals the syntax of the block helper. Use of the if helper conveniently renders our block, in addition to any expressions contained within, only if Expression evaluates as truthy. In other words, if Expression evaluates to null, 0, false, or undefined, the block will be bypassed. Let's apply our if helper to the template from our earlier exercise, in order to prevent the output of contact methods that do not exist. (See Listing 13-24.)

Listing 13-24. Incorporation of the if Helper

```
<script type="application/x-handlebars" id="Handlebar-Employee-Template">
  {{#employees}}
    <div class="employee">
    <p> firstName: {{fName}} </p>
    <p> lastName:  {{lName}} </p>
    {{#contacts}}
    {{#if phone}}
      <p>phone: {{phone}}</p>
    {{/if}}
    {{#if cell}}
      <p>cell: {{ cell }}</p>
    {{/if}}
    {{#if email}}
      <p>email: {{email}}</p>
    {{/if}}
  {{/contacts}}
  </div>
 {{/employees}}
</script>
```

As shown in bold, the if helper is used to devise a block that may or may not render. This, of course, depends on the resulting evaluation of each expression: phone, cell, and email. Remember that if an expression evaluates to null, 0, false, or undefined, each if block helper will be skipped. Executing the previous template with the data set from Listing 13-24 results in the same output as that shown in Figure 13-9.

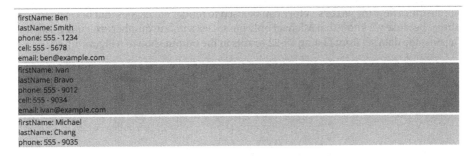

Figure 13-9. *Rendering of a member, if it possesses a value*

The unless Helper

The unless helper is used to render a block only if the expression succeeding it evaluates to falsy. The syntax for the unless helper can be seen in Listing 13-25.

Listing 13-25. Syntax of the unless Helper

```
{{#unless Expression}}
    //evaluate against the current context Expression
{{/unless }}
```

The unless helper is used inversely to that of our if helper, in that it is used to render a block, if and only if Expression evaluates to null, 0, false, or undefined. You may be asking yourself when might this be useful. However, such a helper is useful when rendering invalid or empty form fields. Listing 13-26 uses the unless helper to output into our directory all contacts that have not supplied an e-mail.

Listing 13-26. Incorporation of the unless Helper

```
<script type="application/x-handlebars" id="Handlebar-Employee-Template">
  {{#employees}}
    {{#unless contacts.email}}
    <div class="employee">
       <p> firstName: {{fName}} </p>
       <p> lastName:  {{lName}} </p>
       {{#contacts}}
          <p>phone: {{phone}}</p>
          <p>cell: {{ cell }}</p>
          <p>email: {{email}}</p>
       {{/contacts}}
    </div>
    {{/unless}}
    {{/employees}}
</script>
```

Listing 13-26 demonstrates how the unless helper can be used to render colleagues that have yet to supply an e-mail address. Because we know that Michael only possesses a phone number, executing the preceding template against the data set from Listing 13-22 results in the output shown in Figure 13-10.

```
firstName: Michael
lastName: Chang
phone: 555 - 9035
cell:
email:
```

Figure 13-10. *Use of the unless block to render a contact whose e-mail is not present*

The else Helper

The else helper is a complementary helper for our two previously discussed helpers, unless and if. This special helper can be incorporated within the body of either if/unless blocks in order to render content, provided the conditions for unless/if are unsuccessfully met. The syntax of our else helper for both unless and if blocks can be seen in Listing 13-27.

Listing 13-27. Syntax of the else Helper

```
{{#if Expression}}
    //Evaluate for the current context if truthy
{{else}}
    //Evaluate for the current context if falsy
{{/if}}

{{#unless Expression}}
    //Evaluate for the current context if falsy
{{else}}
    //Evaluate for the current context if truthy
{{/unless}}
```

Utilizing the else helper offers our templates the ability to provide presentation to an unmet outcome. Consider our previous unless example. If we wanted to highlight for Human Resources those colleagues who currently lack a valid e-mail address, while similarly displaying those that did, utilizing the else helper would make this possible. (See Listing 13-28.)

Listing 13-28. Incorporation of the else Helper

```
<script type="application/x-handlebars" id="Handlebar-Employee-Template">
  {{#employees}}
  {{#unless contacts.email}}
  <div class="lacksEmail">
    <p> requires contact for{{fName}}{{lName}} </p>
  </div>
  {{else}}
  <div class="hasEmail">
    <p> congratulations {{fName}} {{lName}} </p>
  </div>
  {{/unless}}
  {{/employees}}
</script>
```

Listing 13-28 reveals the use of the else helper to render an alternate presentation for when our condition is not met. Executing the preceding template with the data set from Listing 13-22 results in the same output as that shown in Figure 13-11.

congratulations Ben Smith

congratulations Ivan Bravo

requires contact forMichael Chang

Figure 13-11. *Use of the* else *helper to render an alternate condition*

EXERCISE 13-2. TEMPLATIZING REMOTE JSON

With the lessons you've learned in this chapter, see if you can revise the exercise in Chapter 8 to incorporate Handlebars. There is no right or wrong answer.

Summary

The Handlebars library makes it easy to combine data with presentation. However, it does so cleanly and semantically, which makes it highly extensible as well as maintainable. In our industry, in which change is constant, the ability to isolate data from presentation allows for things to change independently of one another. Handlebars does this by simply taking advantage of the clear distinctions between design time and runtime.

Key Points from This Chapter

- Handlebars is a templating engine.
- Handlebars templates are encapsulated as text within script tags.
- To prevent our templates from being parsed by the JavaScript engine, we mark the type of script as an unidentifiable language.
- A placeholder is the atomic unit in Handlebars.
- All expressions are references to keys held by JSON data.
- A Handlebars template is converted into a JavaScript function at runtime.
- The JavaScript function accepts JSON data against which all placeholders are evaluated.
- Handlebar templates are logic-less.
- Basic logic can be added to a template in the form of a helper.
- The built-in helpers are used within blocks.
- Block expressions are used to alter the current context.
- Block expressions can be used to traverse arrays.
- {{this}} and {{@key}} are special placeholders that refer to current key/value pairs.

- The each helper can traverse members of an ordered list or collection.

- The if helper is used to add conditional logic to a block.

- The unless helper is used to add conditional logic to a block.

- The else helper can be used when if or unless conditions are unmet.

■ ■ ■

CHAPTER 14

Putting It All Together

Each previous chapter has aimed to discuss the various components of the Web that circulate around JSON. Owing to this common thread, they are typically paired, rather than considered in isolation. In this chapter, I will piece together the various concepts discussed throughout this book as building blocks for an actual project. Each component will play its own critical role.

Within this chapter, I will use JavaScript, JSON, CORS, Node.js, CouchDB, Handlebars, and, finally, Ajax to harness the data from the social media powerhouse that is Twitter.

Twitter

For those who live under a rock, Twitter is the latest social trend enabling users to communicate via a short, 140-character message. For all intents and purposes, Twitter can be thought of as the modern-day soapbox. Registered users can read and respond to other users' messages. But even more important is that unregistered users can still read and search the tweets of all registered users. This is because Twitter stores in a database every tweet and publicizes them, thereby allowing all the world to view the voices of the many.

Furthermore, Twitter has crafted a simple API that welcomes web developers to harness their database, to power the simplest or most complex campaign initiatives. While there are many ways to utilize Twitter's API, this chapter seeks to extract, at near-real-time, broadcast tweets that contain a specific hashtag or phrase. At the time of writing, the iPhone 6 had just been released, and the hashtag #bendgate instantly trended. For this chapter, I will make use of the hashtag #bendgate, but feel free to replace any #bendgate reference with one that is trending today.

Twitter Apps

Much as with all modern-day social APIs, in order to leverage Twitter's API, we must register a Twitter app. This is easily accomplished by visiting http://apps.twitter.com and clicking the Create New App button, as shown Figure 14-1.

Figure 14-1. *Create New App button*

If you are not greeted with a page that resembles that in Figure 14-1, it may be that Twitter has either updated this page or that you have yet to sign in with your Twitter account. Take this opportunity to click "Sign in to twitter," if you have an existing account with Twitter, or click "Sign up now" to create one. As a registered Twitter user, you are allowed to create as many apps as you see fit. Let's begin by creating an app. Clicking Create New App will direct us to a page enabling us to create an application, as seen in Figure 14-2.

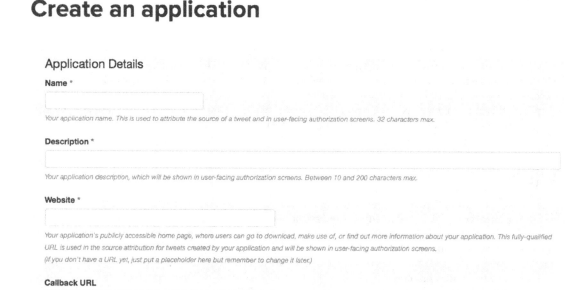

Figure 14-2. *Application Details form*

In the fields shown in Figure 14-2, we will need to provide some required information. First is the provision of a name for our application. Normally this field is presented to the end user, to approve the application to use the Twitter account. However, the app we will be creating is strictly for our own purposes. That being said, you can fill out any name that is not already in use by other Twitter developers. I have labeled my application "BeginningJSON."

The second field seeks a description defining the behavior of our application. What is it for? What are its intentions? Again, this is another user-facing field. However, as it's an internal project, we can call it whatever we wish. I have supplied the following description: "crawls the search API."

The third field is used to provide authority to the source of the application. If your application creates tweets on behalf of a user who authorized your app, the URL you provide here will be listed as the source attribute for the tweet. Our app will not be making any tweets on anyone's behalf; therefore, we can provide a placeholder, in order to satisfy the requirement of the field. I have listed http://127.0.0.1 as my web site.

The final field, which is not required, is mandated by the OAuth authorization protocol. As we will not be making use of this field, we can leave it blank.

The last step in creating a Twitter app requires that we read and acknowledge the policies surrounding the use of the Twitter API. If you agree to the rules laid out by Twitter, then click "Yes, I agree," then click the button labeled "Create your Twitter application."

If the form did not possess any errors, upon its submission, you will be navigated to a portal from which you can manage the particulars of your app. The landing page for your application is the Details page, which provides the overview of your application. Your details should reflect those shown in Figure 14-3.

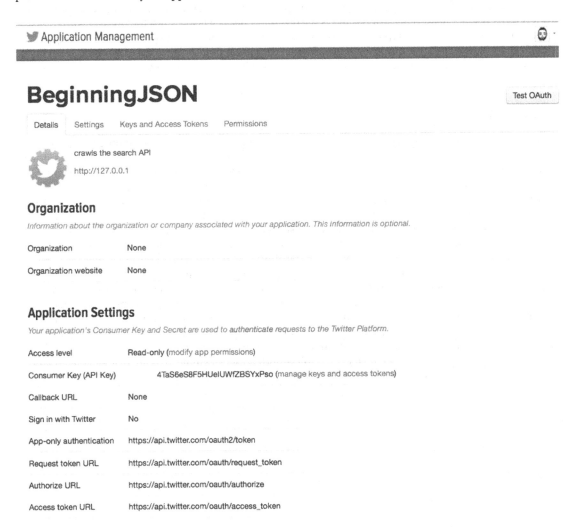

Figure 14-3. Application Details page

Figure 14-3 displays the basic details for our recently created application. The major difference between your app and mine begins with the presented name of the application. In the top left-hand corner, you can see that my app is labeled "BeginningJSON." Further below, our application's settings are listed. Here is yet another obvious difference between your app and mine. Where it states Consumer Key (API Key), the number that appears on your Details page is guaranteed to be that of a different value. This is necessary for your app and my app to be recognized as two separate applications. I'll talk more about this shortly.

By default, all applications are enabled to provide "Read-only" status from Twitter. This is evident, as the first field within the Application Settings section reveals our access level. To the right of "Access level" are the following words: "Read-only." This is always the default value, as it is the safest for any user who wants to use your application. If your application requires write privileges, the existing permissions will require modification. However, for the purposes of this chapter, we will continue to leave the permission set to Read-only. At this point, let's click the Keys and Access Tokens tab within the topmost navigation.

Keys and Access Tokens

This section pertains to our application/user tokens and is integral to a Twitter application. In fact, it's integral to nearly every API out there today. You see, the Twitter application for which we are creating strictly adheres to the OAuth 2.0 protocol. As the topic of OAuth is far beyond the topic of this book, I will simply explain that OAuth is an industry standard for allowing a third party access to your first-party data, while ensuring that the service requesting your data remains ignorant of your credentials. In this particular case, that service would be Twitter. In order to keep all parties isolated, thereby not exposing a user's password to the application creator, a series of access tokens are used and exchanged instead.

Every Twitter application is provided a Consumer Key upon its creation. It is this Consumer Key that distinguishes my application from your application. Furthermore, it is used to establish the identity of my application with Twitter. Much like a Twitter handle, I have the option of changing my application name at any point in time. However, the Consumer Key will always remain the same, that is, unless I regenerate them or change the app permissions, which would provide my app with a brand-new Consumer Key. A change in Consumer Keys, then, represents a different app and, therefore, requires anyone who has previously authorized your app to do so once again. This ensures that users who authorize your read-only app today cannot be taken advantage of tomorrow, without having to authorize any changes made to your app.

While the Consumer Key is intended to be public information, all Public Keys are paired with a secret key that must be safeguarded at all times. For this reason, I have blurred mine out from Figure 14-4.

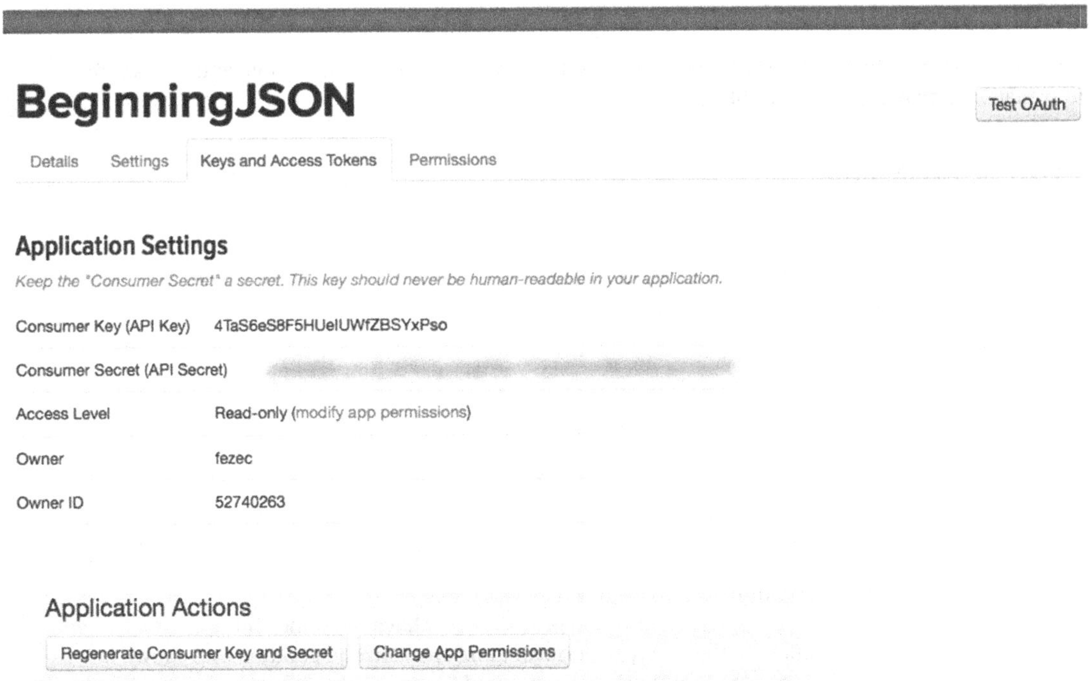

BeginningJSON

Test OAuth

Details   Settings   **Keys and Access Tokens**   Permissions

Application Settings

Keep the "Consumer Secret" a secret. This key should never be human-readable in your application.

Consumer Key (API Key)   4TaS6eS8F5HUeIUWfZBSYxPso

Consumer Secret (API Secret)

Access Level   Read-only (modify app permissions)

Owner   fezec

Owner ID   52740263

Application Actions

[Regenerate Consumer Key and Secret]   [Change App Permissions]

Figure 14-4. *Application Keys and Access Tokens tab*

If anyone ever obtains a secret key, he/she can impersonate your app. These two keys, when paired, establish the rightful ownership. Therefore, make certain that the Private Key you are provided remains a secret from anyone.

■ **Tip**   The safest way to utilize the Private Key is on the server side.

At this point, we have successfully registered a read-only Twitter application that can be used to begin interacting with the Twitter API. All that is required is the understanding of the Twitter API. The Twitter API is bountiful and has loads of methods for us to tap into. To cover them all requires a book in itself; however, now that we have created an app, you may find it interesting to discover the potential that Twitter can offer. Feel free to learn about the various API methods from the online documentation at `https://dev.twitter.com/overview/documentation`.

The clear and concise documentation outlines the methods we can make use of, the type of authorization required, whether or not there is a limit to how many times it can be called, and the response format to be expected. While not every method will provide different answers, what remains a constant is that all response formats will be provided as JSON.

273

Public Stream

The interaction that this chapter will make use of is the public stream's statuses/filter, and its resource information is provided in Figure 14-5.

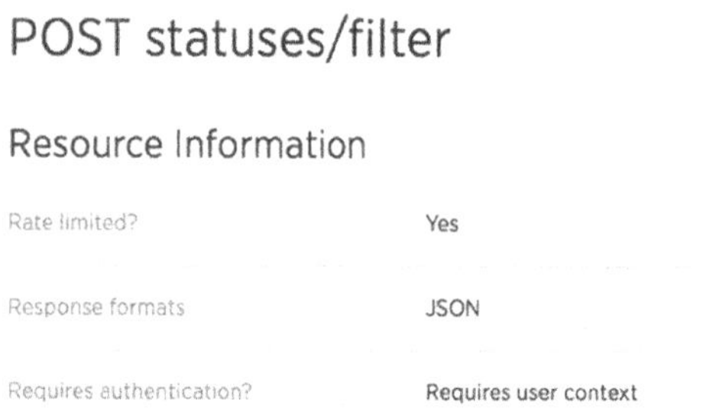

POST statuses/filter

Resource Information

Rate limited?	Yes
Response formats	JSON
Requires authentication?	Requires user context

Figure 14-5. *Public stream's Resource Information page*

The pubic stream, as defined on the Twitter web site, provides "developers low latency access to Twitter's global stream of tweet data." This is achieved by devising a socket between our server and Twitter's, so they can post to our servers public tweets as they receive them.

As I mentioned earlier, both registered and unregistered users have the same ability to view Tweets. However, only registered users have the ability to perform more specialized operations. As shown in Figure 14-5, you can see that the type of authorization required for the public stream is that of a user context. Unlike the Consumer Keys, which we currently have, in order to use this interface, we will require a User Key as well. Fortunately for us, in order to create a Twitter application, one must have access to a registered Twitter account. In other words, we can generate a User Key for our account and pair it to work with our Twitter application.

Your User Access Token

One thing that Twitter provides us from the Keys and Access Tokens menu is the ability to generate an access token that can be authorized to work with our application. In order to obtain an access token, simply click "Create my access token," just below the CTA "Token Actions," shown in Figure 14-6. This will generate an access key for this particular application, thereby satisfying the requirements of the public stream interface.

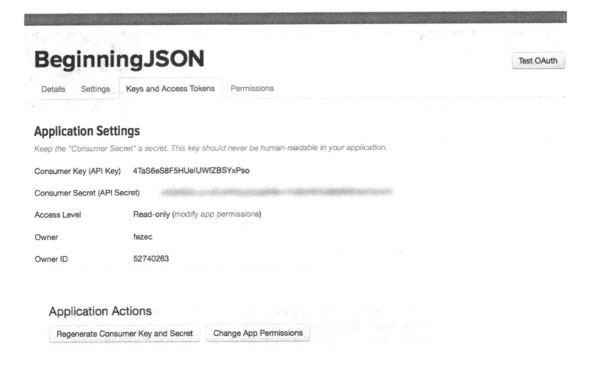

Figure 14-6. *Generated user token*

As shown in Figure 14-6, clicking "Create my access token" will generate an access token as well as its access token secret counterpart. Never reveal this access token secret to anyone; otherwise, he/she can use it to access your account via the Twitter API. By clicking "Generate My Access Token," Twitter will authorize your account with your Twitter app. If you were to navigate to `https://twitter.com/settings/applications`, you would find a list of all the applications that you have authorized. The most recent application should reflect yours, just as Figure 14-7 reveals mine.

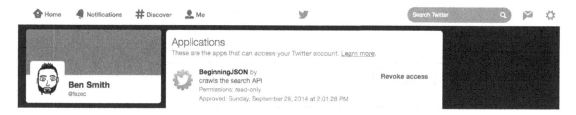

Figure 14-7. *Authoring our account to make use of our application*

At this point, we have all the credentials we require to monitor in near-real time the Twitter database for the tweets of our choosing.

#Trending

Now that we have the required keys to consume data from the Twitter stream, all that remains is the implementation for our application. But what exactly are we building? you ask. We are going to build an application that monitors, as close to real time as possible, a topic that is currently trending. Furthermore, because the trend may be gone tomorrow, we will store within a database the data received from the stream. This will allow us the ability to filter, sort, or search for particular tweets even after the trend subsides.

Last, because the data will be locked away within a database, we will devise a way to extract the data and incorporate it within an HTML document. In order to present the data as a tweet, we will stylize the extracted data upon its inclusion within the HTML document. For this, you will have to use your gleanings from each preceding chapter.

Node.js

The first piece of the puzzle is creating a server from which we can interchange data between our application and Twitter. In order to make our lives easier, we will leverage a Node module, which will conceal our application from the nitty-gritties of the Twitter API. For this challenge, we will leverage the npm Twitter module. You can read more about it at the following site: `www.npmjs.org/package/twitter`.

Twitter Module

In order to utilize the Twitter module, we must first install it as a module with Node.js. In order to do so, we will follow the practices similar to those that were employed with Cradle, discussed in Chapter 12.

Simply use the command-line interface to navigate to the top directory, which contains the `chapter14` source code. For me, that would be the following locations:

```
//PC
C:\Users\UrZA\Documents\Aptana Studio 3 Workspace\BeginningJSON\chapter14\
//Mac
/Users/FeZEC/Documents/Aptana Studio 3 Workspace/BeginningJSON/chapter14/
```

Open Terminal for Mac or CMD for PC, and simply type cd, followed by the location of your `chapter14` directory and hit Enter. Next, type in the following command and hit Return on your keyboard.

`npm install twitter`

This will initiate the installation process for our Twitter module. Remember that to install a module, you may require administration rights.

Incorporating the Twitter Module

Once the Twitter module has been successfully installed into our top-level directory, we can begin working with it, by incorporating it into a Node application via require(). As outlined at www.npmjs.org/package/twitter, the setup for our Twitter application requires a mere eight lines of code, as shown in Listing 14-1.

Listing 14-1. Twitter Module Setup

```
1 var util = require('util');
2 var twitter = require('twitter');
3 var twitr = new twitter({
4     consumer_key        : "REPLACE_WITH_YOUR_CONSUMER_KEY",
5     consumer_secret     : "REPLACE_WITH_YOUR_CONSUMER_KEY_SECRET",
6     access_token_key    : "REPLACE_WITH_YOUR_CONSUMER_ACCESS_TOKEN",
7     access_token_secret : "REPLACE_WITH_YOUR_CONSUMER_ACCESS_TOKEN_SECRET"
8 });
```

As I hinted at earlier, a Twitter application relies on an exchange among keys. This is why the setup requires us to insert the appropriate keys that reflect the application we are devising. The module then utilizes these keys to generate the proper calls to Twitter's API. Because this logic is complex, we are leveraging our module to perform this labor.

Now, as it currently stands, the code from Listing 14-1 simply configures our application to properly access the Twitter API with the appropriate credentials. It does not begin to make any requests or receive any data. For that, we must utilize the relevant methods of the module.

Streaming API (Stable)

The Twitter module has a few methods that we can tap into; however, for the purposes of this chapter, we will make sole use of the Streaming API. The Streaming API is a wrapper to accessing Twitter's public streams. As you can learn from Twitter's documentation on public streams, https://dev.twitter.com/streaming/public, there are three possible end points. We will use statuses/filter.

Statuses/Filter

The documentation for the statuses/filter URI states: "Returns public statuses that match one more filter predicates." In other words, the end point, stream.twitter.com/1.1/statuses/filter, will monitor for public tweets that match any of the delimited terms or hashtags that we specify. Furthermore, because our application will be listening to a stream, Twitter will provide us data in near real time.

In order to specify the terms or tags that our application requires, we will use the track property. Simply put, track is a parameter that can be provided phrases or keywords. Multiple phrases or keywords can be separated by the comma (,) token. Listing 14-2 reveals the eight lines of code required to devise a connection to the status/filter stream.

Listing 14-2. Incorporating the Stream API

```
 8 //..truncated code
 9 var hashTag= "REPLACE_WITH_A_COMMA_DILIMITED_SET_OF_HASHTAG(s)";
10 twitr.stream('statuses/filter', {
11     track : hashTag
12 }, function(stream) {
13     stream.on('data', function(data) {
14         console.log(data);  //outputs JSON
15     });
16 });
```

Listing 14-2 shows all the code we will require for devising a stream for the chosen list of hashtags or phrases. I, however, have chosen to monitor the single hashtag knows as "#BendGate" (the latest trend following the iPhone 6). Incorporating Listing 14-2 with Listing 14-1 and replacing all references appropriately is all that remains to make this Node application fully operational.

If you were to execute the code from the command-line interface, via the node command, depending on the topic you had chosen to monitor, you would notice JSON being output to the console immediately. If the topic was truly trending, you might find it impossible to determine one tweet from another. Remember: We are streaming data, which means that everything is happening in real time or as close to it as it can.

■ **Note**   The stream outputs JSON and not raw data, because the Twitter module parses it.

Because it's coming in at near-real time, we will have to save the incoming data, lest it never reappear in our application, that is, unless it is re-tweeted by another user. In order to ensure that we retain the incoming tweets of the stream, we must incorporate a database on which we can persist them.

CouchDB

There is an expression, "You could not step twice into the same river," that is used to imply that things change. The tweets provided to our application may wind up being deleted by the originator of the tweet moments after they are published. This tweet will, for all intents and purposes, no longer be obtainable by public searches. By applying the preceding expression to our Twitter stream, the incoming tweets will be lost to our HTML document unless we devise a way to capture and store them for later use. For this, we will incorporate CouchDB.

Incorporating the Cradle Module

As you should already have CouchDB installed on your machine, the only thing that will be required of our application is the installation of the Cradle module into our current working directory. This can be achieved by typing cd, followed by the location of your chapter14 directory, and hitting Enter. Next, type in npm install twitter. Remember: You may require administration privileges to do so.

Once the Cradle module is installed, all that remains is to incorporate it into our existing Node application. Listing 14-3 reflects in bold the code required.

Listing 14-3. Incorporation of Cradle into Our Node Application

```
1 var util = require('util');
2 var twitter = require('twitter');
3 var cradle = require('cradle');

4 var twitr = new twitter({
    consumer_key        : "REPLACE_WITH_YOUR_CONSUMER_KEY",
    consumer_secret     : "REPLACE_WITH_YOUR_CONSUMER_KEY_SECRET",
    access_token_key    : "REPLACE_WITH_YOUR_CONSUMER_ACCESS_TOKEN",
    access_token_secret : "REPLACE_WITH_YOUR_CONSUMER_ACCESS_TOKEN_SECRET"
  });

5 var hashTag= "REPLACE_WITH_A_COMMA_DILIMITED_SET_OF_HASHTAG";

6 var couchDB = new (cradle.Connection)('127.0.0.1', 5984, {
     cache : true,
     raw : false,
    forceSave : true
  });
7 var twitterDataBase = couchDB.database('twitter');
8 twitterDataBase.exists(function(err, exists) {
9     if (err) {
10        console.log('error', err);
11    } else if (exists) {
12        console.log('the twitter db exists');
13    } else {
14        console.log('twitter database does not exists.');
15    twitterDataBase.create();
16    }
17 });
18 twitr.stream('statuses/filter', {
       track : hashTag
     }, function(stream) {
        stream.on('data', function(data) {
           twitterDataBase.save( data, function(err, res) {
              if (!err) {
                 console.log(res);  //logs out saved couchDB _id
              }
           });
        });
   });
```

Listing 14-3 outlines in bold the inclusion of CouchDB via the Cradle module. As you can see in lines 5 through 16, we establish a connection to our CouchDB service and determine the existence of the database labeled "twitter." If a database of that name does not currently exist, we create it via the create method.

Once our database is devised, and with a reference to it, we can pipe the incoming JSON into our database. Because the Twitter module converts any data read from the stream into JSON, we can simply provide it as the body to Cradle's save method.

If you don't currently have the CouchDB service running on port 5984, take this opportunity to start the CouchDB application. Once you have verified that CouchDB is running via the Futon interface, go ahead and restart our Node application. In lieu of Twitter data being outputted to the console, you should now be viewing JSON data returned by CouchDB. This data, as you may remember, represents the individual documents used to persist the provided JSON. Feel free to allow this application to run for a short while, in order to fill our `twitter` database. Before long, you will surely see an abundant amount of tweets that will have been saved to our database.

When you are satisfied, navigate your browser to the Futon Overview (`http://127.0.0.1:5984/_utils`) to bear witness to the fruits of your labor. As revealed in Figure 14-8, I managed to receive a total of 7,173 tweets before deciding to shut down my application. This amounted to nearly 50 megs in saved documents. While hard-drive space is nearly infinite for the penny these days, my desire to save 50 megs' worth of people complaining about their bent phone is sadly finite.

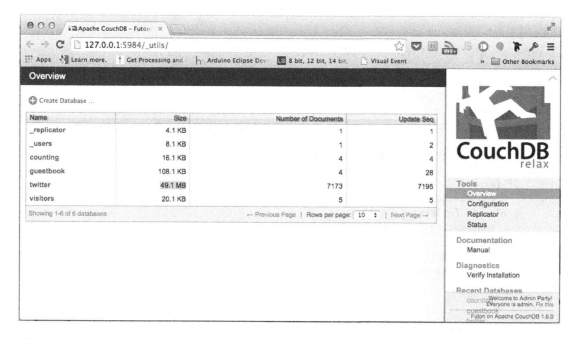

Figure 14-8. *Overview of my Twitter database*

Because Twitter does not understand what attributes our app may or may not wish to utilize, each JSON document saved possesses an exuberant amount of information. Such information addresses whom the tweet is in reply to or the location from which the tweet originated, etc. Feel free to delve into your Twitter database and observe at random a single document. As you will undoubtedly find, there is an expansive amount of information pertaining to the captured tweet. As this will be less than ideal for HTTP transport, we will have to create a view that reflects the sole aspects required by this chapter.

Creating a View

As was seen in Chapter 12, creating a view entails the creation of a design document, for which the `map` function we devise will reflect the rows for this particular view. For the purpose of our application, we will require a mere fraction of the values held within each JSON document. These values are the following: `message`, `profile_pic`, `handle`, `full_name`, `created_time`, `media`, and `tweet_id`. Each of these aforementioned labels will play an integral role in the presentation of the tweet.

Last, as the key that will be used to sort our results, our map function will reference the captured timestamp of the tweet. Referencing this value as the primary key to our view will enable the ability to sort tweets by their creation time. Currently, the creation time is represented as a string rather than as a number. However, we can easily convert the timestamp to a number via the built-in JavaScript function Number(string), as seen in Listing 14-4.

Listing 14-4. Devising a Tweet map Function

```
function(doc) {
var mediaURL=undefined;
if(doc.extended_entities){
   mediaURL=doc.extended_entities.media[0].media_url;
};
emit( Number(doc.timestamp_ms), {
                            "message"      :doc.text,
                            "profile_pic"  :doc.user.profile_image_url,
                            "handle"       :doc.user.screen_name,
                            "full_name"    :doc.user.name,
                            "created_time" :doc.created_at,
                            "media"        : mediaURL,
                            "tweet_id"     :doc.id_str
                        });
}
```

Listing 14-4 reveals the map function that will be used to create the data set that will be used within our HTML document. As you can see, the emit function obtains the reference to our document and, from it, captures only the properties our application requires. Because media will not accompany every tweet, I have also created a condition in which the mediaURL is set to undefined if media does not exist. This will effectively remove the media key from the returned JSON. This will be important to remember when we devise our template.

With our map function devised, click the Run button to extract our data set against the entries within our Twitter database. Once the operation completes, you should witness the results of your query, as shown in Figure 14-9. The amount of time required to query the existing database will vary. Remember that the initial render is the slowest, and subsequent rendering of the same query only occurs on recently added/removed or updated documents.

Figure 14-9. *Specialized query*

Once your view has successfully resulted in a valid data set, you will want to save it. You may recall that this is achieved by clicking the Save As... button, which will display the Save View As... dialog box shown in Figure 14-10.

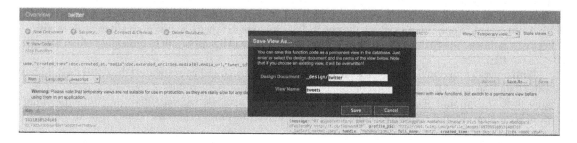

Figure 14-10. *Save dialog for a temporary view*

I have labeled my design document "twitter" and the view's name "tweets." Once the fields are properly filled in, click Save, so that we can now reference our view via the following URL: `http://127.0.0.1:5984/twitter/_design/twitter/_view/tweets`. Visiting this URL reveals JSON to be the data set captured by our query.

Enabling CORS

If we wish our HTML application to obtain and utilize the preceding JSON resource, we will require the use of Ajax. However, because CouchDB runs on a specific port, any and all Ajax requests that do not get initiated from within Futon will be denied, per the same-origin policy.

However, as CouchDB invites us to modify its configurations, we can enable CORS with ease. Navigating to `http://127.0.0.1:5984/_utils/config.html` reveals, via a Futon interface, the ability for us to modify, add, and alter the default configurations of CouchDB.

By default, CouchDB disables CORS, to ensure that data captured within remains safeguarded. However, enabling CORS is as simple as scrolling to the httpd section and locating the enable_cors option. While it may appear that the value is uneditable, double-clicking the value will reveal an input box, thereby allowing us to replace the current value with that of true. (See Figure 14-11.)

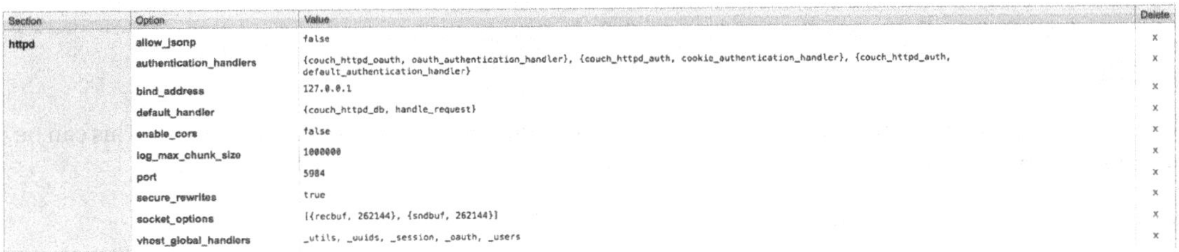

Section	Option	Value	Delete
httpd	allow_jsonp	false	x
	authentication_handlers	{couch_httpd_oauth, oauth_authentication_handler}, {couch_httpd_auth, cookie_authentication_handler}, {couch_httpd_auth, default_authentication_handler}	x
	bind_address	127.0.0.1	x
	default_handler	{couch_httpd_db, handle_request}	x
	enable_cors	false	x
	log_max_chunk_size	1000000	x
	port	5984	x
	secure_rewrites	true	x
	socket_options	[{recbuf, 262144}, {sndbuf, 262144}]	x
	vhost_global_handlers	_utils, _uuids, _session, _oauth, _users	x

Figure 14-11. Configuring CouchDB with CORS capability

Once we have configured CouchDB to utilize CORS, we will have to include the proper CORS headers within the CORS section. By default, the CORS section does not possess any CORS headers as an option and, therefore, will have to be added. This is achieved by locating, at the bottom of the interface, the button labeled "Add a new section," as seen in Figure 14-12.

Overview	Configuration			
	verify_ssl_certificates	false		x
stats	rate	1000		x
	samples	[0, 60, 300, 900]		x
uuids	algorithm	sequential		x
	max_count	1000		x
vendor	name	The Apache Software Foundation		x
	version	1.6.0		x
view_compaction	keyvalue_buffer_size	2097152		x
Add a new section				

Figure 14-12. Adding a new section button

On clicking this button, a dialog box will appear, as shown in Figure 14-13, and to it, we specify a key/value pair into a given section.

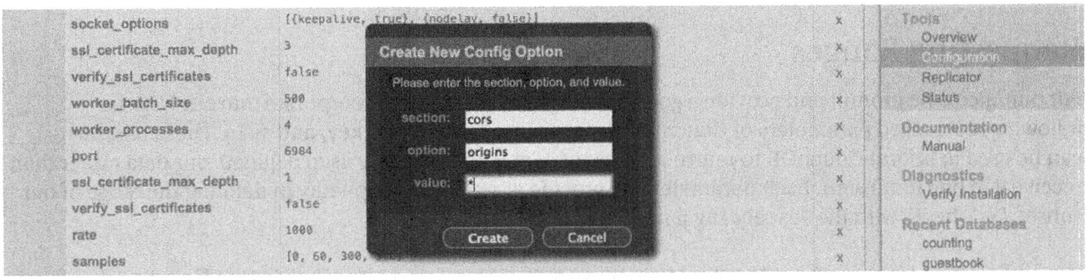

Figure 14-13. Configuring the origins header

283

For the purposes of this chapter, our application will only initiate a GET request for the Twitter view. Per the CORS specification, in order to authorize GET requests for data from origin A to a source origin B, we must use the origins header. As its value, we must configure any and all approved origins. To make things easy, we can use the wildcard after all the information we are exposing is already public on Twitter. On clicking Create, we will have successfully configured our data set from being obtained via varying origins.

Ajax

In order to fetch the JSON data from CouchDB, we must configure the Ajax request accordingly. This can be as simple as configuring an xhr object and defining the request line, as shown in Listing 14-5.

Listing 14-5. Ajax Request to Obtain Tweets

```
var ajax = new XMLHttpRequest();
    ajax.open("GET", "http://127.0.0.1:5984/twitter/_design/twitter/_view/tweets");
    ajax.responseType = "json";
    ajax.onload = function() {
        console.log(this.response);
    };
    ajax.send();
```

Listing 14-5 initializes an XMLHttpRequest object and configures the request line to make a GET request for the Twitter design document. Submission of the request, provided the CORS headers are properly configured in CouchDB, should result in the output of the received JSON data to the developer's console. At this point, all that would remain is to append our JSON to the document.

▪ **Note** To keep things simple, Listing 14-5 solely makes use of XMLHttpRequest Level 2.

If you were to open a simple HTML document, make reference to the external Ajax.js file, and run it within a browser with the developer's network pane opened, you would be able to witness a successful Ajax request. If your database is as bountiful as mine, you might have witnessed that your request received an incredibly large number of tweets. Receiving this many tweets will require the viewer of our document to wait until the transmission/parsing of JSON has been fulfilled, which is less than ideal.

Requesting Ranges

For our Ajax to be prompt and provide a good user experience, we will incorporate into our URI the following recognized parameters of CouchDB: descending, limit, startkey, and skip. These parameters can be used to inform CouchDB to return a subset of data. This will allow us to paginate our data rather than receive it in one lump sum. Each parameter will provide a specific functionality in defining the range of our subset. Let's begin with the descending parameter.

```
var url="http://127.0.0.1:5984/twitter/_design/twitter/_view/tweets?descending=true";
ajax.open("GET",url);
```

As you can see from the preceding code, I have appended the `descending` parameter to the end of our resource URI. Furthermore, I have specified the value of the `descending` parameter as `true`. This will ensure the sorting order of the original data set, from which we will define our subset. Next, we will utilize the parameter `limit`.

```
var url="http://127.0.0.1:5984/twitter/_design/twitter/_view/tweets?descending=true&limit=20;
ajax.open("GET",url);
```

Appending the `limit` parameter to our resource will allow us to cap the amount of rows returned by the view. In this particular case, I have specified the value of 20. If you were to navigate to the preceding URI, you would note that only 20 rows are presented. Furthermore, those 20 rows are sorted in the order they were extracted, that order being descending order.

By default, the 20 values being returned will simply reflect the first 20 rows that appear, beginning with the most recent. However, we can manipulate the starting index with the incorporation of our next parameter, `startkey`.

```
var url="http://127.0.0.1:5984/twitter/_design/twitter/_view/tweets?descending=true&limit=20
        &startkey=1412433722297";
ajax.open("GET",url);
```

Use of `startkey` invites us to specify a known key as the index from which our subset begins. In this case, I have specified the key 1412433722297. However, as you may or may not have a tweet that reflects this key, it's best to make this value dynamic. This, of course, can be obtained easily from each Ajax request. We simply obtain the key from the very last row of JSON in our data set. I will demonstrate this shortly.

Because we will use the last key to indicate the key from which we begin our subset, we will undoubtedly obtain in each subset a tweet that has already been provided in our previous subset. Therefore, the final parameter we will utilize will inform CouchDB to skip over a specified number before beginning our subset. That parameter is, of course, `skip`.

```
var url="http://127.0.0.1:5984/twitter/_design/twitter/_view/tweets?descending=true&limit=20
        &startkey=1412433722297&skip=1";
ajax.open("GET",url);
```

Providing the value of 1 to our `skip` parameter informs CouchDB to offset our subset by one from the established `startkey`. This will effectively skip the row identified by the `startkey` from being provided in this data set.

Now that we have a firm understanding of the parameters involved, all that remains are the operations that can manipulate our URI accordingly. Such operations can be seen in Listing 14-6.

Listing 14-6. `js/mylibs/ajaxRange.js` Incorporates the Pagination of Tweets

```
1 var url = 'http://127.0.0.1:5984/twitter/_design/twitter/_view/tweets';
2 var lastKey = null;

3 function render() {
4 var ajax = new XMLHttpRequest();
5     ajax.open("GET", incrementRange( lastKey ));
6     ajax.responseType = "json";
7     ajax.onload = function() {
8         var data = (this.response);
```

```
 9           var rows = data.rows;
10           lastKey = rows[rows.length - 1].key;
11           console.log(data);
12       };
13       ajax.send();
14 }

15 function incrementRange(lastCount) {
16   var range = "?descending=true";
17   var limit = 20;
18   if (lastCount) {
19     range += "&startkey=" + lastCount.toString()+"&skip=1";
20   };
21   range += "&limit=" + limit;
22   return url + range;
23 };
```

Listing 14-6 incorporates the use of two functions to append the appropriate parameters and their values that enable the appropriate and linear subset of the original data contained in our twitter database.

The first function, labeled "render," is the main entry into our Ajax request. This function is responsible for the actual request that will take place. However, the render function will defer to our second function, labeled "incrementRange," which is responsible for appending the appropriate parameters for the Ajax call. As discussed earlier, three of our four parameters are known constants. We will always work in descending order; we will limit our data set to 20 rows; and, last, we will always skip one. However, what varies is the key that will represent our starting index, from which our subset is derived.

In order to satisfy the startkey parameter, we must retain the key value from the last row provided in each data set to a variable that can be referenced by the incrementRange function. The variable that will be assigned the key value is that of lastKey (line 10). With each data set returned, we must access the final collection in the array and obtain the value of key.

With each call to render, lastKey will be provided as an argument to incrementRange, where, if and only if the value is not null, will it be set as the value to startkey. Next, startkey and the skip parameter are appended to the current URI, along with limit.

With each invocation to render, the data set will continue to be incremented by the next 20 rows in the database. To make it easy to request a data set, we could easily bind the render function to that of a button in our HTML, as shown in Listing 14-7.

Listing 14-7. HTML Document's Incorporation of Our ajaxRange Script

```
<!DOCTYPE html>
<html lang="en">
 <head>
  <meta charset="utf-8">
 </head>
 <body>
  <input type="submit" value="load tweets"  onclick="return render()"/>
  <script src="js/mylibs/ajaxRange.js"></script>
 </body>
</html>
```

286

▨ **Tip**   Scripts should always be referenced at the end of your document, to increase page load.

If we were to run the document from Listing 14-7, we would only be able to witness on the page a Submit button that reads "load tweets." Although clicking the button does initiate the appropriate Ajax request, we have yet to perform any options that would insert the returned data into our page.

Handlebars

The final piece of the puzzle is the incorporation of our template, which will not only apply presentation to our data but also insert our data into the document. To assist in our template creation, it will be of great use to know exactly what the composition of our data is. Listing 14-8 reveals the composition of a data whose range is limited to the return of two rows.

Listing 14-8. A Subset of Our Data Context Received from CouchDB

```
{
  "total_rows":3976,
  "offset":0,
  "rows":[
    {
      "id":"83f4b7105a3aad630fb06e036600176b",
      "key":1412433722297,
      "value":{
        "message":"truncated",
        "profile_pic":"truncated.jpeg",
        "handle":"truncated",
        "full_name":"truncated",
        "created_time":"truncated",
        "media":truncated.jpg",
        "tweet_id":"518410721529307136"
      }
    },{
      "id":"83f4b7105a3aad630fb06e03660016cb",
      "key":1412433721956,
      "value":{
        "message":"truncated",
        "profile_pic":"truncated.jpeg",
        "handle":"truncated",
        "full_name":"truncated",
        "created_time":"truncated",
        "media":truncated.jpg",
        "tweet_id":"518410719986216960"}
    }
  ]
}
```

Listing 14-8 reveals that each tweet is a collection of key/value pairs, held sequentially within the ordered list labeled rows. Because our context is made up of collections and ordered lists, our template will have to rely on block expressions and block helpers to traverse the contexts appropriately. Listing 14-9 reflects the template I have chosen to represent our tweets.

Listing 14-9. index.html Handlebar-Tweet-Template

```html
<!DOCTYPE html>
<html lang="en">
<head>
<meta charset="utf-8">
 <link href='css/tweet.css' rel='stylesheet' type='text/css'>
</head>
<body>
<section id="tweets">
 <script type="application/x-handlebars" id="Handlebar-Tweet-Template">
   {{#each rows}}  //for each item contained within rows
   {{#value}}        //set the current context to value
   <div class="social-article">
    <a target="_blank" href="{{profile_pic}}" class="profile-pic">
      <img alt="twitter icon" src={{profile_pic}}>
    </a>
    <div class="social-text">
     <p class="socialprofilelink">
      <a target="_blank" href="https://twitter.com/{{handle}}">{{full_name}}</a>
      <a target="_blank" href="https://twitter.com/{{handle}}">{{handle}}</a>
     </p>
     <a target="_blank" href="https://twitter.com/{{handle}}/status/{{tweet_id}}"
            class="created-time">{{created_time}}</a>
     <p>{{message}}</p>
    </div>
    {{#if media}}   //if a media is supplied add it
     <a href={{media}} target="_blank"><img class="media" src="{{media}}"></a>
    {{/if}}
    <div id="twitter-actions">
     <a target="_blank" href="https://twitter.com/intent/tweet?in_reply_to={{tweet_id}}"
            title="Reply" id="intent-reply" class="intent"></a>
     <a target="_blank" href="https://twitter.com/intent/retweet?tweet_id={{tweet_id}}"
            title="Retweet" id="intent-retweet" class="intent"></a>
     <a target="_blank" href="https://twitter.com/intent/favorite?tweet_id={{tweet_id}}"
            title="Favorite" id="intent-fave" class="intent"></a>
    </div>
   </div>
   {{/value}}     //return to the original context
   {{/each}}
 </script>
</section>
<input type="submit" value="load tweets"  onclick="return render()"/>
<script src="js/libs/handlebars-v2.0.0.js"></script>
<script src="js/mylibs/ajaxRange.js"></script>
</body>
</html>
```

If you were to open the HTML document within a browser, all that would be shown at this point is what appears in Figure 14-14. Furthermore, clicking the "load tweets" button continues to make Ajax requests; however, it will not insert any tweets into our page.

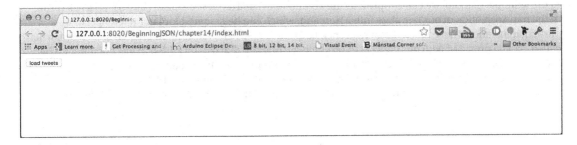

Figure 14-14. *Only a "load tweets" button is rendered to the page*

This is because we have yet to supply our data to our template. However, before we are able to do so, we must compile our template, so that we can reference it as a function, as seen in Listing 14-10.

Listing 14-10. js/mylibs/engine.js Incorporates the Template with ajaxRange.js

```
1  var initialTemplateWrapper = document.getElementById("Handlebar-Tweet-Template");
2  var initialTemplateContent = initialTemplateWrapper.innerHTML;
3  var templateFunction = Handlebars.compile(initialTemplateContent);

4  var url = 'http://127.0.0.1:5984/twitter/_design/twitter/_view/tweets';
5  var lastKey = null;

6  function render() {
7   var ajax = new XMLHttpRequest();
9   ajax.open("GET", incrementRange(lastKey));
10  ajax.responseType = "json";
11  ajax.onload = function() {
12   var data = (this.response);
13   var rows = data.rows;
14   lastKey = rows[rows.length - 1].key;
15   document.getElementById("tweets").innerHTML += templateFunction( data );
16  };
17  ajax.send();
18 }

19 function incrementRange(lastCount) {
20  var range = "?descending=true";
21  var limit = 20;
22  if (lastCount) {
23   range += "&startkey=" + lastCount.toString() + "&skip=1";
24  };
25  range += "&limit=" + limit;
26  return url + range;
27 };
```

Listing 14-10 begins by prepending into our `ajaxRange` JavaScript file the necessary lines both to obtain and compile our `Handlebar-Tweet-Template` into a JavaScript function. We begin first by obtaining a reference to the HTML `<script>` element whose ID is that of `Handlebar-Tweet-Template` (**line 1**). From there, we extract the value within via the element's `innerHTML` attribute (**line 2**). Once we have a reference to the template markup, we can supply it as the argument to `Handlebars.compile` (**line 3**). This will result in the transformation of our template into a function, which can be assigned for later reference. In this particular instance, I have labeled that reference `templateFunction`. The variable `templateFunction`, when called, can be provided with our data set to produce the markup that can be added to our document. The final touch is then to invoke the `templateFunction` with our returned JSON data (**line 15**).

At this point, if we were to open our HTML document within a browser and click the "load tweets" button, our document would render each returned tweet with the appropriate presentation, as seen in Figure 14-15.

Figure 14-15. *Handlebars automates the presentation*

As you can see from Figure 14-15, each tweet is clearly added to the document. All that remains is the incorporation of the appropriate styling. The styling, much like the template, can take on any form. The styling I have chosen to apply can be seen in Listing 14-11, resulting in the rendering of Figure 14-16.

Listing 14-11. `css/tweet.css` Provides Style to Coincide with Our Template

```
@import url("//fonts.googleapis.com/css?family=Open+Sans+Condensed:300|Open+Sans");

#tweets {
    font-family: 'Open Sans' sans-serif;
    width: 30%;
    margin: auto;
    overflow: hidden;
}
.recent-activity img, img {
    border: 0 none;
}
a img.media {
    width: 100%;
    height: auto;
    margin: 10px 0;
    -webkit-border-radius: 7px;
    -moz-border-radius: 7px;
    border-radius: 7px;
}
.social-article {
    border-top: 1px slategray dotted;
    width: 100%;
    padding: 8px 0px 8px 0px;
    margin: 0 0 10px 0;
    position: relative;
    overflow: hidden;
}
.social-article .profile-pic a {
    position: absolute;
    z-index: 99;
    float: left;
}

.profile-pic {
    position: absolute;
}
.profile-pic img {
    float: left;
    border: none;
    -webkit-border-radius: 20px;
    -moz-border-radius: 20px;
    border-radius: 20px;
    width: 42px;
    height: 42px;
}
```

```css
.social-article .social-text {
    width: 100%;
    float: left;
    font-size: 11px;
    padding-left: 52px;
    -moz-box-sizing: border-box;
    -webkit-box-sizing: border-box;
    box-sizing: border-box;
    position: relative;
}
.social-article .social-text p {
    margin: 0px;
    min-height: 1em;
    line-height: 15px;
    -ms-word-break: break-all;
    word-break: break-all;
    /* Non standard for webkit */
    word-break: break-word;
    -webkit-hyphens: auto;
    -moz-hyphens: auto;
    -ms-hyphens: auto;
    hyphens: auto;
}
.social-article .social-text a, .social-article .social-text h1 a {
    color: #00acee;
    text-decoration: none;
}
.social-article .social-text a:hover, .social-article .social-text h1 a:hover {
    text-decoration: underline;
    color: #00acee;
}

.created-time {
    font-size: 10px;
    color: #878787;
    clear: both;
    display: block;
    margin: 0 0 5px 0;
}
.created-time a, .created-time a:hover {
    color: #878787;
}
.socialprofilelink a, .socialprofilelink a:hover {
    color: #444;
}
```

```
/* -------- FEED  ACTIONS ------*/
#twitter-actions {
    width: 75px;
    float: right;
    position: relative;
    margin-right: 5px;
    display: block;
}
.intent {
    width: 16px;
    height: 16px;
    float: left;
}
.intent a {
    width: 16px;
    height: 16px;
    display: block;
    background-image: url(../img/everything-spritev2.png);
    float: left;
}

#intent-retweet a { background-position: 48px 0px; }
#intent-retweet a:hover { background-position: 32px 0px; }
#intent-fave a { background-position: 95px 0px; }
#intent-fave a:hover { background-position: 79px 0px; }
#intent-reply a { background-position: 0px 0px; }
#intent-reply a:hover { background-position: -16px 0px; }
```

Figure 14-16. Fully stylized #bendgate tweets

Summary

As this chapter has shown, JSON is not simply a data format but, rather, the kernel from which modern-day applications blossom. Owing to its convenience, simplicity, and ability to maintain the hierarchical structure of data, JSON has become the substance that fuels the Web.

It is true that we could have transmitted XML in lieu of JSON. However, the convenience of working with JSON far outweighs the tediousness and bloat that comes with XML.

Index

Get the eBook for only $10!

Now you can take the weightless companion with you anywhere, anytime. Your purchase of this book entitles you to 3 electronic versions for only $10.

This Apress title will prove so indispensible that you'll want to carry it with you everywhere, which is why we are offering the eBook in 3 formats for only $10 if you have already purchased the print book.

Convenient and fully searchable, the PDF version enables you to easily find and copy code—or perform examples by quickly toggling between instructions and applications. The MOBI format is ideal for your Kindle, while the ePUB can be utilized on a variety of mobile devices.

Go to www.apress.com/promo/tendollars to purchase your companion eBook.